CONCISE
ELEVENTH
EDITION

YOUR
COLLEGE
EXPERIENCE

Strategies for Success

CONCISE
ELEVENTH
EDITION

YOUR
COLLEGE
EXPERIENCE
Strategies for Success

John N. Gardner

President, John N. Gardner Institute for Excellence in Undergraduate Education
Brevard, North Carolina

Distinguished Professor Emeritus, Library and Information Science
Senior Fellow, National Resource Center for
  The First-Year Experience and Students in Transition
University of South Carolina, Columbia

Betsy O. Barefoot

Senior Scholar
John N. Gardner Institute for Excellence in Undergraduate Education
Brevard, North Carolina

Bedford/St. Martin's
Boston ▪ New York

For Bedford/St. Martin's

Vice President, Editorial, Macmillan Higher Education Humanities: Edwin Hill
Publisher for College Success: Erika Gutierrez
Senior Executive Editor for College Success: Simon Glick
Developmental Editor: Jennifer Jacobson of Ohlinger Publishing Services
Associate Editor: Bethany Gordon
Senior Production Editor: Christina M. Horn
Senior Production Supervisor: Dennis J. Conroy
Senior Marketing Manager: Christina Shea
Production Assistant: Erica Zhang
Copy Editor: Kathleen Lafferty
Indexer: Schroeder Indexing Services
Photo Researcher: Sue McDermott Barlow
Director of Rights and Permissions: Hilary Newman
Senior Art Director: Anna Palchik
Text Design: Jerilyn Bockorick and Carie Keller, Cenveo Publisher Services
Cover Design: William Boardman
Cover Photo: © 4x6/Getty Images
Composition: Cenveo Publisher Services
Printing and Binding: RR Donnelley and Sons

9 8 7 6 5 4
f e d c b a

For information, write: Bedford/St. Martin's, 75 Arlington Street, Boston, MA 02116
   (617-399-4000)

ISBN 978-1-4576-7252-1   (Student Edition)
ISBN 978-1-4576-9045-7   (Loose-leaf Edition)

Acknowledgments
Data from all *First-year students report* . . . features from *The American Freshman: National Norms, 2012.* Running-head photos: Chapter 1, Photodisk/Punchstock; Chapter 2, Maksim Kabakou/ Shutterstock; Chapter 3, © james steidl/istockphoto; Chapter 4, Digital Vision/Punchstock; Chapter 5, © Vincenzo Lombardo/age fotostock; Chapter 6, Freer/Shutterstock; Chapter 7, Hank Frentz/ Shutterstock; Chapter 8, Digital Vision/Punchstock; Chapter 9, © fStop/Alamy; Chapter 10, simple stock shots/Punchstock; Chapter 11, dutourdumonde/Shutterstock; Chapter 12, pterwort/Shutterstock

Dear Student,

More than ever before, a college education is an essential step in preparing you for almost any career. While only a few years ago many well-paying jobs required only a high school diploma, most employers today require that job applicants have some form of education beyond high school. This can be an associate's or bachelor's degree, or a diploma or certificate of competency in a particular vocation.

As the cost of higher education increases, some people are questioning whether a college degree is worth the cost. Yes, college is expensive. We know, however, that the benefits of a college education far outweigh the price tag—not only monetary benefits like a better salary but overall improvement in the quality of life such as better overall physical health, more confidence, and greater earning potential for children you have or might have in the future. Of course we can all name a few exceptions: World-famous entrepreneurs Mark Zuckerberg of Facebook and Steve Jobs of Apple were college dropouts who still managed to be highly successful. Such success stories are rare; most of us can't depend on a combination of luck and brilliance to catapult us into fame and fortune.

While you might have many reasons for being in college, we hope your primary goal is graduation. And you will be more likely to graduate if you have a successful first year. When we were in our first year of college, college success courses were, by and large, nonexistent. Colleges and universities just allowed new students to sink or swim. As a result, some students made it through their first year successfully, some barely survived, and some dropped out or flunked out.

Today, most colleges and universities offer college success courses to provide essential help to students in navigating their way through the first year and charting a path toward graduation. You are likely reading *Your College Experience* because you are enrolled in a college success course. Although this book might seem different from your other textbooks, we believe that it could be the most important book you read this term because it's all about improving your chances for success in college and beyond. This book will help you identify your own strengths as well as your needs for improvement.

As college professors, researchers, and administrators with many years of experience working with first-year students, we're well aware that starting college can be challenging. But we also know that if you apply the ideas in this book to your everyday life, you are more likely to enjoy your time in college, graduate, and achieve your life goals. Welcome to college!

John N. Gardner

Betsy O. Barefoot

ABOUT THE AUTHORS

John N. Gardner brings unparalleled experience to this authoritative text for first-year seminar courses. He is the recipient of the University of South Carolina's highest award for teaching excellence. He has twenty-five years of experience directing and teaching in the most respected and most widely emulated first-year seminar in the country, the University 101 course at the University of South Carolina. He is recognized as one of the country's leading educators for his role in initiating and orchestrating an international reform movement to improve the beginning college experience. He is also the founding leader of two influential higher education centers that support campuses in their efforts to improve the learning and retention of beginning college students: the National Resource Center for The First-Year Experience and Students in Transition at the University of South Carolina (**www.sc.edu/fye**) and the John N. Gardner Institute for Excellence in Undergraduate Education (**www.jngi.org**) based in Brevard, North Carolina. The experiential basis for all of John Gardner's work is his own miserable first year of college on academic probation, an experience that he hopes to prevent for this book's readers.

Betsy O. Barefoot is a writer, researcher, and teacher whose special area of scholarship is the first year of college. During her tenure at the University of South Carolina from 1988 to 1999, she served as codirector for research and publications at the National Resource Center for The First-Year Experience and Students in Transition. She taught University 101, in addition to special-topics graduate courses on the first-year experience and the principles of college teaching. She conducts first-year seminar faculty training workshops around the United States and in other countries, and she is frequently called on to evaluate first-year seminar outcomes. She currently serves as Senior Scholar in the Gardner Institute for Excellence in Undergraduate Education. In her Institute role she led a major national research project to identify institutions of excellence in the first college year. She currently works with both two- and four-year campuses in evaluating all components of the first year.

BRIEF CONTENTS

CONTENTS

1 Why Go to College?   1

6 Reading to Learn 117

7 Getting the Most Out of Class 137

8   **Studying**   161

9   **Test Taking**   179

10 Information Literacy and Communication 205

11   Diversity   237

PREFACE

Anyone who teaches beginning college students knows how much they have changed in recent years. Today's students are increasingly job-focused, technologically adept, and concerned about the future. And more than ever, students are worrying about how they will pay for college. Recently, popular media sources such as *USA Today* have raised questions about whether the money spent on a college degree would be better invested in a start-up business or travel.[1] While it is tempting to focus on the few individuals who can chart an alternate path to a successful future, we know that for the overwhelming majority of individuals, a college degree is more essential than ever before.

Today, we see diverse students of all ages and backgrounds enrolling in both two- and four-year institutions, bringing with them the hopes and dreams that a college education can help fulfill as well as expectations that may or may not be realistic. The Concise Edition of *Your College Experience* is designed specifically to give all students the practical help they need to gain self-knowledge, set goals, succeed, and stay in college so that those hopes and dreams have a better chance to become realities.

While maintaining its hallmark approach on goal setting, the Concise eleventh edition of this text reflects a renewed emphasis on providing skills and strategies in areas where students often need the most support. These skills, such as time management, academic reading, and research, can be applied to all college courses and even to the workplace. At a time when institutions are increasing class sizes and mainstreaming developmental students, students will need more, not less, individual attention and the skills so that they can ask for this attention. And of course concerns about student retention remain, as do pressures on first-year experience administrators to do more with less. These realities of college and university life mean that giving students strategies for immediate use is more important than ever.

To help you meet the challenges of engaging and retaining today's students, we have created a complete package of support materials, including an Instructor's Annotated Edition, an Instructor's Manual and Test Bank, PowerPoint slides, and videos. In the Instructor's Annotated Edition, you will find clearly marked retention strategies and activities to help you engage and retain students. These activities, and all of the instructor support materials, will help both new and experienced instructors as they prepare to teach the course.

What has not changed in the forty years since the inception of the college success course is our level of commitment and deep understanding of our students. Although this Concise Edition of *Your College Experience* has been significantly revised, it is still based on our collective knowledge and experience in teaching first-year students, as well as on feedback from

[1]Oliver St. John, "Kids Skip College—Not Worth the Money," *USA Today* online, April 22, 2013.

generations of users. It is grounded in the growing body of research on student success and retention and includes many valuable contributions from leading experts in the field. Our contributors were chosen for their knowledge and currency in their fields as well as their own deep commitments to their students and to the discipline. Most of all, it is a text born from our devotion to students and to their success. Simply put, we do not like to see students fail. We are confident that if students both read and heed the information herein, they will become engaged in the college experience, learn, and persist to graduation.

We have written this text for students of any age in both two- and four-year residential and commuter institutions. Our writing style is intended to convey respect and admiration for students while recognizing their continued need for challenge and support. We have addressed every topic that our experience, our research, and our reviewers tell us is a concern for students at any type of school with any kind of educational background.

Your College Experience uses a simple and logical organization. The introductory chapters set the foundation for success by challenging students to explore their purpose for attending college and by helping them learn how to apply that purpose to both short- and long-term goal setting. Students are also introduced to strategies for academic and career planning and gaining valuable work and educational experiences during college. In Chapter 2, students are provided with solid time-management strategies before exploring the topics of emotional intelligence and learning styles. Chapters 5 through 10 enumerate essential study skills like critical thinking, reading, note taking, and test taking, and these chapters guide students in communicating and finding information. Chapters 11 and 12 emphasize practical and realistic considerations about diversity and money management that students can use during their first year of college and beyond.

Whether you are considering this textbook for use in your first-year seminar or have already made a decision to adopt it, we thank you for your interest, and we trust that you will find it to be a valuable teaching aid. We also hope that this book will guide you and your campus in understanding the broad range of issues that can affect student success.

A REVISION FOCUSED ON PRACTICAL STRATEGIES TO HELP STUDENTS BE SUCCESSFUL FROM THE START

Substantive features throughout the text increase the probability of your students' success in college.

The hallmark Gardner and Barefoot focus on self-assessment of strengths and goal setting helps students focus on purpose and motivation and combats disengagement in this course. A section on goal setting in Chapter 1 gets students thinking immediately about this important skill. Assessing Your Strengths and Setting Goals boxes in each chapter ask students to set goals, and Stay on Track exercises at the end of each chapter ask students to assess how to apply strengths to current and future academic work.

Powerful LearningCurve online assessment system is available with every new book. When it comes to retaining new information, research shows that self-testing with small, bite-sized chunks of information works best. *LearningCurve for College Success*, a new adaptive online quizzing program, helps students focus on the material they need the most help in learning. With LearningCurve, students receive as much practice as they need to master a given concept and are provided with immediate feedback and links back to online instruction. A personalized study plan with suggestions for further practice gives your students what they need to thrive in the college success course, in their college career, and beyond!

Chapter-opening profiles help students see themselves in the text. Each chapter of the text opens with a story of a recent first-year student who has used the strategies in the chapter to succeed in college. The profiled students come from diverse backgrounds and attend all kinds of colleges around the country. The Concise eleventh edition features several new profiles.

Thought-provoking images and exercises in every chapter encourage critical thinking. Features, photos, and exercises include activities to help students master concepts and think critically about the material.

Coverage of technology and learning is highlighted in a Tech Tip feature in every chapter, many of which are new in the eleventh edition. These features introduce critical technology skills that span the classroom and real life, such as "E-mail Etiquette" in Chapter 1, "Say Yes to Twitter" in Chapter 3, "Research Wisely" in Chapter 5, "Embrace the Cloud" in Chapter 8, and "Fear Not the Online Test" in Chapter 9.

Models (including **digital models**) let students see principles in action. Because many students learn best by example, full-size models—more than in any competing book—show realistic examples of annotating a textbook, creating a mind map, multiple styles of note taking, and other strategies for academic success. This edition includes digital models to reflect the tools students will be using in their everyday lives.

***Where to Go for Help* boxes connect the student to campus, faculty, and other students.** To help students take more control of their own success, every chapter includes a quick overview of further resources for support, including learning-assistance centers, books, Web sites, and fellow students—with a prompt for students to add their own ideas.

***Your Turn* collaborative learning activities foster peer-to-peer communication, collaboration, and critical thinking.** These activities can be used in class, as homework, or as group activities to strengthen the bond between students and their college communities. They are organized into four types based on what students are asked to do: Work Together, Write and Reflect, Think about It, and Discuss.

New! *Is This You?* boxes speak directly to students who are likely taking first-year experience courses. Look for these special messages to first-generation college students, returning students, veterans, students with children, exchange students—as well as students encountering common first-year issues such as the temptation to cheat, anxiety over writing papers, financial problems, and the clash of new ideas with old beliefs. The feature points to specific content in the chapter these students should read and heed.

New! *First-year students report...* **charts help students assess their own college experience.** Data from the Higher Education Research Institute's 2012 Your First College Year survey is presented in pie charts. Each chapter poses questions that allow students to find common ground among their peers, such as "Do you frequently feel overwhelmed by all you have to do?," "How often do you use the Internet for research or homework?," or "Do you have any concerns about your ability to finance your college education?"

New! *In the Media* **features in many chapters encourage students to think critically about a current topic.** These boxes use examples from movies, television, articles, books, or the Web. For instance, the In the Media feature in Chapter 3 uses the film *Silver Linings Playbook* to discuss handling emotions, and the In the Media feature in Chapter 5 looks at how advertising often appeals to false authority.

Skills-based practice exercises provide hands-on, point-of-use reinforcement of major concepts. Students use these exercises to practice skills that they can then apply to their other academic courses. For instance, the time-management chapter includes a tool for students to calculate their Procrastination Self-Assessment; and the test-taking chapter includes a new Test Anxiety Quiz.

Retention Strategies in every chapter of the Instructor's Annotated Edition (IAE) offer best practices from John Gardner and Betsy Barefoot to help students persist in the first year. In addition, a 12-page insert at the beginning of the IAE includes chapter-specific exercises and activities designed as retention strategies to support writing, critical thinking, working in groups, planning, reflecting, and taking action.

KEY CHAPTER-BY-CHAPTER REVISIONS

In addition to new features that appear across all chapters of the book, each chapter also features key new and updated content:

Chapter 1, Why Go to College?, has been revised to focus on helping students identify their purpose for being in college and setting goals for a successful college experience. Chapter 1 includes an In the Media feature that looks at a 2013 study from the Georgetown University Center on Education and the Workforce about the benefits of a college education. The chapter includes answers to questions that commonly are on students' minds, such as "Why should I take this course?" and "Hasn't this all been covered already in high school?" This chapter also offers clear strategies for academic and career planning, exploring potential career paths, and gaining valuable experience while in college.

Extensive revisions to Chapter 2, Time Management, address the tools today's students use to stay organized. This chapter includes new research on procrastination, including a tool for students to measure how much they procrastinate; an activity to increase awareness about distractions; and a wealth of new information about digital tools to get organized and clear strategies to manage time.

The organization of Chapter 3, Emotional Intelligence, has been improved, and the chapter includes a brand-new student profile and a new Tech Tip, "Say Yes to Twitter," that includes a new diagram of a Tweet.

In Chapter 4, How You Learn, wording in the VARK questionnaire and scoring instructions and the MBTI content have all been simplified.

Chapter 5, Critical Thinking, features new content and a visual on Bloom's taxonomy, streamlined coverage of logical fallacies, and a new scenario on vending machines in schools. Students can use this scenario to practice their critical-thinking and argument skills.

Chapter 6, Reading to Learn (formerly covered in Chapter 7), organizes the chapter's strategies in bulleted lists so that students read and understand them easily.

Chapter 7, Getting the Most Out of Class (formerly Chapter 6), has been retooled to focus on how students can get the most out of class through listening, participating, and note taking.

Chapter 8, Studying (formerly covered in Chapter 7), includes a new tool to help students make changes so that study time is more efficient, and a new Tech Tip feature on using Cloud storage sites like Dropbox.

The test-taking strategies in Chapter 9 (formerly Chapter 8) are delivered in a more streamlined fashion, and a new test-anxiety quiz allows students to evaluate how serious an issue this is for them and create a plan to overcome it. The content on cheating has been expanded, while the coverage of plagiarism has been moved into Chapter 10.

A new Chapter 10, Information Literacy and Communication, connects writing and speaking to research and combines content from Chapters 9 and 10 in the previous edition. This chapter covers topics such as effective use of the library; working with librarians; narrowing and researching topics for writing assignments, using keywords, and finding and evaluating both traditional and electronic sources; expanded coverage on plagiarism; and streamlined coverage of moving from research to writing and speaking.

Chapter 11, Diversity, features a rewritten section on gender, a rewritten section on sexuality, and a new section on economic status. A new Is This You? feature poses challenges for a student who has recently come to the United States from another country.

Chapter 12, Money, features simplified information on budgeting and an In the Media feature directing students to free online budgeting tools.

EXTENSIVE RESOURCES FOR INSTRUCTORS

- *LearningCurve for College Success.* LearningCurve for College Success is an online, adaptive, self-quizzing program that quickly learns what students already know and helps them practice what they don't yet understand. LearningCurve motivates students to engage with key concepts before they come to class so that they are ready to participate and offers reporting tools to help you discern your students' needs. To package *LearningCurve for College Success* for **free** with this title, use ISBN 978-1-319-01292-2. To order the standalone product, use ISBN 978-1-4576-7999-5.

- **Instructor's Annotated Edition.** A valuable tool for new and experienced instructors alike, the Instructor's Annotated Edition includes the full text of the student edition with abundant marginal annotations, chapter-specific exercises, and helpful suggestions for teaching, fully updated and revised by the authors. In this edition are numerous Retention Strategy tips and exercises to help you help your students succeed and stay in school.

- **Instructor's Manual and Test Bank.** The Instructor's Manual and Test Bank includes chapter objectives, teaching suggestions, a sample lesson plan for each chapter, a guide to teaching with YouTube, and various case studies that are relevant to the topics covered. It also includes test questions for each chapter, a midterm, and a final exam. New to this edition are sample syllabi and final projects for the end of the course. The Instructor's Manual and Test Bank is available online.

- **Computerized Test Bank.** The Computerized Test Bank contains more than 600 multiple-choice, true/false, short-answer, and essay questions designed to assess students' understanding of key concepts. The questions appear in Microsoft Word format and in easy-to-use test bank software. This allows instructors to add, edit, resequence, and print questions and answers. Instructors can also export questions into a variety of formats, including Canvas and Blackboard. An answer key is included.

- *French Fries Are Not Vegetables.* This comprehensive instructional DVD features multiple resources for class and professional use. Also available online. ISBN 978-0-312-65073-5.

- **Custom Solutions.** Bedford/St. Martin's Custom Publishing offers the highest-quality books and media, created in consultation with publishing professionals who are committed to the discipline. Make *Your College Experience* more closely fit your course and goals by integrating your own materials, including only the parts of the text you intend to use in your course, or both. Contact your local Macmillan Education sales representative for more information.

- **CS Select custom database.** The CS Select database allows you to create a textbook for your college success course that reflects your course objectives and uses just the content you need. Start with one of our core texts, and then rearrange chapters, delete chapters, and add additional content—including your own original content—to create just the book you're looking for. Get started by visiting **macmillanhighered.com/csSelect**.

- **TradeUp.** Bring more value and choice to your students' first-year experience by packaging *Your College Experience* with one of a thousand titles from Macmillan publishers at a 50 percent discount from the regular price. Contact your local Macmillan Education sales representative for more information.

STUDENT RESOURCES

- *LearningCurve for College Success. LearningCurve for College Success* is an online, adaptive, self-quizzing program that quickly learns what students already know and helps them practice what they don't yet understand. For more information, see Extensive Resources for Instructors above.

- **College Success Companion Site.** The College Success Companion Site offers a number of tools to use in class, including videos with quizzing, downloadable podcasts, flashcards of key terms, and links to apps which students can use on their phones or computers to reinforce success strategies. From the companion Web site, you can also access instructor resources whenever you need them. Visit **macmillanhighered.com/ collegesuccess/resources.**

- *VideoCentral: College Success* is a premiere collection of videos for the college success classroom. The site features the 30-minute documentary *French Fries Are Not Vegetables and Other College Lessons: A Documentary of the First Year of College,* which follows five students through the life-changing transition of the first year of college. *VideoCentral* also includes access to the following:

  - 16 brief *Conversation Starters* that combine student and instructor interviews on the most important topics taught in first-year seminar courses.
  - 16 accompanying video glossary definitions with questions that bring these topics to life.

  Learn more about packaging *VideoCentral* with this text at **macmillanhighered.com/videosuccess/catalog.**

- **Bedford e-Book to Go for *Your College Experience*.** For roughly half the cost of a print book, **Bedford e-Book to Go** offers an affordable alternative for students. To learn more, visit **macmillanhighered.com/ aboutebooks.**

- **Additional e-Book formats.** You can also find PDF versions of our books when you shop online at our publishing partners' sites: CourseSmart; Barnes & Noble NookStudy; Kno; CafeScribe; or Chegg.

- *The Bedford/St. Martin's Planner* includes everything that students need to plan and use their time effectively, with advice on preparing schedules and to-do lists, along with blank schedules and calendars (monthly and weekly) for planning. Integrated into the planner are tips and advice on fixing common grammar errors, taking notes, and succeeding on tests; an address book; and an annotated list of useful Web sites. The planner fits easily into a backpack or purse, so students can take it anywhere.

To package *The Bedford/St. Martin's Planner* for **free** with the text, use ISBN 978-1-319-01291-5. To order the planner standalone, use ISBN 978-0-312-57447-5.

■ *Bedford/St. Martin's Insider's Guides.* These concise and student-friendly booklets on topics that are critical to college success are a perfect complement to your textbook and course. One Insider's Guide can be packaged with *any* Bedford/St. Martin's textbook at no additional cost. Additional Insider's Guides can also be packaged for additional cost. Topics include:

- **New!** *Insider's Guide to College Etiquette,* 2e
- **New!** *Insider's Guide for Returning Veterans*
- **New!** *Insider's Guide to Transferring*
- *Insider's Guide to Academic Planning*
- *Insider's Guide to Beating Test Anxiety*
- *Insider's Guide to Building Confidence*
- *Insider's Guide to Career Services*
- *Insider's Guide to College Ethics and Personal Responsibility*
- *Insider's Guide to Community College*
- *Insider's Guide to Credit Cards,* 2e
- *Insider's Guide to Getting Involved on Campus*
- *Insider's Guide to Global Citizenship*
- *Insider's Guide to Time Management,* 2e

For more information on ordering one of these guides with the text, go to **macmillanhighered.com/collegesuccess**.

■ *Journal Writing: A Beginning.* Designed to give students an opportunity to use writing as a way to explore their thoughts and feelings, this writing journal includes a generous supply of inspirational quotes placed throughout the pages, tips for journaling, and suggested journal topics. ISBN 978-0-312-59027-7.

ACKNOWLEDGMENTS

Special thanks to the reviewers of this edition, whose wisdom and suggestions guided the creation of the eleventh edition of the text:

Chris Benson, Madonna University
Andrea Berta, University of Texas at El Paso
Margaret Garroway, Howard Community College
Court Merrigan, Eastern Wyoming College
Cyndee Moore, National College
Donna Musselman, Santa Fe College
Alan Pappas, Santa Fe College

We would also like to continue to thank our reviewers from the eighth, ninth, and tenth editions, as they helped to shape the text you see today. **Tenth Edition:** Nichelle DeNeen Acrum, Augusta State University; Peter Conrath, Professional Business College; Stella Fox, Nassau Community College; Lauren

Grimes, Lorain County Community College; Elizabeth Hammett, College of the Mainland; Alice Lanning, University of Oklahoma; Rajone A. Lyman, Houston Community College; Judith A. Lynch, Kansas State University; Gail Malone, South Plains College; Court Merrigan, Eastern Wyoming College; Louise Mitchum, Louisburg College; Carolyn Poole, San Jacinto College Central; Rajan M. Shore, Blue Ridge Community College; Kerri Sleeman, Michigan Technological University; Jim West, St. Philip's College; Robert Whitley, Caldwell Community College and Technical Institute. **Ninth Edition:** Darby Johnsen, Oklahoma City Community College; Steve Lindgren, Minnesota State Community and Technical College; Deborah Lanza, Sussex County Community College; Miranda Miller, Gillette College; SusAnn Key, Midwestern State University; Pamela R. Moss, Midwestern State University. **Eighth Edition:** Rachel A. Beech, Arizona State University–Polytechnic; Paula Bradberry, Arkansas State University; Khalida I. Haqq, Mercer County Community College; Elizabeth Hicks, Central Connecticut State University; Debra Olsen, Madison Area Technical College.

As we look to the future, we are excited about the numerous improvements to this text that our creative Bedford/St. Martin's team has made and will continue to make. Special thanks to Edwin Hill, Vice President of Editorial, Humanities; Erika Gutierrez, Publisher for College Success; Simon Glick, Senior Executive Editor for College Success; Jennifer Jacobson, Development Editor of Ohlinger Publishing Services; Bethany Gordon, Associate Editor; Christina Shea, Senior Marketing Manager; and Christina Horn, Senior Production Editor.

Most of all, we thank you, the users of our book, for you are the true inspirations for our work.

CONTRIBUTORS

Although this text speaks with the voices of its two authors, it represents contributions from many other people. We gratefully acknowledge those contributions and thank these individuals, whose special expertise has made it possible to introduce new students to their college experience through the holistic approach we deeply believe in.

Lea Susan Engle rewrote and updated the chapter on information literacy and incorporating the topics of writing and speaking. Lea is a former instructor and first-year experience librarian at Texas A&M University and current Ph.D. student at The School of Information at The University of Texas at Austin. Lea earned a B.A. in Women's Studies from the University of Maryland, College Park, and holds an M.S. in Information Studies and an M.A. in Women's and Gender Studies from the University of Texas at Austin.

Her professional interests include first-year experience, creative approaches to library outreach, feminist pedagogy, library service to GLBTQ users, formative assessment, taking risks, and fostering cross-campus collaborations. She works in libraries because they are important and empowering community spaces where all people are welcome to participate in free and equal access to information.

Casey Reid is credited with vastly updating the chapter on time management for today's students. Casey graduated in 2002 from Missouri State University with a B.A. in Anthropology and Professional Writing and in 2004 with an M.A. in Writing. From 2004 through 2011, she served on the English faculty at Metropolitan Community College (MCC) in Kansas City. After taking on the time-management challenge of grading papers for 16–17 English classes every year, she took on a new challenge as the College Orientation Coordinator at MCC. Now, she coordinates a mandatory first-year seminar class for MCC's 6,000–7,000 new students, which includes supervising over 100 instructors and managing the associated Peer Leader program. When she isn't working, volunteering, or helping with the various associations in which she holds positions (Midwest Regional Association for Developmental Education, Heartland College Reading and Learning Association, 49/63 Neighborhood Coalition), she adds balance to her life by running, biking, hiking, reading, spending time with her three rescued dogs, and hanging out with friends and family.

The greatly expanded content on majors and careers in Chapter 1 is thanks to **Heather N. Maietta**. Heather is Associate Vice President of Career and Corporate Engagement at Merrimack College. Heather has presented or co-presented more than thirty times nationally on topics related to career and professional preparation and is a Certified Career Development Facilitator Instructor through the National Career Development Association.

Heather has authored articles and research reports in several publications, including *About Campus; Career Convergence;* and *ESource.* Heather has also coauthored three textbooks for Kendall/Hunt Publishers. Most recently, she coauthored and edited *The Senior Year: Culminating Experiences and Transitions*, published by The National Resource Center on the First-Year Experience and Students in Transition.

Heather also serves on the Notre Dame Education Center Board of Directors, an organization that provides education and support services for adult learners in the Greater Lawrence Community.

Chris Gurrie is Assistant Professor of Speech at the University of Tampa. Chris is an active public speaker and participates in invited lectures, workshops, and conferences in the areas of faculty development, first-year life and leadership, communicating effectively with PowerPoint, and communication and immediacy. He contributed the first generation of Tech Tips that were new to the tenth edition and wrote the *Guide to Teaching with YouTube,* available online and as part of the Instructor's Manual.

We would also like to acknowledge and thank the numerous colleagues who have contributed to this book in its previous editions:

Chapters 2, 6, 7, 8, 9: Jeanne L. Higbee, University of Minnesota, Twin Cities
Chapter 3: Catherine Andersen, Gallaudet University

Chapter 4: Tom Carskadon, Mississippi State University
Chapter 7: Mary Ellen O'Leary, University of South Carolina at
    Columbia
Chapter 9: Christel Taylor, University of Wisconsin at Waukesha
Chapter 11: Charles Curran, University of South Carolina at Columbia
Chapter 11: Rose Parkman Marshall, University of South Carolina at
    Columbia
Chapter 11: Margit Watts, University of Hawaii, Manoa
Chapter 12: Philip Gardner, Michigan State University
End-of-chapter materials: Julie Alexander

CONCISE
ELEVENTH
EDITION

YOUR
COLLEGE
EXPERIENCE
Strategies for Success

1 Why Go to College?

> " Working twenty-two hours and taking sixteen credits mean that I rarely get enough sleep because I have to stay up late studying. So my biggest goal for now is to find a way to better manage my time.

Rontavius Jamal Snipes, 23
Biology major
Clayton State University, Georgia

Setting goals—both long- and short-term goals—has always been important to Rontavius Snipes. After high school, when he found himself living in Atlanta working at a dead-end job, he set his sights on going to college and enrolled at Clayton State. Now that he's in college, he's majoring in biology with the goal of attending dental school after graduation, and he knows that getting good grades and staying involved on campus will help him achieve that ultimate goal.

Like many students, Rontavius also needs to balance working (he works at a pharmacy 30 miles from campus) with attending and participating in school, so many of his goals have involved small steps. "I am currently the president of the pre-dental student association," he explains. "The group is small, but this semester

Rontavius Jamal Snipes ▶

I plan to attend a leadership seminar to get some extra motivation to be able to lead a successful student organization." He also gets involved on campus in smaller ways by promoting concerts and plays, which helps him stay connected with other students. He acknowledges, however, that working while attending school does have its challenges, ones that he's still looking for solutions to. "Working twenty-two hours and taking sixteen credits mean that I rarely get enough sleep because I have to stay up late studying. Finding a social life away from my roommates and my girlfriend can be difficult too, so my biggest goal for now is to find a way to better manage my time." Still, Rontavius knows that the hard work will pay off. "Prior to attending college, I never thought about things deeply and took everything at face value. I have a greater intuition now and definitely feel that the price I pay for education is well worth it," he says.

In the future Rontavius hopes to travel the world tackling issues such as poverty, cultural barriers, and the economic glass ceiling that many people face, and his favorite class so far, Sociology 1101, plays nicely into those goals. "That class pushes my life message," he says, "that we should try to understand other cultures and not be so closed-minded. I have been the subject of negative stereotypes, and I just love how this class shows how these ways of thinking came about."

———

In 1900 fewer than 2 percent of Americans of traditional college age attended college. Today, new technologies and the information explosion are changing the workplace so drastically that to support themselves and their families adequately, most people will need some education beyond high school. College is so important that more than 67 percent of high school graduates (approximately eighteen million students) attend. Because higher education can be essential to your future earning power and your overall well-being, we are committed to providing a set of strategies you can use to do your best.

Rontavius knows how important a college education is to his future economic status, but he also knows that going to college presents him with many learning opportunities that he couldn't access any other way. He has already discovered how important it is to think deeply, and he has recognized that he has leadership skills. Rontavius is also encountering challenges, primarily time management, a challenge facing most college students. He has to work and also wants a personal life. Therefore, he wants strategies to help him better manage his limited time and maintain good grades.

This book is designed to help you explore all that higher education has to offer, discover your own strengths, and learn to be a good thinker, but it will also help you deal with common struggles. As you're settling into your new college routine, we want to welcome you to the challenging and rewarding world of higher education.

Why This Course and This Textbook Are Important

Since you are reading this textbook it probably means that you are enrolled in a first-year seminar or "college success" course. Both the course—possibly the most important course you will take—and this textbook—possibly the

ASSESSING YOUR STRENGTHS

Think about the topic of this chapter. Do you already have a good understanding of the benefits of college? Do you have a clear sense of purpose? What personal and career goals do you want to pursue in college? Describe the experience you have with setting goals and reaching them. If you are not quite ready to answer these questions yet, return to them as you read through the chapter.

_____

_____

_____

_____

SETTING GOALS

What are your most important objectives in learning the material in this chapter? Think about challenges you have had in the past with understanding what college is all about or setting personal goals. List three goals that relate to chapter material (e.g., I will be able to list reasons why college is important for me).

1. _____

_____

2. _____

_____

3. _____

_____

most important textbook you will read—are all about improving your chances for success in college and beyond. Before you start reading, however, you probably have some questions.

WHY SHOULD I TAKE THIS COURSE?

Research conducted by colleges and universities has found that first-year students are far more likely to be successful if they participate in courses and programs designed to teach them how to succeed in college. This course is designed to help you avoid some of the pitfalls—both academic and personal—that trip up many beginning students.

AREN'T ALL THE TOPICS IN THIS BOOK COMMON SENSE?

Whether you're living with your family or have a family of your own, college will challenge you to manage your time, get the most out of class, research and write good papers, take tests and exams well, and study effectively. So, although some of this information may be common sense, this book will provide new insights and information to help you make decisions that will lead to success.

WHAT AM I GOING TO GET OUT OF THIS COURSE?

This course will provide a supportive environment in which you can share your successes and your frustrations, get to know others who are beginning college, develop a lasting relationship with your instructor and some other students, and begin to think about your plans for life after college.

As college professors, researchers, and administrators with many years of experience working with first-year students, we're well aware that starting college can be challenging. We also know that if you apply the ideas in this book to your everyday life, you are likely to enjoy your time in college, graduate, and achieve your life goals. We'll also help you explore the purposes of college and your purposes for being here.

Let's stop and think about what purpose means. A firefighter who enters a burning building with people trapped inside has a clear purpose: He has been trained to get those people out safely. He is resolved and determined to fulfill the commitment of the job. The reason to go into the burning building is clear: to accomplish the objective of rescuing the people.

These words—determination, resolve, goal, reason, and objective—all relate to purpose. What will the training and education that you get in college teach you how to do? How will succeeding in college help you succeed in the job and life that you envision yourself having? What do you feel determined to be, to have, and to accomplish? As you consider your answers to these questions, you'll get closer to understanding your purpose for being in college and setting the right goals to achieve this purpose. And the more you keep the answers to these kinds of questions in the front of your mind, the more purposeful you will feel in what you do and the more motivated you will be to do it. In this course and in this book, we'll help you answer questions about purpose and equip you with strategies to help you achieve your goals.

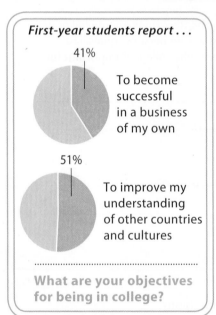

First-year students report . . .

41% To become successful in a business of my own

51% To improve my understanding of other countries and cultures

What are your objectives for being in college?

Data from all *First-year students report . . .* features from *The American Freshman: National Norms*, 2012

The College Experience

YOUR TURN

Work Together

Talk with a classmate to discover whether college life is what each of you thought it would be. Share what you have experienced and times when you have been pleasantly or unpleasantly surprised.

What is the college experience? Depending on who you are, your life circumstances, and why you decided to enroll, college can mean different things. College is often portrayed in books and movies as a place where young people live away from home in ivy-covered residence halls. We frequently see college depicted as a place with a major focus on big-time sports, heavy drinking, and partying. Yes, you'll find some of that at some colleges, but most students today don't move away from home, don't live on campus, and don't see much ivy. College is far more than

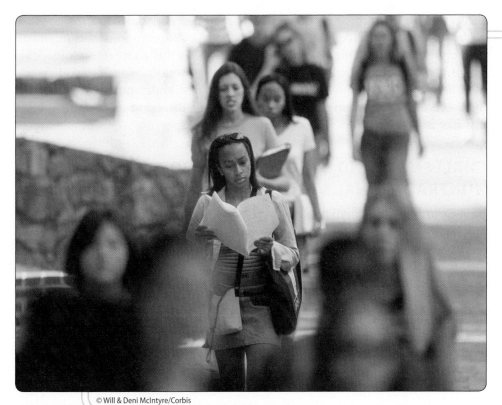
© Will & Deni McIntyre/Corbis

Little Fish in a Big Sea

In your first weeks in college you may feel alone. There may be more students on campus than in your home town. But your college will offer many ways for you to connect with other students, and soon you'll find new friends with whom you'll share much in common.

any single image you might carry around in your head. And college students today come from more walks of life than ever before.

TRADITIONAL STUDENTS: MAKING THE TRANSITION

If you are a traditional student, meaning that you just graduated from high school, the transition you are making means that you have to adjust to some distinct differences between high school and college. For instance, you will probably be part of a more diverse student body, not just in terms of race but also in terms of age, religion, political opinions, and life experiences. If you attend a large college or university, you might feel like a "number" and not as special as you felt in high school. You will have more potential friends to choose from, but familiar assumptions about people based on where they live, where they go to church, or what high school they attended might not apply to the new people you're meeting.

Now, you can choose from many more types of courses, managing your time is sure to be more complex because your classes will meet on various days and times, and you will have additional commitments, including work, family, activities, and sports. Your college classes might have many more students in them and meet for longer class periods than your high school classes. Tests are given less frequently in college—sometimes only twice a term—and you will most likely be required to do more writing in college than in high school. You will be encouraged to do original research and to investigate differing points of view on a topic. You will be expected to study outside of class, prepare assignments, do assigned reading, and be ready for in-class discussions. Your instructors might rely far less on textbooks and far more on lectures than your high school teachers did. As this chapter explores, college is also the time when you will begin making serious plans for your work life after college. Although you may have thought about potential careers in high school, determining a particular career direction takes on special urgency in college.

CHALLENGES AND OPPORTUNITIES FOR NONTRADITIONAL STUDENTS

Nontraditional students are adult students who might have experience in the job market and are likely to have a spouse or partner and children. They might be returning to college or beginning college for the first time. Nontraditional students face a set of challenges, such as trying to relate to younger students and juggling the responsibilities of work, caring for a family, and being in college. These students are likely facing a challenging lack of freedom in dealing with so many important competing responsibilities. Nontraditional students tend to have intrinsic motivation that comes with maturity and experience and an appreciation of the value of an education. They tend to approach being in college with a very clear purpose for why they are here.

Both traditional-aged students and older students bring certain strengths to their college experiences and can help each other. Older students have a lot of determination and a set of real-life experiences that they can relate to what they're learning. Eighteen- and nineteen-year-olds are comfortable with technology and social media and are pop culture experts. These kinds of strengths are important to the learning process in that they make it relevant to the lives of different kinds of students.

Is This You?

Are you an older or "adult" student? Are you having trouble juggling all your responsibilities and finding a time and place to do your out-of-class assignments? Pay extra attention to this section. Even with all the challenges, you'll find that college can be a life-changing experience for you.

COMMUNICATING WITH YOUR INSTRUCTORS

In college, whether you're a nontraditional student adjusting to less freedom than you've been used to or a traditional student adjusting to more freedom, you will find that your instructors are not going to tell you what, how, or when to study. In addition, they will rarely monitor your progress—you're on your own—but you will have more freedom to express views that are different from theirs. They will usually have private offices and keep regular office hours to be available to you. Check with your instructors to find out if you need to make an appointment before coming to their office. (Read the Tech Tip: E-Mail Etiquette, which shows you how to communicate with your instructors appropriately with e-mail.) You might be able to ask your instructors a quick question before or after class, but you will be able to get far more help by actually visiting their offices. By taking advantage of office hours, you will also let the instructor know that you are serious about learning. You can ask the instructor for direct help with any question or

TECH TIP E-MAIL ETIQUETTE

Whether your class is online or face to face, at some point you will need to communicate with your instructor via e-mail. Although you may prefer to use Facebook or Twitter, use e-mail to communicate with your instructors unless they tell you otherwise. Writing e-mails to your instructors is different from writing e-mails to your friends.

1 ▶ THE PROBLEM

You need help with an assignment and have to send your professor an e-mail, but you've never sent an e-mail to any kind of teacher before.

2 ▶ THE FIX

Take a few minutes to figure out what exactly you need to ask, jot down your main points, and then construct a clear and concise e-mail.

3 ▶ HOW TO DO IT

1. **Use a professional e-mail address.** Look at the example shown here and follow its format in your e-mail. It's best to use your college e-mail address so that your professor immediately recognizes you as a student. If you have to use another e-mail address, use a professional, simple address that includes your name.

2. **Make the subject line informative.** Your instructor might receive hundreds of e-mails every day, and a relevant subject like the name of the course or the assignment helps him or her prioritize your e-mail. A subject line like "Class" or "Question" isn't helpful, and a blank subject line usually goes to the instructor's spam folder.

3. **Address your instructor with respect.** Think about how you address your instructor in class, or look at your syllabus to see his or her preference. If an instructor uses *Doctor*, you should use *Doctor*. If you don't know the proper title, you can never go wrong with *Dear Professor*, plus your instructor's last name.

4. **Sign every e-mail with your full name, course number, and e-mail address.**

5. **When attaching files to your e-mail (a skill you should have), use widely accepted file formats like .doc, .docx, or .pdf.** Also, be sure that your last name is included in the file name you use. See the example shown.

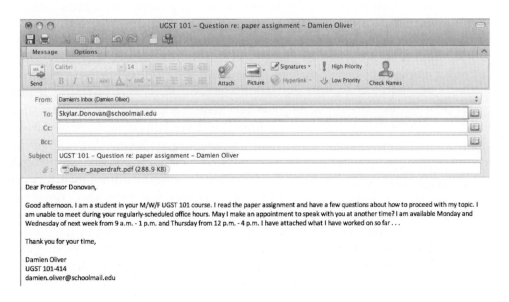

UGST 101 – Question re: paper assignment – Damien Oliver

| Message | Options |

From: Damien's Inbox (Damien Oliver)
To: Skylar.Donovan@schoolmail.edu
Cc:
Bcc:
Subject: UGST 101 – Question re: paper assignment – Damien Oliver
📎 : oliver_paperdraft.pdf (288.9 KB)

Dear Professor Donovan,

Good afternoon. I am a student in your M/W/F UGST 101 course. I read the paper assignment and have a few questions about how to proceed with my topic. I am unable to meet during your regularly-scheduled office hours. May I make an appointment to speak with you at another time? I am available Monday and Wednesday of next week from 9 a.m. - 1 p.m. and Thursday from 12 p.m. - 4 p.m. I have attached what I have worked on so far . . .

Thank you for your time,

Damien Oliver
UGST 101-414
damien.oliver@schoolmail.edu

misunderstanding that you have. You might also want to ask some questions about the instructor's educational career and particular research interests. Many students develop close relationships with their instructors, relationships that can be important to all, both now and in the future.

WHY COLLEGE IS IMPORTANT TO OUR SOCIETY

College is an established process designed to further formal education so that students who attend and graduate will be prepared for certain roles in society. Today, those roles are found especially in what has become known as the "information economy," which means that most college graduates are going to be earning their living by creating, managing, and using information. Because the amount of available information expands all the time, your college classes can't possibly teach you all you need to know for the future. The most important skill you will need to learn in college is how to keep learning throughout your life.

American society values higher education, which explains why the United States has so many colleges and universities, currently more than 4,400. College is the primary way in which people achieve upward social mobility or the ability to attain a higher standard of living. That might accurately describe your purpose for being in college: to attain a higher standard of living. In earlier centuries a high standard of living was almost always a function of family background. Either you were born into power and money or you spent your life working for others who had power and money. In most countries today, however, receiving a college degree helps level the playing field for everyone. A college degree can minimize or eliminate differences due to background, race, ethnicity, family income level, national origin, immigration status, family lineage, and personal connections. Simply put, college participation is about ensuring that more people have the opportunity to be evaluated on the basis of merit rather than family status, money, or other forms of privilege. It makes achieving the American dream possible. See the information in Figure 1.1.

College is also important because it is society's primary means of preparing citizens for leadership roles. Without a college degree, a person will find it difficult to be a leader in a community, a company, a profession, or a military unit.

Another reason students get a four-year college degree is to prepare them for continuing their education in a graduate or professional school. If you want to become a medical doctor, dentist, lawyer, or college professor, a four-year college degree is just the beginning, but it is a required step on the path to such professions. Let's say you aspire to be a pharmacist and are planning to get a bachelor's degree in chemistry. Your primary purpose for your degree in chemistry is to gain admittance into pharmacy school. Perhaps you have also considered that if your plans should change, having a degree in chemistry will get your foot in the door in several different industries, so another purpose for your degree is having an edge in the job market upon graduation.

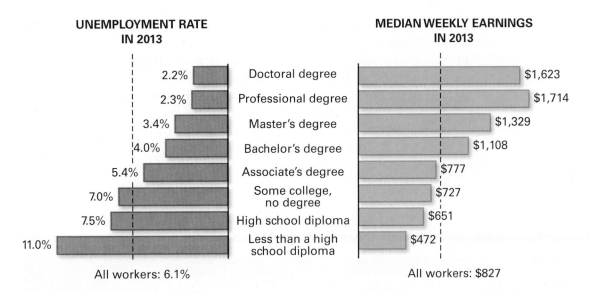

FIGURE 1.1

Education Pays

Earning a college degree will improve your earning potential. This figure breaks down the unemployment rates and weekly earnings according to education level. Use this information as motivation for making the most of college. The more education you have, the more likely you are to be employed, and the higher your earnings will be.

Source: U.S. Department of Labor, Bureau of Labor Statistics, *Current Population Survey*, 2013.

WHY COLLEGE IS IMPORTANT FOR YOU

College is about thinking, and it will help you understand how to become a "critical thinker," someone who doesn't believe everything that he or she hears or reads but instead looks for evidence before forming an opinion. Developing critical-thinking skills will empower you to make sound decisions throughout your life.

Although college is often thought of as a time when traditional-age students become young adults, we realize that many of you are already adults. Whatever your age, college can be a time when you take some risks, learn new things, and meet new and different people, all in a relatively safe environment. It's OK to experiment in college, within limits, because that's what college is designed for.

College will provide numerous opportunities for developing a variety of social networks, both formal and informal. These networks will help you make friends and develop alliances with faculty members and fellow students who share your interests and goals. Social networking sites (such as Facebook and Twitter) provide a way to enrich your real-life social networks in college.

College definitely can and should be fun, and we hope it will be for you. You will meet new people, go to athletic events and parties, build camaraderie with new friends, and feel a sense of school spirit. Many college graduates relive memories of college days throughout their lives, fanatically root for their institution's athletic teams, return for homecoming and class reunions, and encourage their own children to attend their alma mater. In fact, you might be a legacy student, someone whose parents or grandparents attended the same institution as you do.

In addition to being fun, college is a lot of work. Being a college student means spending many hours studying each week, staying up late at night, taking high-stakes exams, and possibly working harder than you ever have. For many students college becomes much like a job, with defined duties, expectations, and obligations. Most important is that college will be a set of experiences that will help you to further define your goals and achieve your own purpose.

OUTCOMES OF THE COLLEGE EXPERIENCE

In its report "Education Pays 2013," the College Board includes the following as outcomes of having a college education:

> You will be more marketable professionally, have a more stable job history, achieve more promotions, be more likely to receive health insurance and pension benefits from employers, and be less likely to be involuntarily unemployed than those without a college education.

> During a forty-year full-time working life, you will earn 65 percent more than high school graduates. You will have an increased chance of moving up the socioeconomic ladder.

> You will learn how to accumulate knowledge.

> You will be more likely to seek appropriate information before making a decision. You are less likely to be duped, conned, or swindled. Seeking information will also help you realize how our lives are shaped by global, local, political, social, psychological, economic, environmental, and physical forces.

> You will grow intellectually through interactions with cultures, languages, ethnic groups, religions, nationalities, and socioeconomic groups other than your own. You will participate more in and enjoy the arts.

> You will gain self-esteem and self-confidence, which will help you realize how you might make a difference in the world. You are more likely to become a leader in your community and employment settings.

> You will tend to be more flexible in your views, more future-oriented, more willing to appreciate differences of opinion, and more interested in political and public affairs. You will be more likely to be elected to public office.

> If you have children, you will likely have fewer than nongraduates, be more involved with their school lives and spend more time with them, and your children will be more likely to have greater learning potential, which in turn will help them achieve more in life. You will be more likely to stay married longer to the same person.

> You will be an efficient consumer, save more money, make better investments, and be more likely to spend money on your home and on intellectual and cultural interests as well as on your children.

> You will be better able to deal with bureaucracies, the legal system, tax laws, and advertising claims.

> You will be more involved in education, hobbies, and civic and community affairs.

> You will be more concerned with wellness and preventive health care and incur fewer health care costs. Through diet, exercise, stress management, a positive attitude, and other factors, you will live longer and suffer fewer disabilities. You will be less likely to be obese, use tobacco products, or become dependent on alcohol or drugs.

Source: trends.collegeboard.org/education-pays.

Exploring Purpose and Setting Goals

You might think that you know exactly what you want to do with your life and where you want to go from here. Or, like many students, you might be struggling to balance being in college, working, and having a life. It is possible that as you discover more about yourself and your abilities, your purpose for coming to college will change. In fact, the vast majority of college students change their academic major at least once during the college years, and some students find that they need to transfer to another institution to meet their academic goals.

How would you describe your reasons for being in college and at this particular college? Perhaps you, like the vast majority of college students, see college as the pathway to a good job. Maybe you are in college to train or retrain for an occupation, or maybe you have recently experienced an upheaval in your life. Perhaps you are here to fulfill a lifelong dream of getting an education, or maybe you are bored or in a rut and see college as a way out of it. As it happens, many students enter college without a purpose that has been clearly thought out. They have just been swept along by life's events, and now here they are.

GETTING STARTED

Think about how you define success. Is success about money, friendship, or power? Is it about achieving excellence in college and beyond or about finding a sense of purpose in your life? For most people, success is a combination of all these factors and more. Although luck or "who you know" may play a role in success, first and foremost it will be the result of intentional steps you take. So, in your quest for success, where do you start?

Identify Your Personal Strengths.   Do you like to talk, deal with conflict, and stand up for yourself? Are you a good reader? If your answers to these questions are "yes," you may want to consider a career in the legal profession. Are you a good science student, and do you enjoy working with your hands? If so, you might want to think about dentistry. Your campus career center can help you discover your own unique strengths—and weaknesses—which can influence your direction as you explore career choices.

Ask Yourself Tough Questions.   Am I here to find out who I am and to study a subject that I am truly passionate about, regardless of whether it leads to a career? Am I here to engage in an academic program that provides an array of possibilities when I graduate? Am I here to prepare myself for a graduate program or for immediate employment? Am I here to obtain specific training in a field that I am committed to? Am I here to gain specific skills for a job I already have?

Establish Goals for Today, This Week, This Year, and Beyond.
Although some students prefer to "go with the flow" and let life happen to them, those students are more likely to flounder and less likely to achieve success in college or in a career. So, instead of "going with the flow" and simply reacting to what college and life present, think instead about how you can take more control over the decisions and choices you make now that lay the foundation for

Score!

Do you have friends who are lucky or have a knack for getting what they want? What seems to be luck can often be a function of careful planning and setting short- and long-term goals.

the achievement of future life goals. Even though it is easy to make vague plans for the future, you need to determine which short-term steps are necessary if those plans are to become a reality.

College is an ideal time for you to begin setting and fulfilling short- and long-term goals. A short-term goal might be to read twenty pages from your history text twice a week, anticipating an exam that will cover the first hundred pages of the book. A long-term goal might be to begin predicting which elective college courses you could choose that would help you attain your career goals.

Thinking about a career might seem unrelated to some of the general education courses you are required to take in your first year. Sometimes it's hard to see the connection between a history or literature course and what you want to do with the rest of your life. If you're open to learning, however, you may discover potential areas of interest that you may never have considered before, areas of interest that may lead you to discover a new career path.

SETTING SMART GOALS

Follow these guidelines to set some short-term goals and consider how they fall within the framework of setting goals that are *specific, measurable, attainable, relevant,* and achievable within a given *time* (SMART).[1] (Figure 1.2 gives you a chance to practice.)

1. Be specific about what you want to achieve and when.
2. State your goal in measurable terms.
3. Be sure that the goal is attainable. Allow enough time to pursue it. If you don't have the necessary skills, strengths, and resources to achieve your goal, change it to one that is more appropriate for you. Be sure that you really want to reach the goal. Don't set out to work toward something only because you want to please others.
4. Know how the goal is relevant to your life and why the goal matters. Be sure that your goal helps your larger plan and can give you a sense of moving forward.
5. Consider the time frame and whether the goal is achievable within the period you desire. Consider the difficulties you might have. Plan for ways

[1]T. Doran, "There's a S.M.A.R.T. Way to Write Management's Goals and Objectives," *Management Review* 70, no. 11 (1981): 35–36.

Goal Navigator

FIGURE 1.2

Practice Setting SMART Goals

Using this chart, try to set one goal in each of the areas listed: academic, career, personal, and financial. Follow the goal through time, from immediate to long term. An example is provided for you.

Types of Goals	Immediate (this week)	Short Term (this term)	Long Term (this year)
Example: Academic	I will list all of my tests and project due dates on my academic calendar.	I will make a file folder to keep my own test and exam grades in case there is a discrepancy with my final course grades.	I will search online for graduate school programs in my field to determine if I have the grades and scores to be admitted.
Academic			
Career			
Personal			
Financial			

you might deal with problems. Decide which goal comes next. How will you begin? Create steps and a time line for reaching your next goal.

For instance, let's assume that after you graduate you think that you might want to work in an underdeveloped country, perhaps spending some time in the Peace Corps. What are some short-term goals that would help you reach this long-term objective? One goal might be to take courses focused on different countries or cultures, but that goal isn't very specific and doesn't state a particular time period. A much more specific goal would be to take one course each year to help you build a body of knowledge about other countries and cultures. An even more specific goal would be to review the course catalog, identify the courses you want to take, and list them on a personal time line.

Before working toward any long-term goal, it's important to be realistic and honest with yourself. Is it your goal—one that you yourself value and desire to pursue—or is it a goal that a parent or friend argued was right for you? Given your abilities and interests, is the goal realistic? Remember that dreaming up long-term goals is the easy part. To reach your goals, you need to be specific and systematic about the steps you will take today, this week, and throughout your college experience.

Academic Planning

If you have a goal to drive across the United States, you could, in theory, hop in a car that hasn't been given a thumbs-up by a mechanic and travel without a map and itinerary and without a carefully packed bag or planned budget.

You could simply follow road signs and hope for the best with weather, lodging, money, and the condition of the car. You might make it to your destination, but what is likely to go wrong? How would some planning have improved the journey? It's the same thing with higher education. Some preparation and a road map will lead to a smooth ride and help you reach your destination.

Academic planning is a vital step in your college career, and it should be an ongoing process that starts on day one. Once you lay a foundation for your studies, you'll save time and money, avoid missing credits, and take ownership of your curriculum. You'll also stay motivated with a clear sense of how each step in your academic plan—each mile of your journey—contributes to your purpose for being in college. It's no coincidence that students who engage in academic planning are more likely to stay in school. They are the people who know where they're going and how to get there. They have set their goals, and they know what it takes to achieve them.

CHOOSING A MAJOR

Even before you have figured out your own purpose for college, you might be required to select a program of study also referred to as a major, an area of study like psychology, engineering, education, or nursing. Selecting a major is one step in academic planning. In every major students take a variety of courses; some are directly related to the area of study, whereas others are general education and elective courses. For example, all students should take college-level math and English courses as part of general education, but they can choose electives depending on their interests.

Many students change majors as they better understand their strengths and weaknesses, learn more about career options, and become interested in different areas of study. Some colleges and universities allow you to be undecided for a while or to select liberal arts as your major until you make a decision about what to study.

Although it's OK to be undecided, planning your major and your college curriculum as soon as possible saves valuable time and resources. Even if you're on financial aid, you're not going to have an unlimited amount of cash. If you randomly take courses without a specific goal in mind, your tuition funds could dry up before your plan takes shape. Therefore, it's essential to have a strategy for your program of study. Start by building a solid base of general courses that could qualify you for a few different majors, but leave time in your schedule to explore other subjects that grab your interest. Do you like math? Try an accounting or economics class. Love *CSI*? Sign up for Criminology 101 or the equivalent. An academic adviser or counselor can provide you with proper information and guidance to make a decision about your major.

WORKING WITH AN ACADEMIC ADVISER

Before you register for classes next term, sit down for a strategy session with your academic adviser. On most campuses, you'll be assigned an adviser (usually an instructor or staff person in your field). Some colleges offer special advisory centers run by professional advisers. A good adviser can help you choose courses, decide on a major, weigh career possibilities, and map

Center on Education and the Workforce, *Hard Times: Not All College Degrees Are Created Equal*

IN THE MEDIA

With a 7.9 percent unemployment rate among college graduates, is getting that degree worth it? "Hard Times," a May 2013 study from the Georgetown University Center on Education and the Workforce, indicates the following:

1. Choice of major substantially affects employment prospects and earnings.

2. People who make technology are better off than people who use technology.

3. In general, majors that are linked to occupations have better employment prospects than majors focused on general skills.

Visit the complete study at **cew.georgetown.edu /unemployment2013/**.

For Reflection: Have you selected a major? If so, is your selection based on the amount of money you're likely to earn in a related career? If you haven't yet chosen a major field, will potential earnings affect your choice? Why or why not?

---

out your degree and certificate requirements. He or she can also recommend instructors and help you simplify all aspects of your academic life. So it's important to meet with your adviser right away. Here are a few ways to make sure that your first meeting is a valuable experience.

- **Prepare by looking at the course catalog, thinking about the available majors, and familiarizing yourself with campus resources.** If you haven't decided on a major, investigate opportunities for taking an aptitude test or self-assessments to help you narrow down your options and ask your adviser about these tests during your meeting. (Read more about self-assessments and self-exploration in this chapter.) The early days of college are critical; once classes start, you might not have time for in-depth research.

- **Prepare materials to bring to the meeting.** Even if you submitted one with your application, take along a copy of your academic transcript. The transcript, your complete high school record, is an important tool. It shows your academic adviser where you've been, your academic strengths, and where your interests lie.

- **Make a list of majors that appeal to you.** Academic advisers love it when students come prepared. It shows that you're passionate and taking your future seriously.

First-year students report . . .

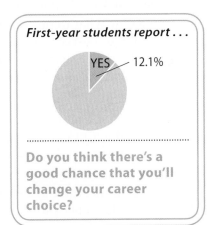

YES — 12.1%

Do you think there's a good chance that you'll change your career choice?

- **Map out your time frame and goals.** Do you plan to enroll full-time or part-time? If you're at a four-year college or university, when do you plan to graduate and with what degree? Are you planning to go to graduate school to finish your studies? If you are at a two-year college, do you want an associate degree or a certificate, and do you plan to transfer to a four-year institution?

- **Know the right questions to ask.** Once you've chosen a major, you'll need to understand how to move forward in your academic program to meet the necessary requirements. Fortunately, the process is straightforward. You will have prerequisites, the core courses that you need to take before you can enroll in upper-level classes in your major. Your major may also have corequisites, courses that you have to take in conjunction with other courses during the same term (a chemistry lab alongside your chemistry class). So, with this knowledge under your belt, here is what you need to find out:

  1. How many credits must I take each term to graduate on time? (Note: If you are on financial aid, are doing a work-study program, or are a college athlete, you may have to take a minimum number of credits per term.)

  2. What are the prerequisites for my major? Corequisites?

  3. If I've taken any Advanced Placement credits or exams, can I use them to fulfill some of my major's requirements?

  4. What career opportunities will I have once I graduate? What will the salary potential look like?

- **Know what to take away from your meeting.** Have in hand a printout of your current course schedule and plans for classes that you might take in the next term and beyond. At many institutions, you and your adviser will set up a five- to seven-term plan online.

- **Know these rules of thumb about selecting your classes:**

  1. Most full-time students take four to six courses a term. Most classes don't meet every day. With that in mind, decide which classes you want to take, find out which days and times they meet, and make sure they don't overlap.

  2. To get the classes you want, make sure to register as early as possible, in person or online.

  3. Resist the temptation to cram all your classes into one or two days. It's better to aim for a manageable workload, so spread your classes over the week.

  4. Go for a mix of hard and easy classes. (Especially at the beginning, you might not realize how challenging college classes can be or how much outside work they entail. If you load up on organic chemistry, Russian 101, and advanced thermodynamics, your grades and general well-being could suffer.)

- **Know what to do if your academic adviser isn't very helpful.** If you think that you and your adviser are not a good match, go to the admissions office and ask to be assigned to a different adviser. Alternately, drop by the campus counseling center for assistance. But whatever you do, don't throw in the towel. Academic planning is so critical to your success in college that it's worth persevering until you find an adviser with whom you feel comfortable.

■ **Set up subsequent meetings with your academic adviser.** Touch base with your adviser at least once a term if not more often. It's important to stay connected and make sure that you're on a positive track. Programs change requirements occasionally, so it's smart to touch base to make any necessary adjustments. Here are some questions to ask your adviser as you check in:

1. Have there been any changes to my program of study?

2. If I want to officially withdraw from a class, will I be penalized down the road?

3. Am I still taking classes in the right order?

4. What courses do I need to take to satisfy the major requirements at the institution where I plan to transfer?

5. For those students who are considering graduate school: Am I meeting the criteria for graduate school, and will my grades qualify me for my program of interest?

> **YOUR TURN**
>
> **Write and Reflect**
>
> Write some synonyms for the word *motivation*. Then describe what have you learned about academic planning that has increased your motivation for working closely with an academic adviser. Finally, describe at least three pitfalls you might fall into when it comes to choosing your major or planning your program of study if you don't take academic planning seriously. How can these possible negative consequences increase your motivation to plan well for your first meeting with your adviser?

The Role of Self-Exploration in Career Planning

Are you self-aware and confident in your skills and abilities? Perhaps you have a friend who always seems to know exactly what he or she wants or can accomplish. How well you know yourself and how effectively you can do the things you need to do are integral to your success, not only as a college student but also as a person. Self-assessment, or the process of gathering information about yourself so as to make an informed career decision, is a good first step in clarifying your academic and career goals. Students enter college at varying levels of self-awareness, and some even have a strong self-image, but most of us continue the process of defining (or redefining) ourselves throughout life. Although you might know some activities you like to do and which activities you are good at doing, you may lack a clear idea of how knowledge of self aligns with different career possibilities.

> **YOUR TURN**
>
> **Discuss**
>
> What kinds of jobs have you had, either for pay or as a volunteer? Which of your jobs was your favorite? Which did you dislike? Be prepared to discuss your ideas in class and offer thoughts about what your previous work experiences tell you about your preferences for work in the future.

FACTORS THAT AFFECT CAREER CHOICES

Engaging in self-exploration is a critical step in the career development process. We will continue the exploration process in several useful ways and consider these attributes with respect to possible careers.

Values.   Values—things that we feel strongly about—are critically important in our lives and careers. Our values are formed through our life experiences. In the context of career planning, values generally refer to things such as job security, money, structure, and a regular schedule, or flexibility, excitement, independence, and variety.

Skills.   The ability to do something well can usually be improved with practice. Each of us has a different skill set that we bring to any situation, and it is important to know both your assets and deficiencies. Skills typically fall into three categories:

1. Personal skills come naturally or are learned. Examples of these skills are honesty, punctuality, being a team-player or motivator, and managing conflict.
2. Workplace skills are gained through work experience, training, or professional development opportunities. Examples include designing Web sites and bookkeeping.
3. As described in more detail on page 21, transferable skills are gained through your previous jobs, hobbies, or even everyday life. Examples include planning events, motivating others, attention to detail, and organization.

In today's job market identifying and improving your existing skills will help you be competitive for new and different positions. By knowing your skill set you can link your skills to career possibilities.

aptitude Natural talent or an ability an individual has acquired through life experience, study, or training.

Aptitudes.   Your inherent strengths, or **aptitudes**, are often part of your biological heritage or are the result of early training. Aptitude is your acquired or natural ability for learning and proficiency in a particular area, which makes it easier for you to learn or do certain things.

Personality.   Your personality makes you who you are, and it can't be ignored when you make career decisions. The quiet, orderly, calm, detail-oriented person will probably make a different work choice than the aggressive, outgoing, argumentative person will.

Life Goals and Work Values.   Each of us defines success and satisfaction in our own way. The process is complex and very personal. Two factors influence our conclusions about success and happiness: (1) knowing that we are achieving the life goals we've set for ourselves and (2) finding that we gain satisfaction from what we're receiving from our work. If your values conflict with the organizational values where you work, you might be in for trouble.

Interests.   From birth we develop particular interests. These interests help shape, and might even define, our career paths. Interests develop from experiences and beliefs and will continue to develop and change throughout our lives. Many people believe that exploring this attribute—interests—is the best path to choosing an academic major and ultimately a career.

EXPLORING YOUR INTERESTS

Most students want their major to lead directly into a career, although it doesn't always happen that way. You might be encouraged to select a major in a subject about which you are really passionate. Most academic advisers would agree. Try a major that you think you'll like and that makes sense given the attributes described above—your values, strengths, aptitudes, skills, personality, goals, and interests—and see what develops. Take advantage of self-assessments available to help you learn more about yourself.

John Holland, a psychologist at Johns Hopkins University, developed a number of tools and concepts that can help you organize the various dimensions of yourself so that you can identify potential career choices (see Table 1.1). Holland suggests that people are separated into six general categories based on differences in their interests, skills, values, and personality characteristics, in short, on their preferred approaches to life. Holland's system organizes career fields into the same six categories. Career fields are grouped according to what a particular career field requires of a person (the skills and personality characteristics most commonly associated with success in those fields) and what rewards those fields provide (interests and values most commonly associated with satisfaction). As you view Table 1.1, highlight or note characteristics you believe that you have as well as those that are less closely matched.

Your career choices ultimately will involve a complex assessment of the factors that are most important to you. To display the relationship between career fields and the potential conflicts people face as they consider them, Holland's model is commonly presented in a hexagonal shape (Figure 1.3). The closer the types, the closer the relationships among the career fields; the farther apart the types, the more conflict between the career fields. Holland's model can help you address the questions surrounding career choice in two ways. First, you can begin to identify many career fields that are consistent with what you know about yourself. Once you have identified potential fields, you can use the career center at your college to get more information about those fields, such as daily activities for specific jobs, interests and abilities required, preparation required for entry, working conditions, salary and benefits, and employment outlook. Second, you can begin to identify the harmony or conflicts in your career choices. Doing so will help you analyze the reasons for your career decisions and be more confident as you make choices.

This book will introduce you to a variety of self-assessments designed to provide a clearer picture of who you are as an individual. These assessments are designed as tools to assist the career exploration process. Never, ever think that you have to make a decision based on the results of only one assessment. Career choices are complex and involve many factors; furthermore, these decisions are reversible. It is important not only to take time to talk over your interests with a career counselor, but also to shadow individuals in the occupations that interest you. Obtaining a better understanding of what an occupation entails in terms of skills, commitment, and opportunity will help you make informed decisions about your own career choices.

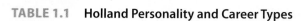

TABLE 1.1 Holland Personality and Career Types

Category	Personality Characteristics	Career Fields
Realistic (R)	These people describe themselves as concrete, down-to-earth, and practical doers. They exhibit competitive/assertive behavior and show interest in activities that require motor coordination, skill, and physical strength. They prefer situations involving action solutions rather than tasks involving verbal or interpersonal skills, and they like taking a concrete approach to problem solving rather than relying on abstract theory. They tend to be interested in scientific or mechanical areas rather than the arts.	Environmental engineer, electrical contractor, industrial arts teacher, navy officer, fitness director, package engineer, electronics technician, Web designer
Investigative (I)	These people describe themselves as analytical, rational, and logical problem solvers. They value intellectual stimulation and intellectual achievement, and they prefer to think rather than to act and to organize and understand rather than to persuade. They usually have a strong interest in physical, biological, or social sciences. They are less apt to be people oriented.	Urban planner, chemical engineer, bacteriologist, flight engineer, genealogist, laboratory technician, marine scientist, nuclear medical technologist, obstetrician, quality-control technician, computer programmer, environmentalist, physician, college professor
Artistic (A)	These people describe themselves as creative, innovative, and independent. They value self-expression and relating with others through artistic expression and are also emotionally expressive. They dislike structure, preferring tasks involving personal or physical skills. They resemble investigative people but are more interested in the cultural or the aesthetic than the scientific.	Architect, film editor/director, actor, cartoonist, interior decorator, fashion model, graphic communications specialist, journalist, editor, orchestra leader, public relations specialist, sculptor, media specialist, librarian, reporter
Social (S)	These people describe themselves as kind, caring, helpful, and understanding of others. They value helping and making a contribution. They satisfy their needs in one-to-one or small-group interaction using strong speaking skills to teach, counsel, or advise. They are drawn to close interpersonal relationships and are less apt to engage in intellectual or extensive physical activity.	Nurse, teacher, social worker, genetic counselor, marriage counselor, rehabilitation counselor, school superintendent, geriatric specialist, insurance claims specialist, minister, travel agent, guidance counselor, convention planner
Enterprising (E)	These people describe themselves as assertive, risk taking, and persuasive. They value prestige, power, and status and are more inclined than other types to pursue it. They use verbal skills to supervise, lead, direct, and persuade rather than to support or guide. They are interested in people and in achieving organizational goals.	Banker, city manager, FBI agent, health administrator, judge, labor arbitrator, salary and wage administrator, insurance salesperson, sales engineer, lawyer, sales representative, marketing manager
Conventional (C)	These people describe themselves as neat, orderly, detail oriented, and persistent. They value order, structure, prestige, and status and possess a high degree of self-control. They are not opposed to rules and regulations. They are skilled in organizing, planning, and scheduling and are interested in data and people.	Accountant, statistician, census enumerator, data processor, hospital administrator, insurance administrator, office manager, underwriter, auditor, personnel specialist, database manager, abstractor/indexer

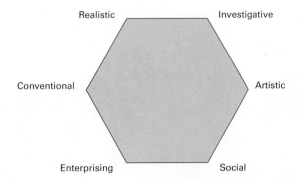

Realistic   Investigative

Conventional   Artistic

Enterprising   Social

FIGURE 1.3
Holland's Hexagonal Model of Career Fields

A Shared Purpose of College Students: Getting the Skills That Employers Seek

One of the many important purposes and outcomes of your college experience is gaining a combination of knowledge and skills. Two types of skills are essential to employment and to life: content skills and transferable skills.

Content skills are intellectual or "hard" skills that you gain in your academic field. They include writing proficiency, computer literacy, and foreign language skills. Computing literacy is now a core skill like reading, writing, and mathematics. You can apply all this specific knowledge to jobs in any field or occupation.

Transferable skills are skills that are general and apply to or transfer to many settings. Included are communication skills such as being a clear and persuasive speaker, listening attentively, and writing well as well as interpersonal skills such as relating to others, motivating others to participate, and easing conflict between coworkers. Transferable skills are valuable to many kinds of employers and professions. They give you flexibility in your career planning because you gain transferable skills through a lot of activities. For

content skills
Cognitive, intellectual, or "hard" skills acquired as one gains mastery in an academic field. They include writing proficiency, computer literacy, and foreign language skills.

transferable skills
General skills that apply to or transfer to a variety of settings. Examples include solid oral and listening abilities, leadership skills, critical thinking, and problem solving.

JOB CANDIDATE SKILLS AND QUALITIES RANKED AS VERY IMPORTANT OR EXTREMELY IMPORTANT BY EMPLOYERS

> Ability to work in a team structure

> Ability to make decisions and solve problems

> Ability to plan, organize, and prioritize work

> Ability to verbally communicate with persons inside and outside the organization

> Ability to obtain and process information

> Ability to analyze quantitative data

> Technical knowledge related to the job

Therefore, the ideal candidate is a team player and good communicator who can make decisions, solve problems, and prioritize.

Source: National Association of Colleges and Employers, *Job Outlook 2014* (Bethlehem, PA: National Association of Colleges and Employers, 2013).

© Sandy Huffaker/Corbis

Making Connections

Some career fairs may be specific to disciplines such as health care, information technology, or business. Others may be specific to the audience such as this career fair for military veterans. Attending these events is part of planning for your career and gives job candidates, present or future, the opportunity to make a strong first impression with potential employers.

example, volunteer work, involvement in a student professional organization or club, and having hobbies or interests can all build teamwork, leadership, interpersonal awareness, and effective communication abilities. Internships and career-related work are also valuable opportunities to practice these skills in the real world.

GETTING EXPERIENCE

One way to develop the skills that employers seek is to get relevant work experience, be it unpaid, paid, or both. Many nontraditional students have an advantage in this regard. To gain some unpaid work experience while you are in college, you can participate in experiential learning opportunities such as service learning, volunteer activities, internships and co-op programs, and competitions and projects designed for students.

service learning Unpaid volunteer service that is embedded in courses across the curriculum.

co-op programs Programs offered at many institutions that allow students to work in their field of study while enrolled in college. They offer valuable experiences and an excellent preview of what work in the chosen field is actually like. Also called cooperative education.

- **Service-learning and volunteer activities. Service learning** allows you to apply what you learn in class to actual practice. Some instructors build service learning into their courses, but if this option isn't available, consider volunteering! A little time spent each week can provide many personal and professional rewards, and it allows you to continue learning about yourself, your interests, and abilities.

- **Internships and co-op programs.** What students learn in the classroom can be applied to the real world through internships and **co-op programs**, giving students an opportunity to gain relevant work experience. As mentioned, employers want to see that you have experience in the professional workplace and have gained an understanding of the skills and knowledge necessary to succeed. Many majors offer academic credit for internships. Check with your academic department and your career center to find out what internships are available in your major. Remember that with one or more internships on your résumé, you'll be a step ahead of students who ignore this valuable experience. Through co-operative education you will alternate work experience and classes. You can also have paid work assignments that provide you with an opportunity to apply what you learn to the workplace.

- **Student projects and competitions.** In many fields students engage in competitions based on what they have learned in the classroom, sometimes competing against teams from other colleges. In the process they learn teamwork, communication, and problem-solving skills.

Paid opportunities to get work experience can support your college goals, provide you with the financial assistance to complete your courses, and help you structure your time so that you are a better time manager. Many options on and off campus allow you to gain work experience and a little cash. For example:

- **Work study.** Work study is a form of federal financial aid that provides part-time employment to help with college expenses. Once you accept the work-study award on your award notification, you will be sent information regarding the steps you should take for getting a job on campus. Generally, you will have to interview for a position. Check with your college's financial aid office or career center to get a list of available jobs and to get help preparing your application materials and getting ready for the interview.

- **On-campus employment.** Often you will see students on campus who are studying while they work. This setup is one benefit of on-campus employment. These positions generally provide more flexibility and more opportunities to connect with instructors and administrators you can later consult as mentors or ask for reference letters. In addition, your "boss" will understand that you occasionally need time off to study or take exams. Students who work on campus are more likely to graduate from college than are students who work off campus, so this benefit in itself is the most rewarding outcome of all!

MCT via Getty Images

Trash or Treasure?

This student intern in the campus recycling department empties a bin of food into a container that will be sent to an off-campus composting center. Imagine what he is learning about the business of recycling, composting, food waste reduction, and the possible applications to areas like environmental studies.

■ **Off-campus employment.** The best places to start looking for off-campus jobs are your campus career center and occasionally your financial aid office. They might have listings or Web sites with off-campus employment opportunities. Feel free to speak to a career counselor for suggestions.

Holding a job while in college has many benefits, but overextending yourself can also interfere with your college success and your ability to attend class, do your homework, and participate in many other valuable parts of college life such as group study. Take some time to determine how involved you are able to be and stay within reasonable limits. Students who work in paid jobs more than fifteen hours a week have a lower chance of success in college than those who work fewer hours.

Although getting a good job when you graduate isn't the only reason to get a college degree, it is a desired outcome for most students and their families. Whatever your career interests may be, start now to investigate related employment trends and prospects. The experts in your campus career center are available to help you to learn more about future employment opportunities and your own interests and aptitudes so that when you graduate you will be prepared for life and work beyond college.

CHECKLIST FOR SUCCESS

GETTING OFF TO THE RIGHT START

☐ **Keep up with your weekly schedule and do your work on time.** Get a paper or electronic calendar and use it consistently to keep track of assignments and appointments.

☐ **Be on time for class.** If you are frequently late, you give your instructors and fellow students the unspoken message that you don't think that the class is important.

☐ **If you are a full-time student, limit the hours you work. If you must work, look for a job on campus.** Students who work a reasonable number of hours per week (about fifteen) and especially those who work on campus are more likely to do well in college than students who work more hours or off campus.

☐ **Improve your study habits.** Find the most effective methods for reading textbooks, listening, taking notes, studying, and using information resources.

☐ **Use the academic skills center, library, and campus career center.** These essential services can help you be a better student and plan for your future.

☐ **Learn to think critically.** If you don't carefully examine and evaluate what you see, read, and hear, you're not really learning.

☐ **Strive to improve your writing and speaking.** The more you write and speak in public, the easier these skills will become now and in the future.

☐ **Speak up in class.** Research indicates that you will usually remember more about what goes on in class when you get involved than when you are not.

☐ **Learn from criticism.** Criticism can be helpful to your learning. If you get a low grade, meet with your instructor to discuss how you can improve.

☐ **Study with a group.** Research shows that students who study in groups often earn the highest grades and have the fewest academic problems.

☐ **Become engaged in campus activities.** Visit the student activities office, join a club or organization that interests you, or participate in community service.

☐ **Meet with your instructors outside the class.** Instructors generally have office hours; successful students use them.

☐ **Find a competent and caring academic adviser or counselor.** Prepare thoroughly for your first meeting with your adviser, know what questions to ask, and keep in touch throughout each term. Doing so will lead to successful academic planning.

☐ **Take your health seriously.** How much you sleep, what you eat, whether you exercise, and how well you deal with stress will affect your college success.

☐ **Set both short-term and long-term goals.** You will be far more likely to succeed in college if your goals for today, tomorrow, and four years from now are clear.

☐ **Have realistic expectations.** If you are disappointed in your grades, remember that college is a new experience and that your grades will probably improve if you continue to apply yourself.

BUILD YOUR EXPERIENCE 1 2 3 4

1 STAY ON TRACK

Successful college students stay focused. They "stay on track." They know what they have to do to be successful, they set goals, and they monitor their progress toward their goals.

Reflect on what you have learned about college success in this chapter and how you are going to apply the chapter information or strategies in college and in your career. List your ideas.

1. _____

_____

_____

2. _____

_____

_____

3. _____

_____

_____

2 ONE-MINUTE PAPER

Chapter 1 explores how deciding to go to college, experiencing college life, and finding your own path can be a unique journey. Sometimes things that seem simple are more complex and interesting if they are given some thought. Take a minute (or several) to think about and note what you found most useful or meaningful during this class. Did anything that was covered in this chapter leave you with more questions than answers?

3 APPLYING WHAT YOU'VE LEARNED

Now that you have read and discussed this chapter, consider how you can apply what you have learned to your academic and personal life. The following prompts will help you reflect on chapter material and its relevance to you both now and in the future.

1. Review the Outcomes of the College Experience box in this chapter. Although landing a lucrative career is probably high on your list of goals after college, take a look at the other possible outcomes of obtaining a college degree. List five outcomes from this box that are most relevant to you. If you think of an outcome that is not noted in the chapter, add it to your top five.

2. College students often feel the stress of trying to balance their personal and academic lives. The ups and downs of life are inevitable, but we can control our choices and attitudes. As a first-year student, you will want to begin developing a personal strategy for bouncing back after a particularly difficult time. Your strategy should include at least three steps you can take to get back on track and move forward.

4 BUILDING YOUR PORTFOLIO

What's in It for Me? Skills Matrix How might the courses in which you are enrolled right now affect your future? Although it might be hard to imagine a direct connection to your career or lifestyle after college, your classes and experiences can play an important role in your future.

Developing a skills matrix will help you reflect on your college experiences and track the skills that will eventually help you land a great summer job, a hard-to-get internship, a scholarship, and a future career.

1. Using Microsoft Excel or another spreadsheet software, develop a skills matrix to identify courses and out-of-class experiences that enhance the following skills: communications, creativity, critical thinking, leadership, research, social responsibility, and teamwork. View an example at the book Web site **macmillanhighered.com/collegesuccess/resources**.

2. Add any additional skills categories or courses you would like to track.

3. Indicate what you did in your courses or activities that helped you learn one of these skills. Be specific about the assignment, project, or activity that helped you learn.

4. Save your skills matrix on your computer or in the Cloud.

5. Update your matrix often. Add new skills categories, courses, and activities. Change the title to indicate the appropriate time period (e.g., Skills Learned in My First Two Years of College).

6. Start an electronic collection of your college work. Save papers, projects, and other relevant material in one location on your computer or on an external storage device. Be sure to back up your work to avoid digital disasters!

For more on this topic watch
French Fries Are Not Vegetables and Other College Lessons

WHERE TO GO FOR HELP . . .

> **Academic Advising Center** Does your institution have an academic advising center, or is advising done by faculty in their offices? If you don't already know, find out this week where you will go to get help in selecting courses, obtaining information on degree requirements, and deciding on a major.

> **Academic Skills Center** Whether you need help or not, explore this facility. One day you might want to take advantage of its services such as tutoring, help in study and memory skills, and help in studying for exams.

> **Adult Reentry Center** If you are an adult or returning student, this service will be your lifeline. Plan to visit this center to learn about programs for returning students, make supportive contacts with other adult students, and gather information about services such as child care.

> **Career Center** You may visit the career center as part of your first-year seminar. If not, put it on your list of important services. Career centers usually feature a career library, interest assessments, counseling, help in finding a major, job and internship listings, co-op listings, interviews with prospective employers, and help with résumés and interview skills.

> **Chaplains** Whatever your faith perspective, learn about the worship services, fellowship, and personal counseling offered by college chaplains. Usually the chaplain's office and worship facilities are in an off-campus but nearby location.

> **Commuter Services** Commuter students are the new majority. If you are a commuter, find the office on your campus that offers lists of off-campus housing and roommates as well as orientation to community, including maps, public transportation guides, and child-care listings.

> **Computer Center** If you would like more experience in using word processing or data programs such as Excel, research what your computer center offers. You will find minicourses as well as handouts on campus computer resources.

> **Counseling Center** Find out about your institution's counseling center and the services it offers, which will probably include confidential counseling for personal concerns and stress-management programs.

> **Financial Aid and Scholarship Office** Be sure to meet with someone in this office to learn about financial aid programs, scholarships, and grants. You may be eligible for a loan or a grant that you didn't know about.

> **Health Center** Don't wait until you need a doctor or a nurse. Locate your campus health center and learn about their services. Your campus health center might also include a pharmacy.

> **Legal Services** Legal help can be expensive and difficult to find. Does your institution have a law school or legal services center? If so, and if you need legal advice or representation, access the Web site for the law school or center and learn about possible legal aid for students. This aid might be provided by law students or interns and available for all students on a low-cost or no-cost basis.

> **Math Center** If your math instructor hasn't already told you about help from the math center, ask whether your college or university has such a center.

> **Writing Center** As you write your first research paper, ask an expert in the writing center to read a first draft to help you with proper grammar, syntax, and punctuation as well as the appropriate method of citing and listing references.

MY INSTITUTION'S RESOURCES

_____

_____

_____

2 Time Management

IN THIS CHAPTER YOU WILL EXPLORE

Common time-management problems in college

The importance of setting priorities and goals and the role time management plays in doing so

Strategies and tools for getting organized

Ways to make sure that your college schedule works for you

> ❝ **It is difficult balancing school, volunteer work, and a job, but as long as you have everything scheduled and planned it is easily achievable and very rewarding.**

Abby York, 19
Economics major
California State University,
Los Angeles

When Abby York started college, she had already begun to build a solid foundation in time-management skills. She was born in New York City and moved to Los Angeles, California, when she was three years old. During her senior year of high school she participated in a college preparation program, which meant taking all her classes at a local college for transferable credit. Part of the curriculum was geared toward learning how to manage time and set priorities. She credits that course with helping her learn how to manage time in her first year of college and beyond. But even with a solid foundation, Abby didn't make it through her first year of college without a few time-management

Abby York ▶

Blend Images—Peathegee, Inc./Getty Images

roadblocks. "Sometimes I just got overwhelmed with school and just wanted to work or hang out with my friends and would put my schoolwork on the back burner. This had some bad side effects. Once I saw the drop in my grades, I knew that I had to reprioritize and get back on track."

One key to Abby's success with time management is organization. "I use both paper and electronic organizational tools. If my computer ever goes down, I still have all my information, plans, and due dates in my planner, and vice versa, if I lose my planner, I still have everything on my computer."

Abby recognizes that prioritizing is key to maintaining her busy schedule and her sanity. "My first priority is school, second comes work, and then everything else—volunteering, exercising, friends, and family," she says. "I find places in my schedule to fit them in every week. All these things are important and essential for me to be successful and happy. It's like each piece of my life is a puzzle piece. If I don't keep making sure that each piece fits, or if there is any piece missing, the puzzle doesn't work and breaks apart."

Abby recently changed her major from Psychology to Economics. She just returned from a semester abroad in England and is looking into transferring to a school more geared toward her new major. After college she hopes to move to the East Coast, find a job in market research or finance, and possibly continue her education in graduate school. Her advice to other first-year students: "Take a class on time management and balancing all your priorities. It definitely helped me ease into college life and balance my life."

———————

As you transition into your college experience, you will discover new and sometimes unanticipated demands on your time, demands that will require new strategies for time management. According to the Bureau of Labor Statistics *American Time Use Survey*, high school students will spend an average of 5.9 to 6.4 hours a day on education, hours spent mostly in school starting early in the morning.[1] In college, however, the average full-time student (ages fifteen to forty-nine) will spend only 3.3 hours a day[2] on educational activities and the peak time when full-time students are engaged in the highest number of educational activities falls around 10:00 a.m. For part-time students, those peak hours extend past 8:00 p.m.![3] In college you will have more control over how many hours you spend on your education and when you will schedule those hours. How you manage those hours corresponds to how successful you will be in college and throughout life.

[1] "Chart: Average Hours per Weekday Spent by High School Students in Various Activities," *American Time Use Survey*. Bureau of Labor Statistics. Web. 16 Nov. 2012.

[2] "Chart: Time Use on an Average Weekday for Full-Time University and College Students," *American Time Use Survey*. Bureau of Labor Statistics. Web. 16 Nov. 2012.

[3] "Chart: Percent of University and College Students Who Did Educational Activities, by Hour of Day on Weekdays," *American Time Use Survey*. Bureau of Labor Statistics. Web. 16 Nov. 2012.

◢ ASSESSING YOUR STRENGTHS

Time management is a challenge for almost all college students. Are you a good time manager? As you begin to read this chapter, list the strengths you have in this area.

_____

_____

_____

_____

◢ SETTING GOALS

What are your most important objectives in learning the material in this chapter? Think about challenges you have had in the past with managing your time. List three goals that relate to time management (e.g., I will keep an hour-by-hour record this week of how I spend my time).

1. _____

_____

2. _____

_____

3. _____

_____

Common Time-Management Problems

As a new college student, one of the most challenging aspects of time management is accurately assessing how much time you will need to complete the diverse range of tasks you will encounter in college and what problems may come up along the way. These problems will be specific to you and your college experience, and they may be recurring time-management challenges in your life. For instance, procrastination is one of the biggest challenges for college students, just as it is for people who are not in college. If you are willing to assess and evaluate your time-management habits on a regular basis, however, you will be able to recognize your time-management challenges and address them before they become serious problems. Only when you have a realistic understanding of these challenges will you be able to set goals and refocus your time—and your life—to maximize your success in college.

PROCRASTINATION

Dr. Piers Steel, who specializes in researching procrastination and motivation, writes that procrastination is on the rise with 80–95 percent of students in college spending time procrastinating.[4] According to Steel, half of college students report that they procrastinate on a regular basis, spending as much as one-third of their time every day in activities solely related to procrastination. All this procrastination takes place even though most people, including researchers who study the negative consequences of procrastination, view procrastination as a significant problem. These numbers, plus the widespread acknowledgment of the negative effects of procrastination, provide evidence that it is a serious issue that trips up many otherwise capable people.

The good news is that, of those people who procrastinate on a regular basis, 95 percent want to change their behavior.[5] As a first step toward initiating change, it is important to understand why people procrastinate. According to Steel, even people who are highly motivated often fear failure, and some people even fear success (although that might seem counterintuitive). Consequently, some students procrastinate because they are perfectionists; not doing a task might be easier than having to live up to your own very high expectations or those of your parents, teachers, or peers. Many procrastinate because they are easily distracted (a topic covered later in this chapter), they have difficulty organizing and regulating their life, they have difficulty following through on goals, the assigned task may seem too far into the future, or they find an assigned task boring or irrelevant[6] or consider it "busy work," believing they can learn the material just as effectively without doing the homework.

Many of the traits most associated with people who chronically procrastinate can make change more difficult. Fortunately, though, there is hope. With certain changes in behaviors and mind-set, you can reduce procrastination and become more effective at managing your time. In college changing how you think about and approach less enjoyable assignments is key to decreasing procrastination and increasing your success.

For instance, simply disliking an assignment is not a good reason to put it off; it's an *excuse*, not a valid *reason*. Throughout life you'll be faced with tasks you don't find interesting, and in many cases you won't have the option not to do them. Whether it is cleaning your house, filing your taxes, completing paperwork, or responding to hundreds of e-mails, tedious tasks will find you, and you will have to figure out strategies to complete these tasks. College is a good time to practice and hone your skills at finishing uninteresting tasks in a timely manner. Perhaps counterintuitively, research indicates that making easier or less interesting tasks more challenging can decrease boredom and increase your likelihood of completing the tasks on time.[7]

When you're in college, procrastinating can signal that it's time to reassess your goals and objectives; maybe you're not ready to make a commitment to academic priorities at this point in your life. Only you can decide, but a counselor or academic adviser can help you sort it out.

---

[4] Piers Steel, "The Nature of Procrastination: A Meta-Analytic and Theoretical Review of Quintessential Self-Regulatory Failure," *Psychological Bulletin* 133, no. 1 (2007): 65–94.
[5] Ibid.
[6] Ibid.
[7] Ibid.

Here are some strategies for beating procrastination:

- Think about ways to make less enjoyable classes and assignments relevant to your interests and goals to decrease boredom and increase motivation.
- Remind yourself of the possible consequences if you do not get down to work. Then get started.
- Create a to-do list. Check off things as you get them done. Use the list to focus on the things that aren't getting done. Move them to the top of the next day's list and make up your mind to do them. Working from a list will give you a feeling of accomplishment.
- Break down big jobs into smaller steps. Tackle short, easy-to-accomplish tasks first.
- Promise yourself a reward for finishing the task, such as watching your favorite TV show or going out with friends. For more substantial tasks, give yourself bigger and better rewards.
- Find a place to study that's comfortable and doesn't allow for distractions and interruptions. Say "no" to friends and family members who want your attention; agree to spend time with them later.
- Don't talk on the phone, send e-mail or text messages, or surf the Web during planned study sessions. If you study in your room, close your door.

If these ideas don't sufficiently motivate you to get to work, you might want to reexamine your purposes, values, and priorities. Keep coming back to some basic questions: Why am I in college here and now? Why am I in this course? What is really important to me? Are these values important enough to forgo some short-term fun or laziness and get down to work? Are my academic goals really my own, or were they imposed on me by family members, my employer, or societal expectations? Use the Procrastination Self-Assessment in Figure 2.1 to evaluate your own procrastination tendencies. But here is the bottom line: If you are not willing to stop procrastinating and get to work on the tasks at hand, perhaps you should reconsider why you are in college and if this is the right time to pursue higher education.

Researchers at Carleton University in Canada have found that college students who procrastinate in their studies also avoid confronting other tasks and problems and are more likely to develop unhealthy habits, such as higher levels of alcohol consumption, smoking, insomnia, a poor diet, or lack of exercise.[8] If you cannot get procrastination under control, it is in your best interest to seek help at your campus counseling service before you begin to feel as though you are also losing control over other aspects of your life.

DISTRACTIONS

For many students, distractions are used as a way to procrastinate. For others who are actively trying to focus on tasks, distractions are simply part of their lives that hinder their time management, and they need coping strategies to help them focus on tasks at hand.

[8] Timothy A. Pychyl and Fuschia M. Sirois, "Procrastination: Costs to Health and Well-Being," presentation at the American Psychological Association convention, Aug. 22, 2002, Chicago.

FIGURE 2.1

Procrastination Self-Assessment

Place a number from 1 to 5 before each statement. (For example, if you "agree" with a statement, place a 4 before the statement.)

1	2	3	4	5
Strongly Disagree	**Disagree**	**Mildly Disagree**	**Agree**	**Strongly Agree**

_____ I have a habit of putting off important tasks that I don't enjoy doing.

_____ My standards are so high that I'm not usually satisfied enough with my work to turn it in on time.

_____ I spend more time planning what I'm going to do than actually doing it.

_____ The chaos in my study space makes it hard for me to get started.

_____ The people I live with distract me from doing my class work.

_____ I have more energy for a task if I wait until the last minute to do it.

_____ I enjoy the excitement of living on the edge.

_____ I have trouble prioritizing all my responsibilities.

_____ Having to meet a deadline makes me really nervous.

_____ My biggest problem is that I just don't know how to get started.

If you responded that you "agree" or "strongly agree" with 0–2 questions ...

You might procrastinate from time to time, but it may not be a major problem for you. Reading this chapter will help you continue to stay focused and avoid procrastination in the future.

If you responded that you "agree" or "strongly agree" with 3–5 questions ...

You may be having difficulties with procrastination. Revisit the questions to which you answered "agree" or "strongly agree" and look in the chapter for strategies that specifically address these issues to help you overcome obstacles. You *can* get a handle on your procrastination!

If responded that you "agree" or "strongly agree" with 6 or more questions ...

You may be having a significant problem with procrastination, and it could interfere with your success in college if you do not make a change. Revisit the questions to which you answered "agree" or "strongly agree" and look in the chapter for strategies that specifically address these issues. Also, if you are concerned about your pattern of procrastination and you aren't having success in dealing with it yourself, consider talking to a professional counselor in your campus counseling center. It's free and confidential, and counselors have extensive experience working with students who have problems with procrastination.

(continued)

Finally: Can you think of the number of times you may have been late (one of the symptoms of procrastination) this week alone? Think back. Take the following quiz.

Situation	Number of Times This Week
How many times were you late to class?	_____
How many times were you late for appointments/dates?	_____
How many times were you late for work, a carpool, or another job and/or responsibility?	_____
How many times were you late returning an e-mail, phone call, or text such that a problem resulted from this lateness?	_____
How many times were you late paying a bill or mailing any important document?	_____
How many times were you late getting to bed or waking up?	_____
TOTAL	_____

Did the total number of times you were late surprise you? Two to five incidences of being late in a week is fairly normal. Everyone is late sometimes. Being late more than eight times this week might indicate that you are avoiding situations and tasks that are unpleasant for you. Or maybe you find it difficult to wait for other people, and so you would rather have others wait for you. Try to think of lateness from the other person's perspective. Getting more organized might help if you find that you don't have enough hours in the day to get everything done in the way you think it should be done. Position yourself for success and develop the reputation for being dependable!

When considering how to deal with distractions, assess the types of distractions you encounter, the times and places you encounter these distractions, and the activities these distractions affect. For instance, where should you study? Some students find it best not to study in places associated with leisure, such as the kitchen table, the living room, or in front of the TV, because these places lend themselves to interruptions and other distractions. Similarly, it might be unwise to study on your bed because you might drift off to sleep when you need to study, or you may learn to associate your bed with studying and not be able to go to sleep when you need to. Instead, find quiet places, both on campus and at home, where you can concentrate and develop a study mind-set each time you sit down to do your work.

Accurately assessing the distractions you will face is especially important if you have significant family obligations at home or plan to take online classes. If you have children at home, assume that they will always want your attention no matter how much others try to help. Online learners may be more tempted by online distractions, such as e-mail or Facebook, because they are already online for their classes. In these instances students tend to struggle with fulfilling their college obligations until they have tried a variety of strategies for minimizing distractions within their studying environment. The chart in Figure 2.2 will help you identify potential distractions and develop strategies to take better control of your time.

© Anderson Ross/Blend Images/Corbis

Better Late Than Never?

Be on time to class, but if you have an emergency situation that causes you to run late, talk to your instructor. He or she will understand a real emergency and help you make up work you missed.

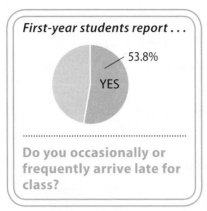

First-year students report . . .

53.8%
YES

Do you occasionally or frequently arrive late for class?

Try to stick to a routine as you study. The more firmly you have established a specific time and a quiet place to study, the more effective you will be in keeping up with your schedule. If you have larger blocks of time available on the weekend, for example, take advantage of that time to review or catch up on major projects, such as term papers, that can't be completed effectively in 50-minute blocks. Break down large tasks and take one thing at a time; you will make more progress toward your ultimate academic goals this way.

OVEREXTENDING YOURSELF

Being overextended is a primary source of stress for college students. Often, students underestimate how much time it will take to earn the grades they want in college and have overscheduled themselves with work and other commitments, leaving them little to no flexible time to use when they need more time.

Even with the best intentions, some students who use a time-management plan overextend themselves. If you do not have enough time to carry your course load and meet your commitments, drop a course before the drop deadline so that you won't have a low grade on your permanent record. If you receive financial aid, keep in mind that you must be registered for a minimum number of credit hours to be considered a full-time student and thereby maintain your current level of financial aid.

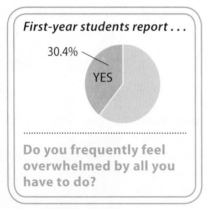

First-year students report . . .

30.4%
YES

Do you frequently feel overwhelmed by all you have to do?

If dropping a course is not feasible or if other activities are lower on your list of priorities, which is likely for most college students, assess your other time commitments and let go of one or more. Doing so can be very difficult, especially if you think you are letting other people down, but it is far preferable to excuse yourself from an activity in a way that is respectful to others than fail to come through at the last minute because you have committed to more than you can possibly achieve.

LOSS OF MOTIVATION

Many of the decisions you make today are reversible. You can change your major, your career, and even your life goals. It is important, however, to take control of your life by establishing your own goals for the future, using those goals to set your priorities, and managing your time and motivation accordingly. Many first-year students, especially recent high school graduates, might temporarily forget their primary purposes for coming to college, lose sight of their goals, and lose motivation during difficult or less engaging parts of their college experience. In other instances they may spend their first term of college engaging in a wide array of new experiences, which is OK to do within limits. Some students, though, spend the next four or five years trying to make up for poor decisions they made early in their college careers, such as

Here are some situations that may or may not distract you. Choose Yes (a problem) or No (not a problem) for each one. Are the problems you identify controllable? If so, as a responsible student, what solutions will help you take control of your time? Use this worksheet to increase your awareness of what distractions are tripping you up and how to overcome them.

Situations	Yes (Y) No (N)	Controllable (C) Uncontrollable (U)	Solutions?
Cell phone			
Internet/Facebook			
Gaming/Videos/Music			
Sports/Hobbies			
Television			
Lack of sleep			
Relationship problems			
Meals/Snacking			
Daydreaming			
Perfectionism			
Errands/Shopping			
Lost items			
Worries/Stress			
Children/Siblings			
Socializing/Friends			
Multitasking			
Illness, self or others			
Work schedule			
Pleasure reading			
Family			

FIGURE 2.2

Possible Distractions

Planning your time is closely associated with planning your goals (see Chapter 1). What you do on a daily basis affects your outcomes for that week, that month, that year, and so on. Things may distract you and push you off course and away from your intended goals, however. In this chapter you will find a weekly timetable to plan your schedule for the week ahead, but what happens when *life happens*? Take control of distractions you know are difficult for you. When you allow distractions to take control of your life, you feel anxiety about the areas of your life you have ignored.

skipping class and not taking their assignments seriously. Such decisions can lead to plummeting grade point averages (GPAs) and the threat of academic probation or, worse, academic dismissal. Staying focused means always keeping your eyes on your most important purposes for being in college. Ask yourself whether what you are doing at any moment contributes to, or detracts from, those purposes.

Many students of all ages question their decision to attend college and might sometimes feel overwhelmed by the additional responsibilities it brings.

Work Study

Did you know that the majority of college students have jobs? If you need to work, try to find a job that is flexible and allows you to study during your off-time. Use every available minute to stay up to date with your classwork.

Courtesy of Sue McDermott Barlow

Prioritizing, rethinking some commitments, letting some things go, and weighing the advantages and disadvantages of attending school part-time versus full-time can help you work through this adjustment period. Again, keep your long-term goals in mind and find ways to manage your stress rather than reacting to it. Although this book is full of suggestions for enhancing academic success, the bottom line is to stay focused and take control of your time and your life. Make a plan that begins with your priorities: attending classes, studying, working, and spending time with the people who are important to you. Then think about the necessities of life: sleeping, eating, exercising, and relaxing. Leave time for fun things such as talking with friends, checking out Facebook, watching TV, and going out, but finish what *needs* to be done before you move from work to pleasure. Also, don't forget about personal time. If you live in a residence hall or share an apartment with other students, talk with your roommates about how you can coordinate your class schedules so that each of you has some privacy. If you live with your family, particularly if you are a parent, work together to create special family times as well as quiet study times.

Time-Management Goals

Now that you have a better picture of common time-management problems in college, you are prepared to move into action and recognize that you are in control of your time. How often do you find yourself saying, "I don't have time"? Once a week? Once a day? Several times a day? The next time you find yourself saying this statement, stop and ask yourself whether it is really true. Do you really not have time, or have you made a choice, consciously or unconsciously, not to make time for that particular task or activity? Once you recognize that you can control and change how you use your time, you'll want to assess your time-management strengths and then set time-management goals and priorities.

The first step in this assessment is to acknowledge that we have control over how we use our time. We have control over many of the commitments we choose to make. We also have control over many small decisions that affect our time-management success, such as what time we get up in the morning, how much sleep we get, what we eat, how much time we spend studying, and whether we get exercise. All these small decisions have a big effect on our success in college and in life.

Being in control means that you make your own decisions. Two of the most often cited differences between high school and college are increased **autonomy**, or independence, and greater responsibility. If you are not a recent high school graduate, you have most likely already experienced a higher level of independence, but returning to school creates responsibilities above and beyond those you already have, whether they include employment, family, community service, or other activities.

Whether you are beginning college immediately after high school or are continuing your education after a break, make sure that the way you spend your time aligns with your most important values. For instance, if you value becoming an expert in a particular academic area, you'll want to learn everything you can in that field by taking related classes and participating in internships. If you value learning about many things and postponing a specific decision about your major, you might want to spend your time exploring many different areas of interest and taking as many different types of courses as possible. To take control of your life and your time and to guide your decisions, begin by setting some goals for the future.

PRIORITIZE

As you consider your time-management strengths and goals, you should think about how to prioritize your tasks, goals, and values. Which goals and objectives are most important to you and most consistent with your values? Which are the most urgent? For example, studying to get a good grade on tomorrow's test might have to take priority over attending a job fair today. Don't ignore long-term goals to meet short-term goals, however. With good time management you can study during the week prior to the test so that you can attend the job fair the day before.

autonomy Self-direction or independence. College students usually have more autonomy than they did in high school.

© N&E Alexandre/Photononstop/Corbis

Five More Minutes

Are you ever tempted to hit snooze on your alarm repeatedly when you shouldn't? In the morning, get up in time to eat breakfast and make it to class without feeling frazzled. Think of an alarm—whether it's on your phone or on a clock—as an important tool for college success.

Skilled time managers often establish priorities by maintaining a to-do list (discussed in more detail later in this chapter) and ranking the items on the list to determine schedules and deadlines for each task.

FIND A BALANCE

Another aspect of setting priorities while in college is finding an appropriate way to balance your academic schedule with the rest of your life. Social activities are an important part of the college experience. Time alone and time to think are also essential to your overall well-being.

For many students, the greatest challenge of prioritizing is balancing school with work and family obligations that are equally important and are not optional. Good advance planning can help you meet these challenges, but you also need to talk with your family members and your employer to make sure they understand your academic responsibilities. Most professors will work with you when conflicts arise, but if you have problems that can't be resolved easily, be sure to seek support from the professionals in your college's counseling center. They will understand your challenges and help you manage and prioritize your many responsibilities.

> ### YOUR TURN
> ....
> **Write and Reflect**
>
> List your current priorities in order of importance. What does your list suggest about why you consider some things more important? Less important? Have you put any items in the wrong place? What should you change, and why? In a journal entry reflect on your current list of priorities, what you should change, and why.

Getting Organized

In college as in life, you will quickly learn that managing time is important to success. Almost all successful people use some sort of calendar or planner, either paper or electronic, to help them keep up with their appointments, assignments or tasks, and other important activities and commitments.

USE A PLANNER

Your college might design and sell a calendar in the campus bookstore designed specifically for your school, with important dates and deadlines already provided. Or, you might prefer to use an online calendar or the calendar that comes on your computer or cell phone. Regardless of the format you prefer (electronic or hard copy), it's a good idea to begin the term by completing a term assignment preview like the one shown in Figure 2.3, which is a template you can use to map your schedule for an entire term.

To create a term assignment preview, begin by entering all your commitments for each week: classes, assignment due dates, work hours, family commitments, and so on. Examine your toughest weeks during the term. If paper deadlines and test dates fall during the same week, find time to finish some assignments early to free up study and writing time. Note this time on your calendar. If you use an electronic calendar, set a reminder for these important deadlines and dates. Consult with tutors or more experienced students to help you break down

	Monday	Tuesday	Wednesday	Thursday	Friday
Week 1	✕	✕	First day of Classes!	Read Ch. 1–2 English	Discuss Ch. 1–2 History in Class Work 2–5
Week 2	English Quiz Ch. 1–2 Work 4–7	Psych Quiz Ch. 1	English Essay #1 Due Work 4–7	History Quiz Ch. 1–2	English Quiz Ch. 1–2 Work 2–5
Week 3	English Quiz Ch. 3–4 Work 4–7	Psych Quiz Ch. 2 Read Bio Ch. 1–2	English Essay Due Work 4–7	Be Ready for Bio Lab Experiment	Discuss English pp. 151–214 Work 2–5
Week 4	Work 4–7	Read English pp. 214–275	English Essay Due Work 4–7 Discuss pp. 214–275	Read English pp. 276–311	Discuss English pp. 276–311 Work 2–5

	Monday	Tuesday	Wednesday	Thursday	Friday
Week 5	Work 4–7	Psych Quiz Ch. 3–4	English Essay Due Work 4–7	Bio Lab Experiment	Prepare Psych Experiment Work 2–5
Week 6	Work 4–7	Present Psych Experiment	English Essay Due Work 4–7	Bio Lab Experiment	Work 2–5
Week 7	Work 4–7	Study for English Mid-Term	English Mid-Term!! Work 4–7	Bio Lab Experiment	Study Psych Mid-Term Work 2–5
Week 8	Study for Psych Mid-Term Work 4–7	Psych Mid-Term!!	Study for History Mid-Term Work 4–7	Bio Lab Experiment Study for History Mid-Term	History Mid-Term!! Work 2–5

FIGURE 2.3

Term Assignment Preview

Using the course syllabi provided by your instructors, create your own term calendar. You can find blank templates on the book's Web site at **macmillanhighered.com /collegesuccess/resources**. For longer assignments such as term papers, remember to divide the task into smaller parts. Then establish your own deadline for each part of the assignment, such as deadlines for choosing a topic, completing your library research, developing an outline of the paper, and writing a first draft.

large assignments (e.g., term papers) into smaller steps. Add deadlines in your term assignment preview for each of the smaller portions of the project.

After you complete your term assignment preview, enter important dates and notes from the preview sheets into your calendar or planner and continue to enter all due dates as soon as you know them. Write down meeting times and locations, scheduled social events (including phone numbers in case you need to cancel), study time for each class you're taking, and so forth. It's best not to rely solely on one calendar. If you are using an electronic device for your calendar, take time to sync that device with others so that you will have an updated calendar in multiple places. Another option is to keep a backup copy on paper in case you lose your phone, you can't access the Internet, or your computer crashes. If you use a print planner, keep it with you in a place where you're not likely to lose it. Your first term of college is the time to get into the habit of using a planner to help you keep track of commitments and maintain control of your schedule. This practice will become invaluable to you in your career. Review your calendar daily at the same time of day for the current week as well as the coming week. It takes just a moment to be certain you aren't forgetting something important, and it helps relieve stress.

CHART A WEEKLY TIMETABLE

Now that you have created a term preview, the weekly timetable model in Figure 2.4 can help you tentatively plan how to spend your hours in a typical week. Here are some tips for creating a weekly schedule:

- As you create your schedule, try to reserve at least two hours of study time for each hour spent in class. This universally accepted "two-for-one" rule reflects faculty members' expectations for how much work you should be doing to earn a good grade in their classes. So, if you take a typical full-time class load of fifteen credits, for example, you should plan to study an additional thirty hours per week. Think of this forty-five-hour-per-week commitment as comparable to a full-time job. If you are also working, reconsider how many hours per week it will be reasonable for you to be employed above and beyond this commitment, or consider reducing your credit load.

- Depending on your **biorhythms**, obligations, and potential distractions, decide whether you study more effectively in the day, in the evening, or with a combination of both. Determine whether you are capable of getting up very early in the morning to study or how late you can stay up at night and still wake up for morning classes.

- Not all assignments are equal. Work with tutors, other students, and instructors to estimate how much time you will need for each one and begin your work early. A good time manager frequently finishes assignments before actual due dates to allow for emergencies.

biorhythms The internal mechanisms that drive our daily patterns of physical, emotional, and mental activity.

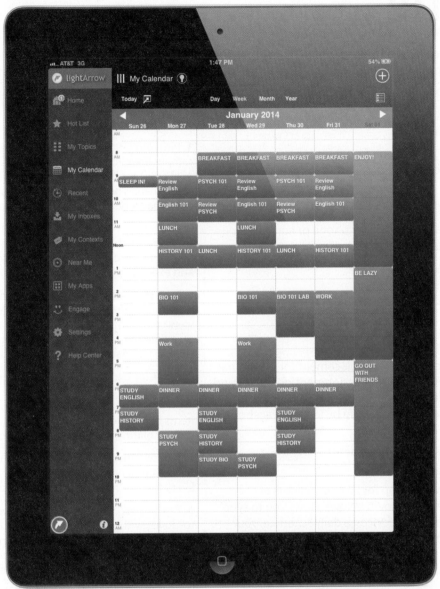

Courtesy of Light Arrow, Inc.

FIGURE 2.4
Weekly Timetable

Using your term calendar, create your own weekly timetable such as the one shown here, which uses the popular app LifeTopix. You can also find blank templates on this book's Web site at **macmillanhighered.com/collegesuccess/resources**. As you complete your timetable, keep in mind the suggestions in this chapter. Track all your activities for a full week by entering into your schedule everything you do and how much time each task requires. Use this record to help you estimate the time you will need for similar activities in the future.

- Each term is different. As you progress through your college experience, the tasks and demands on your time will continue to change. From one term to the next, you will take different (and, typically, more demanding) classes. Throughout each class, you will be required to read a great deal of material, but the work may shift from tests and quizzes to research papers, presentations, and group projects. Be prepared for the additional time and project management these types of assignments involve.

YOUR TURN

Think about It

Make a list of the best and worst times for you to study. Why do you think you are more able to concentrate or be creative at certain times of the day or night?

TECH TIP GET ORGANIZED, DIGITALLY

Mapping out your schedule needn't be a chore. Think of a well-appointed calendar as a compass for a college student. Besides being a guide for navigating your current term, it will also keep you pointed toward your long-term goals.

 THE PROBLEM

You keep forgetting assignments and can't find the paper planner that your college provided.

 THE FIX

Replace the lost print planner with your phone or computer using a free electronic calendar or phone app.

 HOW TO DO IT

First, pick one of the following:

Google calendar

www.google.com/calendar/

Google Calendar is a quick, easy, free replacement for traditional print planners that allows you to input assignment deadlines and reminders, sync with group members' calendars during group projects, and even manage your social life by loading Facebook events.

iStudiez Pro app for Mac, iPhone, and iPad

http://istudentpro.com/

Rated the Best College Student App for 2011 by readers of BestAppEver.com, iStudiez Pro (shown below) allows you to sync the following information across devices: a daily schedule, your calendar by term, assignments, grades, and instructor information.

Courtesy of iStudiez Team

Studious app for Android devices

https://play.google.com/store/apps/details?id=com.young .studious

If you own an Android device and want to ditch your old-school paper planner, try out Studious. It is an all-in-one app for tracking your schedule, including upcoming homework deadlines, and it can also be used for taking and managing notes. Best of all, it's free.

Then, take these steps:

1. Find out if your college sells a special planner in the campus bookstore with important dates or deadlines already marked, or get the academic calendar from your school's Web site. If there is no college calendar, grab a sheet of paper or download a blank calendar page from the Internet.

2. Draw up a plan for the term, entering your commitments for each week: classes, work hours, assignment deadlines, study groups (including contact numbers), and exam and vacation dates.

3. Transfer all the information into the electronic calendar or phone app of your choice, where you can view commitments by day, week, or month. Simply click on a date or time slot, follow the instructions on the toolbar to create a new entry, and start typing.

4. A useful trick is to highlight the most important deadlines and activities. As you type in each new entry, most programs will give you the option to color-code items by category (i.e., school, work, family). Set reminder alarms to keep yourself on track.

5. Use the to-do list function to jot down and prioritize tasks. Start a new to-do list every day or once a week. Every time you complete a task, cross it off the list.

6. Back up everything by syncing your calendar and to-do list with other electronic devices. If you need help, visit your college's computer lab or information technology department. Alternately, turn to a hyperorganized friend for advice or look for an online tutorial.

Now you can file your original paper calendar away for safekeeping in case you experience technical difficulties down the road.

PERSONAL BEST

Set up a calendar with all your classes for the term and create specific to-do lists for your first three assignments.

EXTRA CREDIT

While you're at it, write up a tentative four-year plan, including required classes in your major and the types of internships or volunteer work you'll need to build your résumé. The exercise will help to demystify the college process, even if you change your major six times down the road.

   Keep track of how much time it takes you to complete different kinds of tasks. For example, depending on your skills and interests, it might take longer to read a chapter in a biology text than to read one in a literature text. Keeping track of your time will help you estimate how much time to allocate for similar tasks in the future. How long does it really take you to solve a set of twenty math problems or write up a chemistry lab? Use your weekly timetable to track how you actually spend your time for an entire week.

MAINTAIN A TO-DO LIST

Once you have plotted your future commitments with a term planner and decided how your time will be spent each week, you can stay on top of your obligations with a to-do list, which is especially handy for last-minute reminders. It can help you keep track of errands you need to run, appointments you need to make, e-mail messages you need to send, or anything you're prone to forget. You can keep this list on your cell phone (see Figure 2.5) or in your notebook, or you can post it on your bulletin board. Some people start a new list every day or once a week. Others keep a running list and throw a page

Is This You?

Do you find yourself in class, panicking because of an assignment that you forgot about until your instructor asked for it? How many times do you realize late at night that you have a test or paper due the next day? Are you falling behind in one or more classes because of missed or late work? Read the Tech Tip on page 44, and for at least one week try out a digital solution to your homework assignment woes.

Courtesy of Light Arrow, Inc.

FIGURE 2.5
To-Do Lists

Almost all successful people keep a daily to-do list. The list may be in paper or electronic form. Get in the habit of creating and maintaining your own daily list of appointments, obligations, and activities. Dozens of apps such as the one shown here are available for free for any mobile device.

away only when everything on the list is done. Whichever method you prefer, use your to-do list to keep track of all the tasks you need to remember, not just academics. You might want to develop a system for prioritizing the items on your list: highlight; different colors of ink; one, two, or three stars; or lettered tasks with A, B, C. As you complete a task, cross it off your list. You might be surprised by how much you have accomplished—and how good you feel about it.

Making Your Schedule Work for You

As a first-year student, you might not have had much flexibility in determining your course schedule; by the time you were allowed to register for classes, some sections of the courses you needed might already have been closed. You

ORGANIZE YOUR DAYS

Being a good student does not necessarily mean studying day and night and doing little else. Notice that the Daily Planner (Figure 2.6) includes time for classes and studying as well as time for other activities. Keep the following points in mind as you organize your day:

> **Set realistic goals for your study time.** Assess how long it takes to read a chapter in different types of textbooks and how long it takes you to review your notes from different instructors and schedule your time accordingly. Give yourself adequate time to review and then test your knowledge when preparing for exams. Online classes often require online discussions and activities that take the place of face-to-face classroom instruction, so be prepared to spend additional time on these tasks.

> **Use waiting time to review** (on the bus, before class, before appointments). Prevent forgetting what you have learned by allowing time to review as soon as is reasonable after class. (Reviewing immediately after class might be possible but not reasonable if you are too burned out to concentrate!) Invest in tools (note cards, digital recorders, flash card apps, etc.) to convert less productive time into study time.

> **Know your best times of day to study.** Schedule other activities, such as laundry, e-mail, or spending time with friends, for times when it will be difficult to concentrate. If you have children or significant family obligations at home, plan to complete homework early in the morning or later in the evening when family members are asleep to maximize your concentration.

> **Restrict repetitive, distracting, and time-consuming tasks** such as checking your e-mail, Facebook, or text messages to a certain time, not every hour. This strategy is especially important if you take online classes and complete most of your coursework at home, where distractions abound.

> **Avoid multitasking.** Even though you might actually be quite good at it, or at least think you are,

the reality is (and research shows) that you will be able to study most effectively and retain the most information if you concentrate on one task at a time.

> **Let others help.** Find an accountability partner to help keep you on track. If you struggle with keeping a regular study schedule, find a friend, relative, or classmate to keep you motivated and on course. If you have children, plan daily family homework times and encourage family members to help you study by taking flash cards wherever you go.

> **Be flexible.** You cannot anticipate every disruption to your plans. Build extra time into your schedule so that unexpected interruptions do not prevent you from meeting your goals. Also, be prepared for different time challenges with new classes every term.

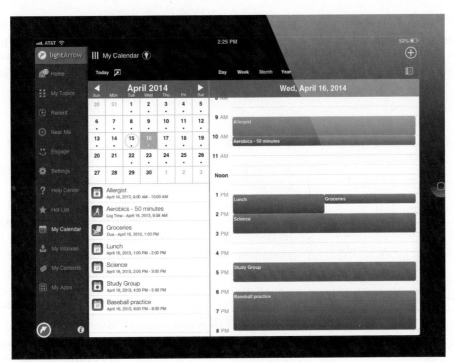

Courtesy of Light Arrow, Inc.

FIGURE 2.6
Daily Planner

On your daily planner be sure to enter times for exercise, obligations, and classes. Also add your personal activities and block out time to study.

also might not have known whether you would prefer taking classes back-to-back or giving yourself a break between classes.

How might you wisely use time between classes? This term may have been your first opportunity to take classes that do not meet five days a week. Do you prefer spreading your classes over five or six days of the week, or would you like to go to class just two or three days a week or even once a week for a longer class period? Your attention span and other commitments should influence your decision. In the future you might have more control over how you schedule your classes. Before you register, think about how to make your class schedule work for you; in other words, consider how you can create a schedule that allows you to use your time more efficiently. Also consider your own biorhythms and recognize the part of the day or evening in which you are most alert and engaged.

> **Is This You?**
>
> Do you find yourself wondering where your time has gone at the end of a long day? Do you spend your time between classes talking with other students, texting, or checking e-mail instead of studying or working on homework? Are you so tired at the end of your classes that you can't make yourself study or do homework after classes? Read this section carefully. Choose one strategy and use this strategy to imagine a better class schedule in upcoming terms.

CREATE A WORKABLE CLASS SCHEDULE

If you live on campus, you might want to create a schedule that situates you near a dining hall at mealtimes or allows you to spend breaks between classes at the library. Alternatively, you might need breaks in your schedule for relaxation, catching up with friends, or spending time in a student lounge, college union, or campus center. You might want to avoid returning to your residence hall room to take a nap between classes if the result is that you could feel lethargic or over-sleep and miss later classes. Also, if you attend a large university, be sure to allow adequate time to get from one class to another.

SCHEDULE YOUR CLASSES IN BLOCKS

> ### YOUR TURN
>
> **Work Together**
>
> Share your current schedule with another student and explain what you like or dislike about it. If your current schedule is not working well, discuss why that might be and identify changes you can make next term.

If you're a commuter student or if you must carry a heavy workload to afford going to school, you might prefer to schedule your classes in blocks without breaks. Although taking back-to-back classes allows you to cut travel time by attending school one or two days a week and might provide for more flexible scheduling of a job or family commitments, it can also have significant drawbacks.

When all your classes are scheduled in a block of time, you run several risks. If you become ill on a class day, you could fall behind in all your classes. You might also become fatigued from sitting in class after class. When one class immediately follows another, it will be difficult for you to have a last-minute study period immediately before a test because you will be attending another class and are likely to have no more than a 15-minute break. Finally, remember that for back-to-back classes, several exams might be held on the same day. Scheduling classes in blocks might work better if you have the option of attending lectures at alternative times in case you are absent, if you alternate classes with free periods, and if you seek out instructors who are flexible with due dates for assignments.

TIME MANAGEMENT: DO IT!

Now that you are aware of common college time-management problems and know some tips for organizing your time and making good use of your schedule, it's time to carry out the priorities and goals that you have set. Here are a few final tips to help as you set forth to successfully manage your time in college:

> Before each term, talk with other students, counselors, tutors, and instructors about the time demands of different classes.

> Determine what a realistic workload is for you.

> Reflect on how even the classes and assignments you enjoy the least are relevant to your interests and goals.

> Remind yourself of the possible consequences if you do not get down to work. Then, get started.

> Create a to-do list. Check off things as you get them done. Use the list to focus on the things that aren't getting done. Working from a list will give you a feeling of accomplishment.

> Break down big jobs into smaller steps. Tackle short, easy-to-accomplish tasks first.

> Promise yourself a reward for finishing the task, such as watching your favorite TV show or going out with friends. For more substantial tasks, give yourself bigger and better rewards.

> Do *not* communicate by phone, e-mail, text, Twitter, or Facebook, and don't go online during planned study and homework sessions. If you study in your room, close your door.

> Turn off the computer, TV, CD or DVD player, iPod, or radio unless the background noise or music really helps you concentrate on your studies or drowns out more distracting noises (e.g., people laughing or talking in other rooms or hallways). Silence your cell phone so that you aren't distracted by incoming calls or text messages.

> Try not to let personal concerns interfere with homework. If necessary, call a friend or write in a journal before you start to study and then put your worries away.

> Develop an agreement with your roommate(s) or family about quiet hours. Say "no" to friends and family members who want your attention; agree to spend time with them later. If that's not possible, find a quiet place where you can go to concentrate or take advantage of time when others in your household are sleeping or gone to focus on academic work.

> Make your academic work your top priority. It should not take a backseat to extracurricular activities or other time commitments.

> Take on only what you can handle. Learn to say "no." Do not feel obligated to provide a reason; you have the right to decline requests that will prevent you from getting your own work done.

> Spend time with your financial aid office mining opportunities for paying for college expenses before adding more hours to your workweek.

> Remember that college should take only a few years of your life, so any shuffling you do with your priorities and commitments will be temporary. College needs to be high on your list of priorities, which means that other priorities will have to shift until you finish.

CHECKLIST FOR SUCCESS

TIME MANAGEMENT

☐ **Quickly identify and address common time-management problems in college before they spiral out of control.** Be aware of problems with procrastination, distractions, overscheduling, and motivation. As you notice them happening, take stock and make changes. If any of these issues becomes a serious problem, seek help from your campus counseling center.

☐ **Make sure that the way you use your time supports your goals for being in college.** All your time doesn't have to be spent studying, but remember the "two hours out of class for each hour in class" rule.

☐ **Get organized by using a calendar or planner.** Choose either an electronic format or a paper calendar. Your campus bookstore will have a campus-specific version.

☐ **Devise a weekly timetable of activities and then stick to it.** Be sure to include special events or responsibilities in addition to recurring activities such as classes, athletic practice, or work hours.

☐ **Create and use day-by-day paper or electronic to-do lists.** Crossing off those tasks you have completed will give you a real sense of satisfaction.

☐ **Use the tips and strategies in this chapter to meet your time-management goals.** Keep the lists in this chapter handy as reminders of what to do and what to avoid.

BUILD YOUR EXPERIENCE 1 2 3 4

1 STAY ON TRACK

Successful college students stay focused. They "stay on track." They know what they have to do to be successful, they set goals, and they monitor their progress toward their goals.

Reflect on what you have learned about college success in this chapter and how you are going to apply the chapter information or strategies in college and in your career. List your ideas.

1. _____

_____

_____

2. _____

_____

_____

3. _____

_____

_____

2 ONE-MINUTE PAPER

Chapter 2 gives you a lot of tips for managing your time. It can be frustrating to realize that you have to spend time organizing yourself just to manage your time effectively. Did any of the time-management tips in this chapter really appeal to you? If so, which ones? Why? Did anything in this chapter leave you with more questions than answers? If so, what are your questions?

APPLYING WHAT YOU'VE LEARNED

Now that you have read and discussed this chapter, consider how you can apply what you have learned to your academic and personal life. The following prompts will help you reflect on chapter material and its relevance to you both now and in the future.

1. Review the procrastination section of this chapter. Think of one upcoming assignment in any of your current classes and describe how you can avoid waiting until the last minute to get it done. Break down the assignment and list each step you will take to complete the assignment. Give yourself a due date for each step and one for completing the assignment.

2. After reading about effective time-management strategies, consider the way in which you manage your own time. If you were grading your current set of time-management skills, what grade (A, B, C, or lower) would you give yourself? Why? What is your biggest challenge to becoming a more effective time manager?

4 BUILDING YOUR PORTFOLIO

Time Is of the Essence   This chapter includes many great tips for effectively managing your time. Those skills are necessary for reducing the stress of everyday life, but have you thought about managing your time over the long term? What are your long-term goals? Preparing yourself for a particular career is probably high on your list, and it's not too early to begin thinking about what kind of preparation is necessary for the career (or careers) you are considering.

First, to help you determine the careers you're most interested in pursuing, schedule an appointment with the career center on your campus and ask for information on career assessments to help you identify your preferences and interests. This portfolio assignment will help you realize that it is important to plan ahead and consider what implications your long-term goals have for managing your time right now.

1. In a Microsoft Word document or Excel spreadsheet, create a table. See an example on the book's Web site at **macmillanhighered.com/collegesuccess/resources**.

2. Choose a career or careers in which you're most interested. In the example on the Web site, a student needs to plan ahead for activities that will help prepare for a future as a CPA. It is OK if you have not decided on just one major or career; you can repeat this process as your interests change. An "action step" is something you need to do within a certain time frame.

3. Talk with someone in the career center, an instructor, an upperclass student in your desired major, or a professional in your chosen career to get an idea of what you need to consider, even now.

4. Fill in the action steps, to-dos, time line, and notes sections of your own chart and update the chart as you learn more about the career you are exploring.

5. Save your work in your portfolio or in the Cloud.

For more on this topic watch
French Fries Are Not Vegetables and Other College Lessons

WHERE TO GO FOR HELP . . .

ON CAMPUS

> **Academic Skills Center** Your campus academic skills center offers more than just assistance in studying for exams. Head here for time-management advice specific to you. For instance, if you are struggling with managing the process of writing a paper, talk with a writing tutor about how to break the process into manageable steps on a timetable to meet course deadlines.

> **Counseling Center** Make an appointment at your campus counseling office if your time-management problems involve emotional issues.

> **Your Academic Adviser or Counselor** If you have a good relationship with your academic adviser, ask him or her for time-management advice or for a referral to another person on campus.

> **A Fellow Student** Don't overlook your closest resources! If you feel your time slipping away, ask a friend who is a good student for advice.

MY INSTITUTION'S RESOURCES

_____

_____

_____

_____

_____

_____

_____

_____

3 Emotional Intelligence

> **Going to college is not only about enjoying success and accomplishments but also about persevering when things get difficult or go wrong.**

Gustavo Mejia, 20
Business Administration major
South Texas College

Growing up in Turmero, Venezuela, Gus Mejia's family always encouraged him to attend college. "I see college as the path to the future," he says, "one that will help me build a better life for my family." Gus began college at Sinclair Community College in Dayton, Ohio, where he took classes full-time while working two days a week at his uncle's restaurant. He quickly learned a few things that helped him succeed. "As an international student, I left important parts of my life behind when I made the decision to go to college, such as family and my country. Being alone for almost a year taught me how important it is to have a positive attitude and an optimistic spirit."

This realization didn't come without hard work and practice. One of the most important things Gus had to learn during his first year of college was how to deal with the stress of managing college, work, and living in a new environment, and Gus

Gustavo Mejia ▶

figured out that having a good sense of his own emotional intelligence helped. Being aware of how these stresses affected him emotionally helped him better understand how to deal with situations and kept him from reacting negatively in stressful situations. Emotional intelligence has also played a big role in Gus's favorite class (so far), organizational behavior, where he had to learn how to work with other students, no matter what their customs and beliefs. "I liked this class not only because it related directly to my major," he says, "but also because it allows me to communicate with others. Being able to work efficiently with different people from different backgrounds was very valuable."

Gus decided to begin the transfer process last year. Transferring to South Texas College represented a new beginning for him, one that came with its own fair share of challenges that he had to face with a clear head. Some of his classes—such as English literature as well as some courses on Microsoft Excel and PowerPoint—didn't transfer because they didn't fit the business program curriculum at his new college. Gus had to find out all the requirements of transferring, including admission tests, and be sure to meet them to make the transition as smooth as possible. His one piece of advice for other first-year students: perseverance. "Going to college is not only about enjoying success and accomplishments but also about persevering when things get difficult or go wrong," he says.

The ability to understand oneself and others and get along with people is vital for success in school, work, and life. Another element of success is the ability to manage time well and get things done. Also, it's important to anticipate potential problems before they occur. Gus's problems with transfer are not uncommon, but he was able to deal with them without letting them become a barrier to his success. Why do some individuals struggle to handle stressful situations while others, like Gus, seem to handle them with ease? Although we tend to think of these abilities as inborn personality traits that can't be changed, social skills and stress-management skills really can be learned and improved.

Particularly in the first year of college, many students who are intellectually capable of succeeding have difficulty establishing positive relationships with others, dealing with pressure, or making wise decisions. Other students exude optimism and happiness and seem to adapt to their new environment without any trouble. Being optimistic doesn't mean that you ignore your problems or pretend they will go away, but optimistic people believe in their own abilities to address problems successfully as they arise. The difference in the way students deal with life's challenges lies not in academic talent but in emotional intelligence (EI), or the ability to recognize and manage moods, feelings, and attitudes. A growing body of evidence shows a clear connection between students' EI and whether or not they stay in college.

As you read this chapter, you will develop an understanding of EI, and you will learn how to use it to become a more successful student and person. You will begin to look at yourself

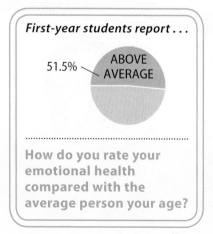

First-year students report . . .

51.5% ABOVE AVERAGE

How do you rate your emotional health compared with the average person your age?

■ **ASSESSING YOUR STRENGTHS** ▮▮▮▮▮▮▮▮▮▮▮

How well you understand and manage your emotions will affect your success in college. As you begin to read this chapter, list what you believe are your current strengths in the area of emotional intelligence.

_____

_____

_____

_____

■ **SETTING GOALS** ▮▮▮▮▮▮▮▮▮▮▮

What are your most important objectives in learning the material in this chapter? Think about challenges you have had in the past with understanding your emotions and managing your reactions to frustrating circumstances. List three goals that relate to emotional intelligence (e.g., This week I will keep a list of interactions with other people that frustrate me and how I react).

1. _____

_____

2. _____

_____

3. _____

_____

and others through an EI lens, observe the behaviors that help people do well, get to know yourself better, and take the time to examine why you are feeling the way you do before you act. Then, as you read each subsequent chapter in this book, try to apply what you have learned about EI and think about how it might relate to the behaviors of successful college students. You can't always control the challenges and frustrations of life, but with practice you *can* control how you respond to them.

What Is Emotional Intelligence?

Emotional intelligence, or **EI**, is the ability to identify, use, understand, and manage emotions. Emotions are a big part of who you are; you should not ignore them. The better the emotional read you have on a situation, the more appropriately you can respond to it. Being aware of your own and others' feelings helps you to gather accurate information about the world around you and allows you to respond in appropriate ways.

There are many competing theories about EI, some of them very complex. Although experts vary in their definitions and models, all agree that

emotional intelligence (EI) The ability to recognize, understand, use, and manage moods, feelings, and attitudes.

AP Photo/Cathleen Allison

Anger Management

Since the 1960s, college students have used their anger about political, social, and campus-specific issues (like tuition increases) in positive ways through organized demonstrations. Such demonstrations have influenced major actions in U.S. history, such as the decision of a president to resign and the end of the Vietnam War. What issues would "bring students to the barricades" today?

YOUR TURN

....

Discuss

Make a list (first names only) of people you know who are "book smart" but don't have good people skills. What kinds of challenges do these people face? Come to class prepared to share your thoughts.

emotions are real, can be changed for the better, and have a profound effect on whether a person is successful.

In the simplest terms, EI is "a person's innate ability to perceive and manage his/her own emotions in a manner that results in successful interactions with the environment and, if others are present, to also perceive and manage their emotions in a manner that results in successful interpersonal interactions. In other words, Emotional Intelligence is about recognizing and managing one's own emotions and the emotions of others."[1]

PERCEIVING AND MANAGING EMOTIONS

Learning how to put yourself in the "right" mood to handle different situations is part of developing your emotional intelligence. Handling emotions involves both perceiving them and managing them.

---

[1] High Performing Systems, Inc., "Leadership Teams Assessments: EQ-i 2.0," 2013, www.hpsys .com/Emotional_Intelligence.htm.

© Weinstein Company/Courtesy Everett Collection

IN THE MEDIA

The 2012 film *Silver Linings Playbook*, which stars Bradley Cooper, Jennifer Lawrence, and Robert DeNiro, explores issues of mental illness and anger management, family, and new beginnings.

For Reflection: If you have seen the film, discuss how the characters attempt to handle their emotions. What works? What doesn't work? What other movies, TV shows, or novels can you think of that feature characters with emotional issues? What can you learn from such fictional accounts?

Perceiving emotions involves the capacity to monitor and label feelings accurately (nervous, happy, angry, relieved, etc.) and to determine why you feel the way you do. It also involves predicting how others might feel in a given situation. Emotions contain information, and the ability to understand and think about that information plays an important role in behavior.

Managing emotions builds on the belief that feelings can be modified and even improved. At times you need to stay open to your feelings, learn from them, and use them to take appropriate action. At other times it is better to disengage from an emotion and return to it later. Anger, for example, can blind you and lead you to act in negative or antisocial ways; used positively, however, the same emotion can help you overcome adversity, bias, and injustice.

Developing an awareness of emotions allows you to use your feelings to enhance your thinking. If you are feeling sad, for instance, you might view the world in a certain way, whereas if you feel happy, you are likely to interpret the same events differently. Once you start paying attention to emotions, you can learn not only how to cope with life's pressures and demands, but also how to harness your knowledge of the way you feel for more effective problem solving, reasoning, decision making, and creative endeavors.

ASSESSING YOUR EMOTIONAL INTELLIGENCE

A number of sophisticated tools can be used to assess emotional intelligence. Some first-year seminars and many campus counseling centers offer the opportunity to complete a professionally administered questionnaire such as the Emotional Quotient Inventory (EQ-i), which provides a detailed assessment of your emotional skills and a graphic representation of where you stand in comparison with other students. Even without a formal test, however, you can take a number of steps to get in touch with your own EI (see the box below). You'll have to dig deep inside yourself and be willing to be honest about how you really think and how you really behave. This process can take time, and that's fine. Think of your EI as a work in progress.

> ### YOUR TURN
> ....
> **Write and Reflect**
>
> After you have completed the EI questionnaire, reflect on your results. Were you surprised about what you learned about yourself? What particular areas would you like to work on? Answer these questions in a journal entry.

EMOTIONAL INTELLIGENCE QUESTIONNAIRE

Your daily life gives you many opportunities to take a hard look at how you handle emotions. Here are some questions that can help you begin thinking about your own EI.

1. What do you do when you are under stress?

- ☐ a. I tend to deal with it calmly and rationally.
- ☐ b. I get upset, but it usually blows over quickly.
- ☐ c. I get upset but keep it to myself.

2. My friends would say that:

- ☐ a. I will play, but only after I get my work done.
- ☐ b. I am ready for fun anytime.
- ☐ c. I hardly ever go out.

3. When something changes at the last minute:

- ☐ a. I easily adapt.
- ☐ b. I get frustrated.
- ☐ c. It doesn't matter, since I don't really expect things to happen as I plan.

4. My friends would say that:

- ☐ a. I am sensitive to their concerns.
- ☐ b. I spend too much time worrying about other people's needs.
- ☐ c. I don't like to deal with other people's petty problems.

5. When I have a problem to solve such as too many things due at the end of the week:

- ☐ a. I write down a list of the tasks I must complete, come up with a plan indicating specifically what I can accomplish and what I cannot, and follow my plan.
- ☐ b. I am very optimistic about getting things done and just dig right in and get to work.
- ☐ c. I get a little frazzled. Usually I get a number of things done and then push aside the things I can't do.

Review your responses. a responses indicate that you probably have a good basis for strong EI. **b** responses indicate that you may have some strengths and some challenges in your EI. **c** responses indicate that your success in life and in school could be negatively affected by your EI.

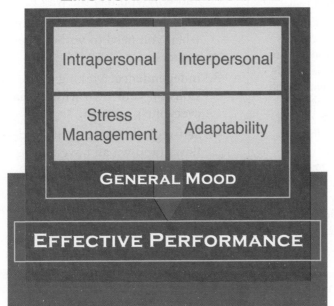

BAR-ON MODEL OF
EMOTIONAL INTELLIGENCE

Intrapersonal | Interpersonal

Stress Management | Adaptability

GENERAL MOOD

EFFECTIVE PERFORMANCE

FIGURE 3.1

Bar-On Model of Emotional Intelligence

Source: "What Is Emotional Intelligence?" from *Bar-On EQ-i Technical Manual*, © 1997, 1999, 2000 Multi-Health Systems, Inc., Toronto, Canada. Reproduced by permission of Multi-Health Systems.

Categorizing the Skills of Emotional Intelligence

Emotional intelligence is divided into different categories. Within each category are several competencies or skills that influence a person's ability to cope with life's pressures and demands. Reuven Bar-On, a professor at the University of Texas at Austin and world-renowned EI expert, developed a model that demonstrates how four categories of EI—intrapersonal, interpersonal, adaptability, and stress management—directly affect general mood and lead to effective performance (see Figure 3.1).

Let's take a closer look at the specific skills and competencies within the categories that Bar-On has identified as the pieces that make up a person's emotional intelligence.[2] It's something like a jigsaw puzzle, and when you have put all the pieces together, you will begin to see yourself and others more clearly.

INTRAPERSONAL SKILLS

The first category, intrapersonal skills, relates to how well you know and like yourself as well as how effectively you can do the things you need to do to stay happy. This category is made up of five specific competencies:

---

[2]Adapted from Reuven Bar-On, "The Bar-On Model of Emotional-Social Intelligence (ESI)," *Psicothema* 18, suppl. 13-25 (2006): 21, www.eiconsortium.org/pdf/baron_model_of_emotional _social_intelligence.pdf.

Is This You?

Are you an older student, maybe in your thirties or forties, who is back in college? As an adult, you probably have a great deal of life experience in dealing with tough times. How are you using your skills at standing up for yourself and negotiating with others as you face the challenges of college? You might want to give some advice to younger students who seem to be struggling with the day-to-day interactions that are part of college life.

1. **Emotional self-awareness.** Knowing how and why you feel the way you do.
2. **Assertiveness.** Standing up for yourself when you need to without being too aggressive.
3. **Independence.** Making important decisions on your own without having to get everyone's opinion.
4. **Self-regard.** Liking yourself despite your flaws (and we all have them).
5. **Self-actualization.** Being satisfied and comfortable with what you have achieved in school, work, and your personal life.

Understanding yourself and why you think and act as you do is the glue that holds all the EI competencies together. Knowledge of self is strongly connected to respect for others and their way of life. If you don't understand yourself and why you do the things you do, it can be difficult for you to understand others. What's more, if you don't like yourself, you can hardly expect others to like you.

INTERPERSONAL SKILLS

Recent studies have shown that people with extensive support networks are generally happier and tend to enjoy longer, healthier lives than those without

Help Yourself

Do you depend on other people to raise your own level of self-esteem? It is easy to allow comments from others to affect how we feel about ourselves. If you have a strong level of emotional intelligence, you will be less vulnerable to insults or empty flattery.

www.CartoonStock.com

www.CartoonStock.com

Think Outside the Bowl

Good problem solvers sometimes have to work alone and be persistent. Help is not always readily available. Harness your own creativity to solve your problems in college. That way you won't feel like a fish out of water.

such networks. Forging relationships and getting along with other people depend on three competencies that form the basis for the second category, interpersonal skills:

1. **Empathy.** Making an effort to understand another person's situation or point of view.
2. **Social responsibility.** Establishing a personal link with a group or community and cooperating with other members in working toward shared goals.
3. **Interpersonal relationships.** Seeking out healthy and mutually beneficial relationships—such as friendships, professional networks, family connections, mentoring, and romantic partnerships—and making a persistent effort to maintain them.

ADAPTABILITY

Things change. Adaptability, the ability to adjust your thinking and behavior when faced with new or unexpected situations, helps you cope and ensures that you'll do well in life, no matter what the challenges. This third category includes three key competencies:

1. **Reality testing.** Ensuring that your feelings are appropriate by checking them against external, objective criteria.
2. **Flexibility.** Adapting and adjusting your emotions, viewpoints, and actions as situations change.
3. **Problem solving.** Approaching challenges step-by-step and not giving up in the face of obstacles.

Don't Blow Your Top

There are good ways and bad ways to vent frustration. Having it out with another person and eating a gallon of ice cream are poor strategies. Going for a walk or a run, doing yoga, or "talking it out" with someone you trust, however, will help you deal with the frustrations that are common to college life without making things worse.

"The key to stress management is knowing how to vent your frustration."

© Randy Glasbergen

STRESS MANAGEMENT

In college, at work, and at home, now and in the future, you'll be faced with what can seem like never-ending pressures and demands. Stress management, the fourth category of the Bar-On Model, depends on two skills:

1. **Stress tolerance.** Recognizing the causes of stress and responding in appropriate ways; staying strong under pressure.
2. **Impulse control.** Thinking carefully about potential consequences before you act and delaying gratification for the sake of achieving long-term goals.

GENERAL MOOD AND EFFECTIVE PERFORMANCE

YOUR TURN

....

Write and Reflect

Select three EI competencies and do an Internet search for each of them. What kinds of information can you find about each of the competencies? Did any Web sites suggest helpful ways to strengthen these competencies? Prepare a short paper discussing your findings.

It might sound sappy, but having a positive attitude really does improve your chances of doing well. Bar-On emphasizes the importance of two emotions in particular:

1. **Optimism.** Looking for the "bright side" of any problem or difficulty and being confident that things will work out for the best.
2. **Happiness.** Being satisfied with yourself, with others, and with your situation in general.

It makes sense: If you feel good about yourself and manage your emotions, you can expect to get along with others and enjoy a happy, successful life.

TECH TIP SAY YES TO TWITTER

Although many considered Twitter to be a fad, it appears that it's here to stay for the foreseeable future. Get off the sidelines and into the world of microblogging.

 1 ▶ **THE PROBLEM**

You've heard people talk about Twitter, but you don't know why you'd join it or what you'd do with it.

 2 ▶ **THE FIX**

Dive in!

3 ▶ **HOW TO DO IT**

Twitter is a microblogging site used by millions of people globally. Microblogging is sending live messages, called "tweets," from Web-enabled devices. It's called "micro" because you have only 140 characters. (The previous sentence contains exactly 140 characters.)

1. Entertainment. You can use Twitter to keep up with your favorite actors, bands, and sports teams. Some people tweet about what they had for lunch; Neil Patrick Harris loves to do so. Some tweet about projects they're working on, some tweet political commentary, and others just share great jokes.

2. Education. Twitter is much more than fun facts about famous people. Twitter is a great way to keep up with professionals and scholars in your chosen discipline. Authors will tweet about their books and often engage in conversations with their readers. People will also share links to news articles, book reviews, Web sites, and videos related to certain careers and areas of study. Following leaders in your chosen field helps you stay up-to-date on current issues and gives you the opportunity to interact with experts.

3. Job hunting. Many career Web sites have Twitter accounts where they post frequent updates. Following the official Twitter feed of a company you want to work for can lead to instant notification of new job opportunities and will give you the chance to get your résumé ready to go!

4. Community involvement. One amazing feature of Twitter is it allows for global conversations on important issues. Twitter was a key component in the Arab Spring of 2011–2012, a period that saw dozens of political demonstrations and revolutionary movements across a wide range of the Arab world. Twitter was a conduit for international exchanges of information in real time. Organizers, protestors, news sources, and anyone curious about the situation were able to follow the story—live—on their computers or smartphones.

Diagram of a tweet

The message in 140 characters or fewer is called a tweet

↓ Tweet author profile image

Sample Person @sampleperson ← Tweet author

Paper Towns by @realjohngreen is my favorite book! #yalit #favoritebook

People mentioned in tweet. Your message will show up in the feed of anyone you've mentioned in your tweet. They'll be able to see what you write.

Hashtags are words preceded by a # that indicate the topic or a keyword related to the tweet. Hashtags are links and clicking on them will take you to all tweets using that hashtag.

Most recent tweets are at the top of the list. The two top tweets are in response to the original tweet at the bottom.

Twitter in Action

Sample King @kingsample

RT @sampleperson Paper Towns by @realjohngreen is my favorite book! #yalit #favoritebook

Sampson McSample @mcsample

.@sampleperson @realjohngreen I love that one too, but Looking for Alaska is my #favoritebook It won the #AWARD

Sample Person @sampleperson

Paper Towns by @realjohngreen is my favorite book! #yalit #favoritebook

Twitter Speak/Symbols
RT – Retweet – sending someone else's exact tweet to your list of followers
MT – Modified Tweet – a retweet with a few changes
. – If a tweet starts with @name, the tweet only shows up in the timeline of people who follow both users. A period is commonly used to make sure the tweet goes to all of a person's followers.

Accentuate the Positive

You probably know people who always find the negative in any situation. Constantly focusing on what's missing or what's not perfect will likely make you the kind of person whom others avoid. Practice looking on the bright side.

YOUR TURN

....

Write and Reflect

Write a description of yourself as a successful person ten years after you graduate. What kinds of skills will you have? Don't just focus on your degree or a job description; include the EI competencies that help explain why you have become successful.

HOW EMOTIONS AFFECT SUCCESS

Emotions are strongly tied to physical and psychological well-being. For example, some studies have suggested that cancer patients who have strong EI live longer than those with weak EI. People who are aware of the needs of others tend to be happier than people who are not. A large study done at the University of Pennsylvania found that the best athletes do well in part because they're extremely optimistic. Even if they face tremendous obstacles or have the odds stacked against them, emotionally intelligent people nonetheless go on to succeed.

EMOTIONAL INTELLIGENCE AND COLLEGE SUCCESS

A number of studies link strong EI skills to college success in particular. Here are a few highlights:

- **Emotionally intelligent students get higher grades.** Researchers looked at students' grade point averages at the end of the first year of college. Students who had tested high for intrapersonal skills, stress tolerance, and adaptability when they entered in the fall did better academically than those who had lower overall EI test scores.

© Quinn Kirk/Terry Wild Stock

Patience Is a Virtue

Delaying gratification when you really want something is tough for people of all ages, but sometimes postponing your desires is the right thing to do. Delaying things you can't afford or don't have time for will help you reach your long-term goals.

- **Students who can't manage their emotions struggle academically.** Some students have experienced full-blown panic attacks before tests, others who are depressed can't concentrate on coursework, and far too many turn to risky behaviors (drug and alcohol abuse, eating disorders, and worse) in an effort to cope. Dr. Richard Kadison, chief of Mental Health Services at Harvard University, notes that "the emotional well-being of students goes hand-in-hand with their academic development. If they're not doing well emotionally, they are not going to reach their academic potential."[3] Even students who manage to succeed academically despite emotional difficulties can be at risk if unhealthy behavior patterns follow them after college.

- **Students who can delay gratification tend to do better overall.** Impulse control leads to achievement. In the famous marshmallow study performed at Stanford University, researchers examined the long-term behaviors of individuals who, as four-year-olds, did or did not practice delayed gratification. The children were given one marshmallow and told that if they didn't eat it right away, they could have another. Fourteen years later, the children who ate their marshmallow immediately were more likely to experience significant stress, irritability, and inability to focus on goals than the children who waited. Those children scored an average of 210 points higher on the SAT; had better confidence, concentration, and reliability; held better-paying jobs; and

---

[3] Richard Kadison and Theresa Foy DiGeronimo, *College of the Overwhelmed: The Campus Mental Health Crisis and What to Do about It* (San Francisco: Jossey-Bass, 2004), p. 156.

THE STANFORD MARSHMALLOW STUDY

Impulse Controlled	Impulsive
> Assertive	> Indecisive
> Cope with frustration	> Overreact to frustration
> Work better under pressure	> Overwhelmed by stress
> Self-reliant, confident	> Lower self-image
> Trustworthy	> Stubborn
> Dependable	> Impulsive
> Delay gratification	> Don't delay gratification
> Academically competent	> Poorer students
> Respond to reason	> Prone to jealousy and envy
> Concentrate	> Provoke arguments
> Eager to learn	> Sharp temper
> Follow through on plans	> Give up in face of failure
> SAT: 610 verbal, 652 math	> SAT: 524 verbal, 528 math

Source: Y. Shoda, W. Mischel, and P. K. Peake, "Predicting Adolescent Cognitive and Self-Regulatory Competencies from Preschool Delay of Gratification," *Developmental Psychology* 26, no. 6 (1990): 978–86.

reported being more satisfied with life than those who did not wait. The chart above details the differences between the two groups of students after fourteen years.

- **EI skills can be enhanced in a first-year seminar.** In two separate studies, one conducted in Australia and another conducted in the United States, researchers found that college students enrolled in a first-year seminar who demonstrated good EI skills were more likely to do better in college than students who did not exhibit those behaviors. A follow-up study indicated that the students who had good EI skills also raised their scores on a measure of EI.

Without strong EI in college, it's possible to simply get by. You might, however, miss out on the full range and depth of competencies and skills that can help you succeed in your chosen field.

Improving Your Emotional Intelligence

Developing your EI is an important step toward getting the full benefit of a college education. Think about it. Do you often give up because something is just too hard or you can't figure it out? Do you take responsibility for what you do, or do you blame others if you fail? Can you really be successful in life if you don't handle change well or if you are not open to diverse groups and their opinions? How can you communicate effectively if you are not assertive or if you are overly aggressive? If you're inflexible, how can you solve problems, get along with coworkers and family members, or learn from other people's points of view?

STRATEGIES TO IMPROVE EI

It might not be easy to improve your EI—old habits are hard to change—but it can definitely be done. Here are some suggestions:

1. **Identify your strengths and weaknesses.** Take a hard look at yourself and consider how you respond to situations. Most people have trouble assessing their own behaviors realistically, so ask someone you trust and respect for insight. If you have an opportunity to take a formal EI test or meet with a behavioral counselor, by all means, do so.

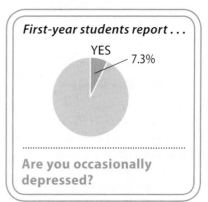

First-year students report . . .

YES — 7.3%

Are you occasionally depressed?

2. **Set realistic goals.** As you identify areas of emotional intelligence that you would like to improve, be as specific as possible. Instead of deciding to be more assertive, for example, focus on a particular issue that is giving you trouble, such as nagging resentment toward a friend who always orders the most expensive thing on the menu and then expects to split the whole check evenly.

3. **Formulate a plan.** With a particular goal in mind, identify a series of steps you could take to achieve the goal and define the results that would indicate success. As you contemplate your plan, consider all the emotional competencies discussed on pages 59–62. You might find that to be more assertive with your friend about the restaurant situation, for instance, you need to figure out why you're frustrated (emotional self-awareness), identify possible causes for your friend's behavior (empathy), and consider what you might be doing to encourage it (reality testing).

4. **Check your progress on a regular basis.** Continually reassess whether or not you have met your goals, and adjust your strategy as needed.

HANDLING STRESS

Suppose you know that you don't handle stress well. When things get tough—too many things are due at once, your roommate leaves clothes and leftover food all over the place, and your significant other seems a bit distant—you begin to fall apart. There's a model on page 68 that you might use for improving the way you handle stress.

EI competency: Stress tolerance

Specific goal: To get control of the things that are causing stress this week

Plan: Identify each stressor and select a strategy for addressing it

- List everything that needs to be done this week. Allot time for each item on the list and stick to a schedule. Reassess the schedule many times during the week.

- Ask yourself whether your roommate is bothering you only because you are stressed. Do you do some of the same things your roommate does? Ask yourself what the next step should be. Should you talk to your roommate? Look for another place to study?

- Ask yourself whether your significant other is acting differently for any reason. Is he or she under stress? Are you overreacting because you feel insecure in the relationship? After answering these questions, decide what the next step will be. Should you talk to your significant other and share your feelings with him or her? Reassess the situation in another week when things calm down?

- Identify what reduces stress for you and still allows you to stay on target to get things done. Exercising? Working in small chunks with rewards when you finish something? Playing a musical instrument?

Success indicator: You are feeling less stressed, and you have accomplished many of the things on your list. You are working out three times a week. Your significant other seems just fine, and your place is still a mess but it's not bothering you. You leave your room and decide to study in the library.

> ## YOUR TURN
> ·····································
> ### Write and Reflect
> Using this example as a model, select an EI competency that you would like to improve, choose a specific goal, and formulate a plan for accomplishing it. What kinds of results do you hope to achieve? How will improving your EI in this area help you become a happier, more confident person? Reflect on these questions in a journal entry.

It's important not to try to improve everything at once. Instead, identify specific EI competencies that you can define, describe, and then set measurable goals for change. Don't expect success overnight. Remember that it took you a while to develop your specific approach to life, and it will take commitment and practice to change it.

CHECKLIST FOR SUCCESS

EVALUATING YOUR EMOTIONAL INTELLIGENCE

☐ **Using the questionnaire in this chapter, assess your emotional intelligence.** Note areas in which your EI is strong and areas that need improvement.

☐ **Be aware of how your emotions affect the way you react to difficult or frustrating situations.** Use your awareness ahead of time to try to control your negative reactions.

☐ **Learn and then practice EI improvement strategies such as:**

- Identifying your strengths and weaknesses
- Setting realistic goals
- Formulating a plan
- Checking your progress on a regular basis

☐ **If you aren't satisfied with your emotional reactions, make an appointment in the campus counseling center to discuss your feelings and get help.** Counselors can help you monitor and understand your emotional responses in a confidential setting.

BUILD YOUR EXPERIENCE 1 2 3 4

1 STAY ON TRACK

Successful college students stay focused. They "stay on track." They know what they have to do to be successful, they set goals, and they monitor their progress toward their goals.

Reflect on what you have learned about college success in this chapter and how you are going to apply the chapter information or strategies in college and in your career. List your ideas.

1. _____

_____

_____

2. _____

_____

_____

3. _____

_____

_____

2 ONE-MINUTE PAPER

Emotional intelligence might be a term that you were not familiar with before reading this chapter. What did you find to be the most interesting information in this chapter? Make a note of any information that was hard to understand or apply to your own life. What kinds of questions do you still have for your instructor?

3 ## APPLYING WHAT YOU'VE LEARNED

Now that you have read and discussed this chapter, consider how you can apply what you have learned to your academic and personal life. The following prompts will help you reflect on the chapter material and its relevance to you both now and in the future.

1. Managing stress is an important skill in college. Take a look through your course syllabi and make a list of assignments, exams, and important dates. Do any of your assignments or exams seem to cluster around the same time in the term? Can you anticipate times when you might be especially likely to get stressed? What can you do in advance to avoid becoming overwhelmed and overstressed?

2. College life offers many opportunities to meet new people and develop a new support network, but finding friends and mentors you can trust is not always easy. What steps have you taken so far to meet new people and build a network of support in college?

4 ## BUILDING YOUR PORTFOLIO

Know Thyself   Understanding your own behavior can sometimes be more difficult than understanding someone else's. Review the questionnaire on page 58. Were you honest in your assessment of yourself?

1. In a Word document, list the questions from page 58 that you answered with a **b** or a **c**. For example, did you rate yourself with a **b** or a **c** on a question about last-minute changes?

2. Next, note the EI competencies that relate to each question. For the example about last-minute changes, the key competency is adaptability, as evidenced in reality testing, flexibility, and problem solving.

3. For each question that you have listed, describe your strategy for improving your response to certain situations. For example, when things change suddenly, you might say, "I am going to take a few minutes to think about what I need to do next. I will remind myself that I am still in control of my actions."

4. Save your responses in your portfolio or in the Cloud. Revisit your responses to the questions listed above as you experience similar situations.

   Pay special attention to how your emotional intelligence affects your daily life. As you become more aware of your emotions and actions, you will begin to see how you can improve in the areas that are most difficult for you.

For more on this topic watch
French Fries Are Not Vegetables and Other College Lessons

WHERE TO GO FOR HELP . . .

If you think you might need help developing some of these EI skills, especially if you think you are not happy or optimistic or you're not handling stress well, do something about it. Although you can look online and get some tips about being an optimistic person, for example, there is nothing like getting some help from a professional. Consider visiting your academic adviser or a wellness or counseling center on campus. Look for any related workshops that are offered on campus or nearby. Remember the good news about EI is that with persistence it can be improved.

MY INSTITUTION'S RESOURCES

_____

_____

_____

_____

_____

_____

4 How You Learn

> **Apply your learning style to your everyday life. Eventually you will learn in a different, smarter, and more efficient way.**
>
> Daniel Graham, 24
> Computer Science major
> Harold Washington College

Although he tells us, "I didn't have much knowledge of learning styles before I started college," Daniel Graham from Harold Washington College in Chicago enrolled in the College Success Seminar in his first semester. There, he took a learning styles inventory called the VARK and learned that he's both a kinesthetic learner, which means that he learns by doing, and a read/write learner, which means that he learns by reading and writing down material from class. Since then he has been able to employ numerous strategies that apply specifically to his form of multimodal learning to help him succeed in class. He does things like rewriting terms and concepts in his own words so that he better understands what they mean, and he uses note cards to help him memorize. He says that knowing

Daniel Graham ▶

eurobanks/Shutterstock

his learning style has improved his performance. "When I take notes, I read them silently on note cards and continue to return to them so I can memorize the meaning," he says.

It's not surprising that Daniel is also a kinesthetic learner as he spends 10 to 15 hours a week working in his family landscaping business. "A hands-on approach has my name written all over it." "I like being able to use my hands and express myself, and I like being able to figure things out just by playing with them for a bit." He translates this hands-on approach to learning by doing things like taking practice exams until he feels ready for the real exam.

Daniel chose to begin higher education at Harold Washington College because it was close to home and because he believed that he would receive more one-on-one attention from instructors by going to a community college for his associate's degree. Daniel is currently taking advantage of the TRIO program, which helps prepare students for a successful transfer to a four-year institution through advising, tutoring, and transfer assistance. After completing his associate's degree at Harold Washington, Daniel plans to transfer to Northeastern Illinois University to pursue a B.S. in computer information systems. Daniel plans to finish his degree and then explore job opportunities as well as master's programs. He ultimately hopes to be working as a computer programmer or software developer, and he plans to continue to rely on his learning styles: "Apply your learning style to your everyday life. Eventually you will learn in a different, smarter, and more efficient way."

Have you ever thought about how you learn, or are you like Daniel and never thought about learning styles before coming to college? People learn differently. This idea is hardly novel, but if you are to do well in college, it is important to become aware of your preferred way, or style, of learning. Experts agree that there is no one best way to learn.

Maybe you have trouble paying attention to a long lecture, or maybe listening is the way you learn best. You might love classroom discussion, or you might consider hearing what other students have to say in class a big waste of time.

Perhaps you have not thought about how college instructors, and even particular courses, have their own inherent styles, which can be different from your preferred style of learning. Many instructors rely almost solely on lecturing; others use lots of visual aids, such as PowerPoint outlines, charts, graphs, and pictures. In science courses, you will conduct experiments or go on field trips where you can observe or touch what you are studying. In dance, theater, or physical education courses, learning takes place in both your body and your mind. And in almost all courses, you'll learn by reading both textbooks and other materials. Some instructors are friendly and warm and others seem to want little interaction with students. It's safe to say that in at least some of your college courses, you won't find a close match between the way you learn most effectively and the way you're being taught. This chapter will help you first understand how you

■ ASSESSING YOUR STRENGTHS ■

Understanding your own preferred style of learning will help you study and earn good grades. Do you know how you learn best? As you begin to read this chapter, list your insights about your own learning styles.

_____

_____

_____

_____

■ SETTING GOALS ■

What are your most important objectives in learning the material in this chapter? Think about challenges you have had with relating to the way some instructors teach and expect you to learn. List three goals that relate to understanding learning styles (e.g., I will make a list of my favorite and least favorite classes and think about how my preferences might relate to my preferred style of learning).

1. _____

_____

2. _____

_____

3. _____

_____

learn best and then think of ways you can create a link between your style of learning and the expectations of each course and instructor. In addition to its focus on learning styles, this chapter will explore learning disabilities, which are very common among college students. You will learn how to recognize them and what to do if you or someone you know has a learning disability.

Tools for Measuring Your Learning Style

There are many ways of thinking about and describing **learning styles**. Some of them will make a lot of sense to you; others might initially seem confusing or counterintuitive. Some learning style theories are very simple, and some are complex. You will notice some overlap between the different theories and tools, but using several of them might help you do a

learning styles Particular ways of learning, unique to each individual. For example, one person prefers reading to understand how something works, whereas another prefers using a "hands-on" approach.

more precise job of discovering your learning style. If you are interested in reading more about learning styles, the library and campus learning center will have many resources.

THE VARK LEARNING STYLES INVENTORY

The VARK Inventory, a sixteen-item questionnaire, focuses on how learners prefer to use their senses (hearing, seeing, writing, reading, experiencing) to learn. The acronym VARK stands for "Visual," "Aural," "Read/Write," and "Kinesthetic." As you read through the following descriptions, see which ones ring true to how you learn.

Is This You?

Have you found that some of your classes aren't as interesting and engaging as you expected? Is one of the problems a mismatch between the way you like to learn and the instructor's teaching method? Perhaps you're a visual learner but are forced to sit through mostly lecture classes, or perhaps you really don't enjoy working with others even though your chemistry course requires you to complete lab assignments with a partner. This chapter will help you understand your own learning style and adapt it to any classroom situation.

- **Visual** learners prefer to learn information through charts, graphs, symbols, and other visual means. If you remember data best that is presented in graphic form or in a picture, map, or video, you are a visual learner.
- **Aural** learners prefer to hear information and discuss it with friends, classmates, or instructors. If talking about information from lectures or textbooks helps you remember it, you are an aural learner.
- **Read/Write** learners prefer to learn information through words on a printed page. During a test, if you can sometimes visualize where information appears in the textbook, you are a read/write learner.
- **Kinesthetic** learners prefer to learn through experience and practice, whether simulated or real. They often learn through their sense of touch. Recopying or typing notes helps them remember the material. They also learn better when their bodies are in motion, whether participating in sports, dancing, or working out. If you are a kinesthetic learner, you may find that even your sense of taste or smell contributes to your learning process.

Two or three of these modes probably describe your preferred ways of learning better than the others. At the college level, faculty members tend to share information primarily via lecture and the textbook, but many students like to learn through visual and interactive means. This difference creates a mismatch between learning and teaching styles. Is it a problem? Not necessarily, if you know how to handle such a mismatch. Later in this chapter you'll learn strategies to adapt lecture material and the text to your preferred modes of learning. First, though, to determine your learning style(s) according to the VARK Inventory, respond to the following questionnaire.

THE VARK QUESTIONNAIRE, VERSION 7.1

This questionnaire is designed to tell you about your preferences for how you work with information. Choose answers that explain your preference(s). Check the box next to those items. For each question, select *as many boxes as apply to you*. If none of the response options applies to you, leave the item blank.

1. You are helping someone who wants to go to your airport, town center, or railway station. You would:

- ☐ a. go with her.
- ☐ b. tell her the directions.
- ☐ c. write down the directions (without a map).
- ☐ d. draw a map or give her one.

2. You are not sure whether a word should be spelled "dependent" or "dependant." You would:

- ☐ a. see the words in your mind and choose by the way they look.
- ☐ b. think about how each word sounds and choose one.
- ☐ c. find it in a dictionary.
- ☐ d. write both words on paper and choose one.

3. You are planning a holiday for a group. You want some feedback from them about the plan. You would:

- ☐ a. describe some of the highlights.
- ☐ b. use a map or Web site to show them the places.
- ☐ c. give them a copy of the printed itinerary.
- ☐ d. phone, text, or e-mail them.

4. You are going to cook something as a special treat for your family. You would:

- ☐ a. cook something you know without the need for instructions.
- ☐ b. ask friends for suggestions.
- ☐ c. look through a cookbook for ideas from the pictures.
- ☐ d. use a cookbook where you know there is a good recipe.

5. A group of tourists want to learn about the parks or wildlife reserves in your area. You would:

- ☐ a. talk about, or arrange a talk for them, about parks or wildlife reserves.
- ☐ b. show them Internet pictures, photographs, or picture books.
- ☐ c. take them to a park or wildlife reserve and walk with them.
- ☐ d. give them a book or pamphlets about the parks or wildlife reserves.

6. You are about to purchase a digital camera or mobile phone. Other than price, what would most influence your decision?

- ☐ a. trying or testing it
- ☐ b. reading the details about its features
- ☐ c. thinking that it is a modern design and looks good
- ☐ d. hearing about its features from the salesperson

7. Remember a time when you learned how to do something new. Try to avoid choosing a physical skill (e.g., riding a bike). You learned best by:

- ☐ a. watching a demonstration.
- ☐ b. listening to somebody explaining it and asking questions.
- ☐ c. referring to diagrams and charts, e.g., visual clues.
- ☐ d. reading the written instructions, e.g., a manual or textbook.

8. You have a problem with your knee. You would prefer that the doctor:

- ☐ a. give you an online source or written materials to read about your problem.
- ☐ b. use a plastic model of a knee to show what was wrong.
- ☐ c. describe what was wrong.
- ☐ d. show you a diagram of what was wrong.

9. You want to learn a new program, skill, or game on a computer. You would:

- ☐ a. read the written instructions that came with the program.
- ☐ b. talk with people who know about the program.
- ☐ c. use the controls or keyboard.
- ☐ d. follow the diagrams in the book that came with it.

(continued)

10. You like Web sites that have:

☐ a. things you can click on, shift, or try.

☐ b. interesting design and visual features.

☐ c. interesting written descriptions, lists, and explanations.

☐ d. audio channels where you can hear music, radio programs, or interviews.

11. Other than price, what would most influence your decision to buy a new nonfiction book?

☐ a. thinking it looks appealing

☐ b. quickly reading parts of it

☐ c. hearing a friend talk about it and recommend it

☐ d. its real-life stories, experiences, and examples

12. You are using a book, CD, or Web site to learn how to take photos with your new digital camera. You would like to have:

☐ a. a chance to ask questions and talk about the camera and its features.

☐ b. clear written instructions with lists and bullet points about what to do.

☐ c. diagrams showing the camera and what each part does.

☐ d. many examples of good and poor photos and how to improve them.

13. You prefer a teacher or a presenter who uses:

☐ a. demonstrations, models, or practical sessions.

☐ b. question and answer, talk, group discussion, or guest speakers.

☐ c. handouts, books, or readings.

☐ d. diagrams, charts, or graphs.

14. You have finished a competition or test and would like some feedback:

☐ a. using examples from what you have done.

☐ b. using a written description of your results.

☐ c. from somebody who talks it through with you.

☐ d. using graphs showing what you had achieved.

15. You are going to choose food at a restaurant or café. You would:

☐ a. choose something that you have had there before.

☐ b. listen to the waiter or ask friends to recommend choices.

☐ c. choose from the descriptions in the menu.

☐ d. look at what others are eating or look at pictures of each dish.

16. You have to make an important speech at a conference or special occasion. You would:

☐ a. make diagrams or get graphs to help explain things.

☐ b. write a few key words and practice saying your speech over and over.

☐ c. write out your speech and learn from reading it over several times.

☐ d. gather many examples and stories to make the talk real and practical.

Scoring the VARK. Now you will match up each one of the boxes you selected with a category from the VARK using the following scoring chart. Circle the letter (V, A, R, or K) that corresponds to each one of your responses (A, B, C, or D). For example, if you marked both B and C for question 3, circle both the V and R in the third row.

Responses to Question 3:	A	B	C	D
VARK letter	K	(V)	(R)	A

Count the number of each of the VARK letters you have circled to get your score for each VARK.

Scoring Chart

Question	a Category	b Category	c Category	d Category
1	K	A	R	V
2	V	A	R	K
3	K	V	R	A
4	K	A	V	R
5	A	V	K	R
6	K	R	V	A
7	K	A	V	R
8	R	K	A	V
9	R	A	K	V
10	K	V	R	A
11	V	R	A	K
12	A	R	V	K
13	K	A	R	V
14	K	R	A	V
15	K	A	R	V
16	V	A	R	K

Total number of **V**s circled = _____   Total number of **A**s circled = _____

Total number of **R**s circled = _____   Total number of **K**s circled = _____

Because there is more than one answer for each question, scoring is not a simple matter of counting. It's like four stepping stones across water. Enter your scores **from highest to lowest** on the stones in the figure, with their V, A, R, and K labels.

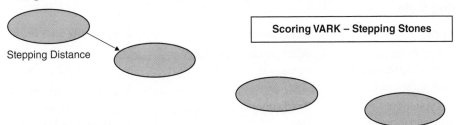

Stepping Distance

Scoring VARK – Stepping Stones

Your stepping distance comes from this table:

The total of my four VARK scores is	My stepping distance is
16–21	1
22–27	2
28–32	3
More than 32	4

Follow these steps to establish your preferences.

1. Your first preference is always your highest score. Check that first stone as one of your preferences.

2. Now subtract your second highest score from your first. If that figure is larger than your stepping distance, you have a single preference. Otherwise, check this stone as another preference and continue with step 3.

3. Subtract your third score from your second one. If that figure is larger than your stepping distance, you have a strong preference for two learning styles (bimodal). If not, check your third stone as a preference and continue with step 4.

4. Last, subtract your fourth score from your third one. If that figure is larger than your stepping distance, you have a strong preference for three learning styles (trimodal). You may also find that you prefer the four learning styles equally. Otherwise, check your fourth stone as a preference, and you have all four modes as your preferences!

Note: If you are bimodal or trimodal or you have checked all four modes as your preferences, you can be described as *multimodal* in your VARK preferences.

> ## YOUR TURN
> ....
> ### Discuss
> Did your VARK score surprise you at all? Did you know what type of learner you were before taking the test? If so, when did you discover that? How do you use your learning modality to your benefit? Be prepared to discuss your results and reflections with the class.

USE VARK RESULTS TO STUDY MORE EFFECTIVELY

How can knowing your VARK score help you do better in your college classes? The following table offers suggestions for using learning styles to develop your own study strategies. Consider also how online course-management systems (see the Tech Tip on page 91) provide opportunities for different types of learners to connect with the material they are studying.

Study Strategies by Learning Style

Visual	Aural	Read/Write	Kinesthetic
Underline or highlight your notes.	Talk with others to verify the accuracy of your lecture notes.	Write and rewrite your notes.	Use all your senses in learning: sight, touch, taste, smell, and hearing.
Use symbols, charts, or graphs to display your notes.	Put your notes on tape and listen or tape class lectures.	Read your notes silently.	Supplement your notes with real-world examples.
Use different arrangements of words on the page.	Read your notes out loud; ask yourself questions and speak your answers.	Organize diagrams or flowcharts into statements.	Move and gesture while you are reading or speaking your notes.
Redraw your pages from memory.		Write imaginary exam questions and respond in writing.	

THE KOLB INVENTORY OF LEARNING STYLES

A learning model that is more complex than the VARK Inventory is the widely used and referenced Kolb Inventory of Learning Styles. While the VARK Inventory investigates how learners prefer to use their senses in learning, the Kolb Inventory focuses on abilities we need to develop so as to learn. This inventory, developed in the 1980s by David Kolb, is based on a four-stage cycle of learning (see Figure 4.1).

According to Kolb, effective learners need four kinds of abilities:

YOUR TURN

Discuss

Think of all your classes this term and list your most favorite and least favorite ones. Then add the instructor's teaching style for each class on your list. Do you think your preferences have anything to do with the way the class is taught? Why or why not? Share your reflections with a small group. On page 90 you can use Figure 4.2 to compare your instructors' teaching styles to your learning style.

1. *Concrete experience* abilities, which allow them to be receptive to others and open to other people's feelings and specific experiences. An example of this type of ability is learning from and empathizing with others.

2. *Reflective observation* abilities, which help learners reflect on their experiences from many perspectives. An example of this type of ability is remaining impartial while considering a situation from a number of different points of view.

3. *Abstract conceptualization* abilities, which help learners integrate observations into logically sound theories. An example of this type of ability is analyzing ideas intellectually and systematically.

4. *Active experimentation* abilities, which enable learners to make decisions, solve problems, and test what they have learned in new situations. An example of this type of ability is being ready to move quickly from thinking to action.

Kolb's Inventory of Learning Styles measures differences along two basic dimensions that represent opposite styles of learning. The first dimension is *abstract-concrete,* and the second is *active-reflective.* See Figure 4.1 to visualize how these polar-opposite characteristics link together to create four discrete groups of learners: *divergers, assimilators, convergers,* and *accommodators.*

Doing well in college will require you to adopt some behaviors that are characteristic of each of these four learning styles. Some of them might be uncomfortable for you, but that discomfort will indicate that you're growing, stretching, and not relying on the learning style that might be easiest or most natural.

If you are a diverger, you are adept at reflecting on situations from many viewpoints. You excel at brainstorming, and you're imaginative, people oriented, and sometimes emotional. On the downside, you sometimes have difficulty making decisions. Divergers tend to major in the humanities or social sciences.

If you are an assimilator, you like to think about abstract concepts. You are comfortable in classes where the instructor lectures about theoretical ideas without relating the lectures to real-world situations. Assimilators often major in math, physics, or chemistry.

FIGURE 4.1
Kolb's Four-Stage Cycle of Learning

Source: "The Experiential Learning Model," from *The Modern American College: Responding to the New Realities of Diverse Students and a Changing Society*, ed. Arthur W. Chickering. Copyright © 1981. Reprinted with permission of John Wiley & Sons, Inc.

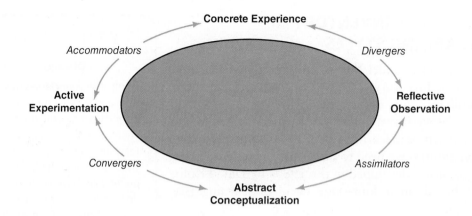

If you are a converger, you like the world of ideas and theories, but you also are good at thinking about how to apply those theories to real-world, practical situations. You differ from divergers in your preference for tasks and problems rather than social and interpersonal issues. Convergers tend to choose health-related and engineering majors.

If you are an accommodator, you prefer hands-on learning. You are skilled at making things happen, and you rely on your intuition. You like people, but you can be pushy and impatient at times, and you might use trial and error, rather than logic, to solve problems. Accommodators often major in business, especially in marketing or sales.[1]

In all your classes, but especially in liberal arts and social science courses, you will need to develop the strengths of divergers: imagination, brainstorming, and listening with an open mind. The abilities that are characteristic of assimilators, developing theories and concepts, are valuable for all students, especially those in the sciences. If you major in the health sciences or in engineering, you will routinely practice the skills of convergers: experimenting with new ideas and choosing the best solution. Finally, whatever your major and ultimate career, you'll need to get things done, take some risks, and become a leader, all skills that are characteristic of accommodators.

> ## YOUR TURN
> ### Write and Reflect
> On the basis of the descriptions we have provided here, where do you see yourself in the Kolb Inventory? Are you more like a diverger, assimilator, converger, or accommodator? How can you use this knowledge in your courses?

THE MYERS-BRIGGS TYPE INDICATOR

One of the best-known and most widely used personality inventories that can also be used to describe learning styles is the Myers-Briggs Type Indicator, or MBTI.[2] Whereas the VARK measures your preferences for using

---

[1]Adapted from David A. Kolb, "Learning Styles and Disciplinary Differences," in *The Modern American College*, ed. Arthur W. Chickering (San Francisco: Jossey Bass, 1981), pp. 232–35.
[2]Isabel Briggs Myers, *Introduction to Type*, 6th ed. (Mountain View, CA: CPP, 1998).

your senses to learn and the Kolb Inventory focuses on learning abilities, the MBTI investigates basic personality characteristics and how they relate to human interaction and learning. The MBTI was created by Isabel Briggs Myers and her mother, Katharine Cook Briggs. The inventory identifies and measures psychological type as developed in the personality theory of Carl Gustav Jung, the great twentieth-century psychoanalyst. The MBTI is given to several million people around the world each year. Employers often use this test to give employees insight into how they perceive the world, go about making decisions, and get along with other people. Many first-year seminar or college success courses also include a focus on the MBTI because it provides a good way to begin a dialogue about human interaction and how personality type affects learning.

All the psychological types described by the MBTI are normal and healthy. There is no good or bad or right or wrong; people are simply different. When you complete the Myers-Briggs survey instrument, your score represents your "psychological type," or the combination of your preferences on four different scales. These scales measure how you take in information and how you then make decisions or come to conclusions about that information. Each preference has a one-letter abbreviation. The four letters together make up your type. Although this book doesn't include the actual survey, you will find a description of the basic MBTI types below. In each case, which sounds more like you?

> ### YOUR TURN
> ....
> **Write and Reflect**
>
> Read the following descriptions of extraverts and introverts. Make a list of your friends and family members and indicate with an "E" or an "I" which are extraverts and which are introverts. How about you? Which type describes you best? Would you like to be different from the way you are? Reflect on these questions in a journal entry.

Extraversion (E) versus Introversion (I): The Inner or Outer World.

The E-I preference indicates whether you direct your energy and attention primarily toward the outer world of people, events, and things or the inner world of thoughts, feelings, and reflections. Personality characteristics of extraverts and introverts are summarized here:

Extraverts	Introverts
Outgoing, gregarious, talkative (may talk too much)	Shy, reflective; careful listeners
People of action (may act before they think)	Consider actions deeply (may think too long before acting or neglect to act at all)
Energized by people and activity	Refreshed by quiet and privacy
Good communicators and leaders	Less likely to voice their opinions; often viewed as unaware of people and situations around them

Jonathan Stark

Take a Time-out
Do you find that you need some occasional time by yourself? Although introverts are more likely to enjoy time alone, even extraverts can benefit from private time to relax or escape from the hustle and bustle of daily life.

Sensing (S) versus Intuition (N): Facts or Ideas. The S-N preference indicates how you perceive the world and take in information: directly, through your five senses; or indirectly, by using your intuition. Personality characteristics of sensing and intuitive types are summarized here:

Sensing Types	Intuitive Types
Interested above all in the facts, what they can be sure of; dislike unnecessary complication; prefer practicing skills they already know	Fascinated by concepts and big ideas; prefer learning new skills over those already mastered
Relatively traditional and conventional	Original, creative, and nontraditional
Practical, factual, realistic, and down-to-earth	Innovative but sometimes impractical; need inspiration and meaning; prefer to look to the future rather than at the present
Accurate, precise, and effective with routine and details; sometimes miss the "forest" for the "trees"	May exaggerate facts unknowingly; dislike routine and details; work in bursts of energy

Thinking (T) versus Feeling (F): Logic or Values. The T-F preference indicates how you prefer to make your decisions: through logical, rational analysis or through your subjective values, likes, and dislikes.

Personality characteristics of thinking types and feeling types are summarized here:

Thinking Types	Feeling Types
Logical, rational, analytical, and critical	Warm, empathetic, and sympathetic
Relatively impersonal and objective in making decisions, less swayed by feelings and emotions; sometimes surprised and puzzled by others' feelings	Need and value harmony; often distressed or distracted by argument and conflict; reluctant to tackle unpleasant interpersonal tasks
Need and value fairness; can deal with interpersonal disharmony	Need and value kindness and harmony
Fair, logical, and just; firm and assertive	Facilitate cooperation and goodwill in others; sometimes unable to be assertive when appropriate
May seem cold, insensitive, and overly blunt and hurtful in their criticisms	Occasionally illogical, emotionally demanding, and unaffected by objective reason and evidence

Judging (J) versus Perceiving (P): Organization or Adaptability.

The J-P preference indicates how you characteristically approach the outside world: by making decisions and judgments or by observing and perceiving instead. Personality characteristics of judging and perceiving types are summarized here:

Judging Types	Perceiving Types
Orderly, organized, punctual, and tidy	Spontaneous and flexible
In control of their own world and sphere of influence	Adapt to their world rather than try to control it; comfortable dealing with changes and unexpected developments
Quick decision makers; like to make and follow plans	Slow to make decisions; prefer a wait-and-see approach
Sometimes judgmental and prone to jump to conclusions or make decisions without enough information; have trouble changing plans	Tendency toward serious procrastination and juggling too many things at once without finishing anything; sometimes messy and disorganized

HOW TO USE YOUR STRONGEST—AND WEAKEST—PREFERENCES

Because each of the four different preferences has two possible choices, sixteen psychological types are possible. No matter what your Myers-Briggs type, all components of personality have value in the learning process. The key to success, therefore, is to use all the attitudes and functions (E, I, S, N, T, F, J, and P) in their most positive sense. As you go about your studies, we recommend this system:

1. *Extraversion:* Take action. Now that you have a plan, act on it. Do whatever it takes. Create note cards, study outlines, study groups, and so on. If you are working on a paper, now is the time to start writing.

2. *Introversion:* Think it through. Before you take any action, carefully review everything you have encountered so far.

3. *Sensing:* Get the facts. Use sensing to find and learn the facts. How do we know facts when we see them? What is the evidence for what is being said?

4. *Intuition:* Get the ideas. Now use intuition to consider what those facts mean. Why are those facts being presented? What concepts and ideas are being supported by those facts? What are the implications? What is the big picture?

5. *Thinking:* Critically analyze. Use thinking to analyze the pros and cons of what is being presented. Are there gaps in the evidence? What more do we need to know? Do the facts really support the conclusions? Are there alternative explanations? How well does what is presented hang together logically? How could our knowledge of it be improved?

6. *Feeling:* Make informed value judgments. Why is this material important? What does it contribute to people's good? Why might it be important to you personally? What is your personal opinion about it?

7. *Judging:* Organize and plan. Don't just dive in! Now is the time to organize and plan your studying so that you will learn and remember everything you need to. Don't just plan in your head, either; write your plan down, in detail.

8. *Perceiving:* Change your plan as needed. Be flexible enough to change something that isn't working. Expect the unexpected and deal with the unforeseen. Don't give up the whole effort the minute your original plan stops working. Figure out what's wrong, come up with another, better plan, and start following that.[3]

YOUR TURN

Write and Reflect

Do a Google search for the term *multiple intelligences debate.* Write a one-page paper that describes different opinions about Howard Gardner's theory. Do you agree with the theory? Why or why not?

MULTIPLE INTELLIGENCES

Another way of measuring how we learn is the theory of *multiple intelligences,* developed in 1983 by Dr. Howard Gardner, a professor of education at Harvard University. Gardner's theory is based on the premise that the traditional notion of human intelligence is very limited. Gardner argues that students should be encouraged to develop the abilities they have and that evaluation should measure all forms of intelligence, not just linguistic and logical-mathematical intelligence. As you might imagine, Gardner's work is controversial because it questions our long-standing

[3]Ibid.

definitions of intelligence. According to Gardner, all human beings have at least eight different types of intelligence:

1. A **verbal/linguistic** learner likes to read, write, and tell stories and is good at memorizing information.

2. A **logical/mathematical** learner likes to work with numbers and is good at problem-solving and logical processes.

3. A **visual/spatial** learner likes to draw and play with machines and is good at puzzles and reading maps and charts.

4. A **bodily/kinesthetic** learner likes to move around and is good at sports, dance, and acting.

5. A **musical/rhythmic** learner likes to sing and play an instrument and is good at remembering melodies and noticing pitches and rhythms.

6. An **interpersonal** learner likes to have many friends and is good at understanding people, leading others, and mediating conflicts.

7. **Intrapersonal** learners like to work alone, understand themselves well, and are original thinkers.

8. A **naturalistic** learner likes to be outside and is good at preservation, conservation, and organizing a living area.

Where do you think you see yourself? Which of these eight intelligences, do you think, best describes you? As you think of your friends and family, what kinds of intelligences do you think they have? Now, take the inventory.

MULTIPLE INTELLIGENCES INVENTORY

Put a check mark next to all the items within each intelligence that apply to you.

Verbal/Linguistic Intelligence

_____ I enjoy telling stories and jokes.

_____ I enjoy word games (e.g., Scrabble and puzzles).

_____ I am a good speller (most of the time).

_____ I like talking and writing about my ideas.

_____ If something breaks and won't work, I read the instruction book before I try to fix it.

_____ When I work with others in a group presentation, I prefer to do the writing and library research.

Logical/Mathematical Intelligence

_____ I really enjoy my math class.

_____ I like to find out how things work.

_____ I enjoy computer and math games.

_____ I love playing chess, checkers, or Monopoly.

_____ If something breaks and won't work, I look at the pieces and try to figure out how it works.

Visual/Spatial Intelligence

_____ I prefer a map to written directions.

_____ I enjoy hobbies such as photography.

_____ I like to doodle on paper whenever I can.

_____ In a magazine, I prefer looking at the pictures rather than reading the text.

_____ If something breaks and won't work, I tend to study the diagram of how it works.

(continued)

Bodily/Kinesthetic Intelligence

_____ My favorite class is gym because I like sports.

_____ When looking at things, I like touching them.

_____ I use a lot of body movements when talking.

_____ I tend to tap my fingers or play with my pencil during class.

_____ If something breaks and won't work, I tend to play with the pieces to try to fit them together.

Musical/Rhythmic Intelligence

_____ I enjoy listening to CDs and the radio.

_____ I like to sing.

_____ I like to have music playing when doing homework or studying.

_____ I can remember the melodies of many songs.

_____ If something breaks and won't work, I tend to tap my fingers to a beat while I figure it out.

Interpersonal Intelligence

_____ I get along well with others.

_____ I have several very close friends.

_____ I like working with others in groups.

_____ Friends ask my advice because I seem to be a natural leader.

_____ If something breaks and won't work, I try to find someone who can help me.

Intrapersonal Intelligence

_____ I like to work alone without anyone bothering me.

_____ I don't like crowds.

_____ I know my own strengths and weaknesses.

_____ I find that I am strong-willed, independent, and don't follow the crowd.

_____ If something breaks and won't work, I wonder whether it's worth fixing.

Naturalist Intelligence

_____ I am keenly aware of my surroundings and of what goes on around me.

_____ I like to collect things like rocks, sports cards, and stamps.

_____ I like to get away from the city and enjoy nature.

_____ I enjoy learning the names of living things in the environment, such as flowers and trees.

_____ If something breaks and won't work, I look around me to see what I can find to fix the problem.

Review your responses. Now, count up the check marks for each intelligence and write the total for each intelligence here. Your score for each intelligence will be a number between 1 and 6:

TOTAL SCORE

_____ Verbal/Linguistic

_____ Logical/Mathematical

_____ Visual/Spatial

_____ Bodily/Kinesthetic

_____ Musical/Rhythmic

_____ Interpersonal

_____ Intrapersonal

_____ Naturalist

Your high scores of 3 or more will help you to get a sense of your own multiple intelligences.

Depending on your background and age, some intelligences are likely to be more developed than others. Now that you know where your intelligences are, you can work to strengthen the other intelligences that you do not use as often. How do college courses measure ways in which you are intelligent? Where do they fall short? Looking to the future, you can use your intelligences to help you make decisions about a major, choose activities, and investigate career options. This information will help you appreciate your own unique abilities and also those of others.

Source: Greg Gay and Gary Hams, "The Multiple Intelligences Inventory." From atsp.atutorspaces.com. Reprinted by permission of Greg Gay.

When Learning Styles and Teaching Styles Conflict

Educators who study learning styles maintain that instructors tend to teach in ways that conform to their own particular styles of learning. So, an introverted instructor who prefers abstract concepts and reflection (an assimilator,

"As we start a new school year, Mr. Smith, I just want you to know that I'm an Abstract-Sequential learner and trust that you'll conduct yourself accordingly!"

William G. Browning, Minneapolis, MN

Learn to Adapt

Do you know your personal learning style? In college you will find that some instructors may have teaching styles that are challenging for you. Seek out the kinds of classes that conform to the way you like to learn, but also develop your adaptive strategies to make the most of any classroom setting.

according to Kolb) and learns best in a read/write mode or aural mode will probably structure the course in a lecture format with little opportunity for either interaction or visual and kinesthetic learning. Conversely, an instructor who prefers a more interactive, hands-on environment will likely involve students in discussion and learning through experience. The Tech Tip in this chapter has great ideas about how a class Web site can help students be successful no matter how learning and teaching styles line up.

Do you enjoy listening to lectures, or do you find yourself gazing out the window or dozing? When your instructor assigns a group discussion, what is your immediate reaction? Do you dislike talking with other students, or is that the way you learn best? How do you react to lab sessions when you have to conduct an actual experiment? Is it an activity you look forward to or one you dread? Each of these learning situations appeals to some students more than others, but each is inevitably going to be part of your college experience. Your college or university has intentionally designed courses for you to have the opportunity to listen to professors who are experts in their field, to interact with other students in structured groups, and to learn through doing. Because they are all important components of your college education, it's important for you to make the most of each situation.

When you recognize a mismatch between how you best learn and how you are being taught, it is important that you take control of your learning process. Use Figure 4.2 as a guide to identify these mismatches and discover strategies for how to handle them. Don't depend on the instructor or the classroom environment to give you everything you need to maximize your learning. Employ your own preferences, talents, and abilities to develop many

FIGURE 4.2
Using the VARK to Adapt

Try to use the VARK to figure out how your instructors teach their classes.

List your classes, your instructor's teaching styles, and then your learning style. Do they match? If not, list a strategy you can use to adapt.

My Classes	Teaching Style	My Learning Style	Match: Yes or No?
Example: Psychology	Loves PowerPoints with her lecture so: Visual and Auditory	I am kinesthetic and visual.	No, but I can ride a stationary bike while looking over my notes.

different ways to study and retain information. Look back through this chapter to remind yourself of the ways in which you can use your own learning styles to be more successful in any class you take. For instance, if you are an aural learner, reviewing and discussing course material in a study group setting will help you retain information.

Learning Disabilities

learning disabilities
Disorders such as dyslexia that affect people's ability to either interpret what they see and hear or connect information across different areas of the brain.

Although everyone has a learning style, a portion of the population has what is characterized as a **learning disability**. In addition to its focus on learning styles, this chapter explores learning disabilities, which are very common among college students. You might know someone who has been diagnosed with a learning disability, such as dyslexia or attention deficit disorder. It is also possible that you have a special learning need and are not aware of it. This section seeks to increase your self-awareness and your knowledge about such challenges to learning. In reading this section, you will learn more about common types of learning disabilities, how to recognize them, and what to do if you or someone you know has a learning disability.

Learning disabilities are usually recognized and diagnosed in grade school, but some students can successfully compensate for a learning problem, perhaps without realizing that's what it is, and reach college without having been properly diagnosed or assisted. Learning disabilities affect people's ability to interpret what they see and hear or to link information across different parts of the brain. These limitations can show up as specific difficulties with spoken and written language, coordination, self-control, or attention. Such difficulties can impede learning to read, write, or do math. The term *learning disability* covers a broad range of possible causes, symptoms, treatments, and outcomes. Therefore, it is difficult to diagnose a learning disability or pinpoint its causes. The types of learning disabilities that most commonly affect college students are attention disorders and disorders that affect the development of academic skills, including reading, writing, and mathematics.

TECH TIP CONNECT

If the thought of a two-hour lecture in an auditorium crammed with two hundred students fills you with a warm glow, chances are you're an auditory learner. What if you're a visual learner who needs charts, graphs, and videos and these are missing from the lecture? Or what if you are a hands-on, group type who thrives best when immersed in a project and has the opportunity to work with others? Many colleges and universities have introduced a course-management system, or CMS. A CMS is a Web site that boosts your ability to connect with the material you're studying—as well as with your instructors and classmates—both in and outside of class.

Courtesy, zengenuity.com

1 ▶ THE PROBLEM

You don't really understand what a CMS is or don't have the slightest clue how to use one, and you aren't so sure that it sounds good to you that a CMS "makes" you learn course material in a whole new way.

2 ▶ THE FIX

Be open-minded about this technology. With patience, you'll learn how to make it work for you. Figure out your learning style (by taking an online survey or test like Myers-Briggs) and look for classes that complement your strengths. At the same time, find ways to adapt to teaching techniques that lie outside your comfort zone.

3 ▶ HOW TO DO IT

To get motivated, think of all the advantages that a CMS offers. A CMS offers lots of other ways to help you connect with your instructors, your classmates, and the material. It lets you keep track of your grades and assignments. It offers a digital drop box for safely submitting your work. It also makes a lot of fun things possible, such as online discussion forums and interactive group projects where you can do things like sketch ideas on whiteboards that other students can view or even collaborate on written assignments in real time. Some CMSs have the excellent advantage of making available to you videos, recorded lectures, or even your instructor's lecture notes. In other words, the basic ingredients of a CMS—video, audio, and text—appeal to different learning styles.

1. If you're an aural learner, you'll love audio recordings. *To get the most from text,* read your notes and textbook passages aloud as you study. (You can even record them to play back to yourself.) While you're at it, listen to books on tape and join a study group for discussions. *To get the most from video clips,* listen to them once and then play them back with your eyes closed.

2. If you're a visual learner, you'll love videos, pictures, maps, and graphs. *To get the most from audio recordings and text,* take notes and illustrate them, playing up key points with colored highlighters, pictures, or symbols. You can also create a graph or chart to display important concepts.

3. If you're a kinesthetic or hands-on learner, you'll love labs, group projects, and any kind of fieldwork. *To get the most from audio, video, and text,* sit in the front row of your classroom, take notes, and read things aloud as you study. Build models or spreadsheets. Take field trips to gather experience. In other words, get creative.

KNOW THIS

Once you learn how to log into the system, do it often. CMS use varies from one department or instructor to another, and you want to make sure you don't miss anything. If you're having trouble logging in or figuring out your username and password, ask your instructor for help.

Figure how much online activity you can handle. If you sign up for face-to-face classes, you might only use a CMS for a few things, such as submitting assignments or swapping essays for peer review. If you enroll in a hybrid course, your instructor may step it up by posting outside reading material or creating online discussions on your CMS. In a fully online course, you'll probably do *everything* on the CMS, including taking exams. Before you register at college, consider which type of course suits your schedule and learning style.

PERSONAL BEST

Your college's CMS is designed to make your life easier, so don't get bogged down by issues that prevent you from taking advantage of it. Turn to your favorite type-A classmate, your instructor or teaching assistant, or the campus computer lab or student success center. College is about finding solutions and learning how to make the most of the resources available to you. So, go out there and embrace your CMS!

ATTENTION DISORDERS

Attention disorders are common in children, adolescents, and adults. Some students with attention disorders appear to daydream excessively, and even after getting their attention, they can be easily distracted. Individuals with attention deficit disorder (ADD) or attention deficit hyperactivity disorder (ADHD) often have trouble organizing tasks, following directions, or completing their work. As a result, their work might be messy or appear careless. Although they are not strictly classified as learning disabilities, ADD and ADHD can seriously interfere with academic performance, leading some educators to classify them along with other learning disabilities.[4]

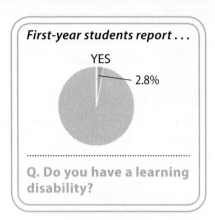

First-year students report . . .

YES

2.8%

Q. Do you have a learning disability?

If you have trouble paying attention or getting organized, you won't really know whether you have ADD or ADHD until you are evaluated. Check out resources on campus or in the community. After you have been evaluated, follow the advice you get, which might or might not mean taking medication. If you do receive a prescription for medication, be sure to take it according to the physician's directions. In the meantime, if you're having trouble getting and staying organized, whether or not you have an attention disorder, you can improve your focus through your own behavioral choices. The National Institute of Mental Health offers the following suggestions (found on its Web site) for adults with attention disorders:

> Adults with ADD or ADHD can learn how to organize their lives by using "props," such as a large calendar posted where it will be seen in the morning, date books, lists, and reminder notes. They can have a special place for keys, bills, and the paperwork of everyday life. Tasks can be organized into sections so that completion of each part can give a sense of accomplishment. Above all, adults who have ADD or ADHD should learn as much as they can about their disorder.[5]

COGNITIVE LEARNING DISABILITIES

Other learning disabilities are related to cognitive skills. Dyslexia, for example, is a common developmental reading disorder. A person can have problems with any of the tasks involved in reading. Scientists have found, however, that a significant number of people with dyslexia share an inability to distinguish or separate the sounds in spoken words. For instance, dyslexic individuals sometimes have difficulty assigning the appropriate sounds to letters, either individually or when letters combine to form words. There is more to reading than recognizing words, though. If the brain is unable to form images or relate new ideas to those stored in memory, the reader can't understand or remember the new concepts. So, other types of

[4]Adapted from Sharyn Neuwirth, *Learning Disabilities* (Darby, PA: National Institute of Mental Health, 1993), 9–10.

[5]http://www.nimh.nih.gov/health/publications/attention-deficit-hyperactivity-disorder/can-adults-have-adhd.shtml. National Institute of Mental Health (2009). "Attention Deficit Hyperactivity Disorder."

reading disabilities can appear when the focus of reading shifts from word identification to comprehension.[6]

"Writing, too, involves several brain areas and functions. The brain networks for vocabulary, grammar, hand movement, and memory must all be in good working order. So, a developmental writing disorder might result from problems in any of these areas."[7] Someone who can't distinguish the sequence of sounds in a word will often have problems with spelling. People who have writing disabilities, particularly expressive language disorders (the inability to express oneself using accurate language or sentence structure), are often unable to compose complete, grammatical sentences.[8]

A student with a developmental arithmetic disorder will have difficulty recognizing numbers and symbols, memorizing facts such as the multiplication table, aligning numbers, and understanding abstract concepts such as place value and fractions.[9]

Anyone who is diagnosed with a learning disability is in good company. The pop star Jewel; Michael Phelps, the Olympic gold medal swimmer; and actors Keira Knightley, Orlando Bloom, Patrick Dempsey, and Vince Vaughn are just a few of the famous and successful people who have diagnosed learning disabilities. A final important message: A learning disability is a learning difference, but in no way is it related to intelligence. Having a learning disability is not a sign that you are stupid. In fact, some of the most intelligent individuals in human history have had a learning disability.

The following questions may help you determine whether you should seek further screening for a possible learning disability:

- Do you perform poorly on tests even when you think you have studied and are capable of performing better?
- Do you have trouble spelling words?
- Do you work harder than your classmates at basic reading and writing?
- Do your instructors tell you that your performance in class is inconsistent, such as answering questions correctly in class but incorrectly on a written test?
- Do you have a really short attention span, or do others say that you do things without thinking?

Although responding "yes" to any of these questions does not mean that you have a disability, the resources of your campus learning center or the office for student disability services can help you address any potential problems and devise ways to learn more effectively.

[6]Ibid., 7.

[7]Quoted ibid., 7–8.

[8]Ibid., 8.

[9]Ibid., 8.

CHECKLIST FOR SUCCESS

USE YOUR LEARNING STYLE TO HELP YOU SUCCEED

☐ **Take a learning styles inventory, either in this chapter or at your campus learning or counseling center(s).** See if the results might explain, at least in part, your level of performance in each class you are taking this term.

☐ **Learn about and accept your unique learning preferences.** Especially make note of your strengths in terms of those things you learn well and easily. See if those skills could be applied to other learning situations.

☐ **Adapt your learning style to the teaching styles of your professors.** Consider talking to your professors about how you might best be able to adapt to their teaching strategies.

☐ **Use your learning style to develop study strategies that work best for you.** You can walk, talk, read, listen, or even dance while you are learning.

☐ **If you need help with making the best use of your learning style, visit your learning center.** Consider taking some courses in the social and behavioral sciences that would help you better understand how humans learn.

☐ **If you think you might have a learning disability, go to your campus learning center and ask for a diagnostic assessment so that you can develop successful coping strategies.** Make sure to ask for a personal interpretation and follow-up counseling or tutoring.

BUILD YOUR EXPERIENCE 1 2 3 4

1 STAY ON TRACK

Successful college students stay focused. They "stay on track." They know what they have to do to be successful, they set goals, and they monitor their progress toward their goals.

Reflect on what you have learned about college success in this chapter and how you are going to apply the chapter information or strategies in college and in your career. List your ideas.

1. _____

_____

_____

2. _____

_____

_____

3. _____

_____

_____

2 ONE-MINUTE PAPER

Recognizing that people have different ways of learning can be a relief. After reading this chapter, do you have a better understanding of your own learning style? What did you find to be the most interesting point in this chapter? What would you like to learn more about?

3 APPLYING WHAT YOU'VE LEARNED

1. It is almost certain that you will find yourself in a class where your learning style conflicts with your instructor's preferred style of teaching. After reading this chapter, describe what you can do to take control and make the most of your strongest learning preferences.

2. It is important to understand various learning styles in the context of education, but it is also important to understand how learning preferences affect career choices. Considering your own learning styles, what might be the best careers for you? Why?

4 BUILDING YOUR PORTFOLIO

Are We on the Same Page?   After reading about the Myers-Briggs Type Indicator in this chapter, can you guess what type you are?

1. Create a Word document and note each type that you think best fits your personality.

   Extravert or Introvert

   Sensing or Intuition

   Thinking or Feeling

   Judging or Perceiving

2. Note what you think your four MBTI letters would be (e.g., ESTP).

3. Using your favorite Internet search engine, search for "suggested careers for MBTI types." You will find several Web sites that suggest specific careers based on specific personality types.

4. Visit one site and list at least two careers that are recommended for the MBTI type you identify. Have you thought about these careers before? Do you think they would be a good fit for you? Why or why not? (Example: Careers recommended for ESTP: sales representatives, marketers, police, detectives, paramedics, medical technicians, computer technicians, computer technical support, entrepreneurs. Suggestions can be found at www.knowyourtype.com.)

5. Save your findings in your portfolio or in the Cloud. Revisit this document as you continue to explore different majors and careers.

For more on this topic watch
French Fries Are Not Vegetables and Other College Lessons

WHERE TO GO FOR HELP . . .

ON CAMPUS

To learn more about learning styles and learning disabilities, talk to your first-year seminar instructor about campus resources. Find out if your college or university has a learning center or a center for students with disabilities. If so, visit the center and learn about its resources. You might also find that instructors in the areas of education or psychology have a strong interest in the processes of learning. Finally, check out both your library and the Internet. A great deal of published information is available to describe how we learn.

BOOKS

> Edward M. Hallowell and John J. Ratey, *Driven to Distraction (Revised): Recognizing and Coping with Attention Deficit Disorder* (New York: Anchor Books, 2011).

> Susan C. Pinsky, *Organizing Solutions for People with Attention Deficit Disorder* (Gloucester, MA: Fair Winds Press, 2006).

> Patricia O. Quinn, MD (ed.), *ADD and the College Student: A Guide for High School and College Students with Attention Deficit Disorder* (Washington, DC: Magination Press, 2001).

ONLINE

> **LD Pride www.ldpride.net/learningstyles .MI.htm**. This Web site was developed in 1998 by Liz Bogod, an adult with learning disabilities. It provides general information about learning styles and learning disabilities and offers an interactive diagnostic tool to determine your learning style.

> **National Center for Learning Disabilities www.ncld.org**. This official Web site of the National Center for Learning Disabilities provides a variety of resources on diagnosing and understanding learning disabilities.

> **Facebook www.facebook.com**. There are groups on Facebook that were created by students who have learning disabilities or ADHD. These groups are a great way to connect with other students with learning disabilities at your college or university or at other institutions. If you have been diagnosed with a disability, the members of these groups can offer support and help you seek out appropriate resources to be successful in college.

> **National Institute of Mental Health http://www.nimh.nih.gov/health/publications /attention-deficit-hyperactivity-disorder/index .shtml**. Adults who have ADD or ADHD—many adults who have this disorder don't know it—can get information about how it is diagnosed and treated in adults from reading this online publication.

MY INSTITUTION'S RESOURCES

_____

_____

_____

_____

_____

_____

_____

_____

_____

5 Critical Thinking

> " Thinking for ourselves and coming up with new conclusions will be really helpful when we enter the workforce.

Alyssa Manning, 18
Psychology major
University of North Carolina
Charlotte

As a psychology student at the University of North Carolina Charlotte (UNCC), Alyssa Manning understands the importance of critical-thinking skills both inside and outside the classroom. When Alyssa arrived on campus last fall, she learned that she would be living in the international residence hall with students from all over the world. She quickly learned that interacting with people who don't know anyone else in the United States and who have different customs, study habits, and food, among other things, presents some welcome challenges and tested her critical-thinking skills. "Some of the questions the international students ask about America make me think in a different way because I never think about my own country in that way." One way she has been able to reach out to the students she lives with is by joining an international student organization, which helps bring new international students to campus and get them settled into campus life.

Alyssa grew up in Philadelphia and decided to attend UNCC because she was interested in the research opportunities available to her as an undergraduate psychology

Alyssa Manning ▶

David Aaron Troy/Getty Images

major (the beautiful campus and location in Charlotte didn't hurt either!). So far, her favorite class has been Social Psychology. She has found critical-thinking skills essential to succeeding in all her classes. "Professors will give you a lot of facts and general information, but they expect you to be able to relate all the information and come up with your own conclusions. Thinking for ourselves and coming up with new conclusions will be really helpful when we enter the workforce," she says.

After Alyssa graduates, she's open to new experiences and opportunities, but she hopes to continue on to graduate school. As an aspiring psychiatrist, she says that "critical-thinking skills will help a lot when dealing with cases and needing to diagnose disorders and develop treatment plans. They will also be helpful in clinical settings." Her advice to other first-year students? Look for ways to recognize problems and come up with their own unique solution.

As Alyssa mentioned, arguably the most important skills you'll acquire in college are the ability and the confidence to think for yourself. Courses in every discipline will encourage you to ask questions, sort through competing information and ideas, form well-reasoned opinions, and defend them.

If you have just completed high school, you might be experiencing an awakening as you adjust to college. If you're an older returning student, discovering that your instructors trust you to find valid answers could be both surprising and stressful. If a high school teacher asked, "What are the three branches of the U.S. government?" there was only one acceptable answer: "legislative, executive, and judicial." A college instructor, on the other hand, might ask, "Under what circumstances might conflicts arise among the three branches of government, and what does this reveal about the democratic process?" There is no simple—or single—answer, and that's the point of higher education. Questions that suggest complex answers engage you in the process of critical thinking.

Most important questions don't have simple answers, and satisfying answers can be elusive. To reach them, you will have to discover numerous ways to view important issues. You will need to become comfortable with uncertainty. You must also be willing to challenge assumptions and conclusions, even those presented by so-called experts. It is natural to find critical thinking difficult and feel frustrated by answers that are seldom entirely wrong or right, yet the complicated questions are usually the ones that are most worthy of study. Also, working out the answers can be both intellectually exciting and personally rewarding. In this chapter we will explain how developing and applying your critical-thinking skills can make the search for truth a worthwhile and stimulating adventure.

What Is Critical Thinking, and Why Is It Important?

For most colleges and universities, helping students become critical thinkers is a central part of their mission and purpose, and measuring whether students actually improve their critical-thinking abilities is a common form of

■ **ASSESSING YOUR STRENGTHS** ■

Critical thinking is one of the most valuable skills you can practice for success in college and in the workplace. Are you a good critical thinker? As you begin to read this chapter, list specific examples of your strengths in critical thinking.

_____

_____

_____

_____

■ **SETTING GOALS** ■

What are your most important objectives in learning the material in this chapter? Do you know the difference between critical thinking and "being critical"? List three goals that relate to developing and practicing critical-thinking skills (e.g., This week I will watch one TV news show, such as *Meet the Press, The O'Reilly Factor,* or *The Daily Show,* and make a list of "facts" I question and why).

1. _____

_____

2. _____

_____

3. _____

_____

student assessment. But figuring out precisely what is meant by the term *critical thinking* is often a challenge for students and professors alike.

DEFINING CRITICAL THINKING

Let's start with what critical thinking is *not*. By "critical," we do not mean "negative" or "harsh." Rather, the term refers to thoughtful consideration of the information, ideas, and arguments that you encounter. Critical thinking is the ability to think for yourself and to reliably and responsibly make decisions that affect your life.

As Richard Paul and Linda Elder of the National Council for Excellence in Critical Thinking explain it, "Critical thinking is that mode of thinking about any subject, content, or problem in which the thinker improves the quality of his or her thinking by skillfully . . . imposing intellectual standards upon [his or her thoughts]."[1] They believe that much of our thinking, left to

[1] Richard Paul and Linda Elder, *The Miniature Guide to Critical Thinking Concepts and Tools* (Dillon Beach, CA: Foundation for Critical Thinking Press, 2008).

itself, is biased, distorted, partial, uninformed, or downright prejudiced. The quality of our life and the quality of what we produce, make, or build, however, depend precisely on the quality of our thoughts.

Paul and Elder also caution that shoddy thinking is costly. How so? You probably know people who simply follow authority. They do not question, are not curious, and do not challenge people or groups who claim special knowledge or insight. These people do not usually think for themselves but instead rely on others to think for them. They might indulge in wishful, hopeful, and emotional thinking, assuming that what they believe is true simply because they wish it, hope it, or feel it to be true. As you might have noticed, such people tend not to have much control over their circumstances or possess any real power in business or society.

Critical thinkers, in contrast, investigate problems, ask questions, pose new answers that challenge the status quo, discover new information, question authorities and traditional beliefs, challenge received dogmas and doctrines, make independent judgments, and develop creative solutions. When employers say that they want workers who can find reliable information, analyze it, organize it, draw conclusions from it, and present it convincingly to others, they are seeking individuals who are critical thinkers.

Whatever else you do in college, make it a point to develop and sharpen your critical-thinking skills. You won't become an accomplished critical thinker overnight. With practice, however, you can learn how to tell whether information is truthful and accurate. You can make better decisions, come up with fresh solutions to difficult problems, and communicate your ideas strategically and persuasively. The rating scale in Figure 5.1 will help you rate yourself as a critical thinker.

FIGURE 5.1

Rate Your Critical-Thinking Skills

Now that you have read about critical thinking, it would be beneficial to rate yourself as a critical thinker. Perhaps at this point in the term, critical thinking may seem unnecessary to you, but it will be interesting to see how you will change in the next few weeks and months.

Circle the number that best fits you in each of the critical situations described below.

Critical Situations	Never			Sometimes				Always		
In class, I ask lots of questions when I don't understand.	1	2	3	4	5	6	7	8	9	10
If I don't agree with what the group decides is the correct answer, I challenge the group opinion.	1	2	3	4	5	6	7	8	9	10
I believe there are many solutions to a problem.	1	2	3	4	5	6	7	8	9	10
I admire those people in history who challenged what was believed at the time, such as "the earth is flat."	1	2	3	4	5	6	7	8	9	10
I make an effort to listen to both sides of an argument before deciding which way I will go.	1	2	3	4	5	6	7	8	9	10

Critical Situations	Never				Sometimes				Always	
I ask lots of people's opinions about a political candidate before making up my mind.	1	2	3	4	5	6	7	8	9	10
I am not afraid to change my belief system if I learn something new.	1	2	3	4	5	6	7	8	9	10
Authority figures do not intimidate me.	1	2	3	4	5	6	7	8	9	10

The more 7–10 scores you have circled, the more likely it is that you use your critical-thinking skills often. The lower scores indicate that you may not be using critical-thinking skills very often or use them only during certain activities, such as an educational class.

Becoming a Critical Thinker

In essence, critical thinking is a search for truth. In college and in life you'll be confronted by a mass of information and ideas. Much of what you read and hear will seem suspect, and a lot of it will be contradictory. (If you have ever talked back to a TV commercial or doubted a politician's campaign promises, you know this already.) How do you decide what to believe?

Paul and Elder remind us that more than one right answer to any given question might exist. The tasks are to determine which of the "truths" you read or hear are the most plausible and then draw on them to develop ideas of your own. Difficult problems practically demand that you weigh options and think through consequences before you can reach an informed decision. Critical thinking also involves improving the way you think about a subject, statement, or idea. To do that, you'll need to ask questions, consider several different points of view, and draw your own conclusions.

> **YOUR TURN**
>
> **Think about It**
>
> Describe in writing a problem you had to solve in the past and how you were able to do it. Think about how you can draw on that experience to solve problems and answer questions in your courses.

ASK QUESTIONS

The first step of thinking critically is to engage your curiosity. Instead of accepting statements and assertions at face value, question them. When you come across an idea or a "fact" that strikes you as interesting, confusing, or suspicious, ask yourself first what it means. Do you fully understand what is being said, or do you need to pause and think to make sense of the idea? Do you agree with the statement? Why or why not? Can the material be interpreted in more than one way?

Don't stop there. Ask whether you can trust the person or institution making a particular claim, and ask whether they have provided enough evidence to back up an assertion (more on this later). Ask who might be likely to agree or disagree and why. Ask how a new concept relates to what you already know, where you might find more information about the subject, and what you could do with what you learn. Finally, ask yourself about the implications and consequences of accepting something as truth. Will you have to change your perspective or give up a long-held belief? Will it require you to do something differently? Will it be necessary to investigate the issue further? Do you anticipate having to try to bring other people around to a new way of thinking?

CONSIDER MULTIPLE POINTS OF VIEW

Once you start asking questions, you'll typically discover a slew of different possible answers competing for your attention. Don't be too quick to latch onto one and move on. To be a critical thinker, you need to be fair and open-minded, even if you don't agree with certain ideas at first. Give them all a fair hearing because your goal is to find the truth or the best action, not confirm what you already believe.

You will often recognize the existence of competing points of view on your own, perhaps because they're held by people you know personally. You might discover them in what you read, watch, or listen to for pleasure. Reading assignments might deliberately expose you to conflicting arguments and theories about a subject, or you might encounter differences of opinion as you do research for a project.

In class discussions your instructors might also present more than one valid point of view. For instance, bilingual education is a hotly debated topic. Your instructor might want you to think about which types of students would or would not benefit from bilingual teaching and provide very specific reasons for your point of view. Instructors themselves often disagree with the experts and will sometimes identify flaws in widely accepted theories. Instructors will also sometimes reinforce your personal views and ask you to elaborate on how your own life experiences help you relate to what you are reading or learning in class.

The more ideas you entertain, the more sophisticated your own thinking will become. Ultimately, you will discover not only that it is OK to change your mind, but that a willingness to do so is the mark of a reasonable, educated person.

DRAW CONCLUSIONS

Once you have considered different points of view, it's up to you to reach your own conclusions, craft a new idea based on what you've learned, or make a decision about what you'll do with the information you have.

This process isn't necessarily a matter of figuring out the best idea. Depending on the goals of the activity, it might be simply the one that you think is the most fun or the most practical, or it might be a new idea of your own creation. For a business decision it might involve additional cost-benefit analysis to decide which computer equipment to purchase for your office. In a chemistry lab it might be a matter of interpreting the results of an experiment. In a creative writing workshop students might collaborate to select the most workable plot for a classmate's short story. Or a social worker might conduct multiple interviews before recommending a counseling plan for a struggling family.

Drawing conclusions involves looking at the outcome of your inquiry in a demanding, critical way. If you are trying to solve a problem, which possible solutions seem most promising after you have conducted an exhaustive search for information? Do some answers conflict with others? Which solutions can be achieved? If you have found new evidence, what does that new evidence show? Do your original beliefs hold up? Do they need to be modified? Which notions should be abandoned? Most important, consider what you would need to do or say to persuade someone else that your ideas are valid. Thoughtful conclusions aren't very useful if you can't share them with others.

Faulty Reasoning: Logical Fallacies

A critical thinker has an attitude—of wanting to avoid nonsense, find the truth, and discover the best action—and it's an attitude that rejects intuiting what is right in favor of requiring reasons. Instead of being defensive or emotional, critical thinkers aim to be logical. Although logical reasoning is essential to solving any problem, whether simple or complex, you need to go one step further to make sure that an argument hasn't been compromised by faulty reasoning. Here are some of the most common missteps, referred to as logical fallacies, that people make in their use of logic:

- **Attacking the person.** It's perfectly acceptable to argue against other people's positions or to attack their arguments. It is not OK, however, to go after their personalities. Any argument that resorts to personal attack ("Why should we believe a cheater?") is unworthy of consideration.

- **Begging.** "Please, officer, don't give me a ticket because if you do, I'll lose my license, and I have five little children to feed and won't be able to feed them if I can't drive my truck." None of the driver's statements offers any evidence, in any legal sense, as to why she shouldn't be given a ticket. Pleading *might* work if the officer is feeling generous, but an appeal to facts and reason would be more effective: "I fed the meter, but it didn't register the coins. Because the machine is broken, I'm sure you'll agree that I don't deserve a ticket."

- **Slippery-slope arguments.** "If we allow tuition to increase, the next thing we know it will be $20,000 a term." Such an argument is an example of "slippery-slope" thinking.

- **Appealing to false authority.** Citing authorities, such as experts in a field or qualified researchers, can offer valuable support for an argument, but a claim based on the authority of someone whose expertise is questionable relies only on the appearance of authority rather than on real evidence.

- **Jumping on a bandwagon.** Sometimes we are more likely to believe something that many others also believe. Even the most widely accepted truths can turn out to be wrong, however. At one time, nearly everyone believed that the world was flat, until someone came up with evidence to the contrary.

John W. McDonough/Sports Illustrated/Getty Images

IN THE MEDIA

Another misstep in the use of logic is **appealing to false authority**. Citing authorities, such as experts in a field or the opinions of qualified researchers, can offer valuable support for an argument, but a claim based on the authority of someone whose expertise is questionable relies on the *appearance* of authority rather than on real evidence. We see this type of logical fallacy all the time in advertising.

For Reflection: How effective do you think retired professional basketball player Charles Barkley is as a Weight Watchers spokesperson? What makes him believable? What examples can you think of where a celebrity is viewed as an authority but whose expertise is questionable?

- **Assuming something is true because it hasn't been proven false.** If you go to a bookstore or online, you'll find dozens of books detailing close encounters with flying saucers and extraterrestrial beings. These books describe the person who had the close encounter as beyond reproach in integrity and sanity. Because critics could not disprove the claims of the witnesses, the events are said to have actually occurred. Even in science, few things are ever proved completely false, but evidence can be discredited.

- **Falling victim to false cause.** Frequently, we make the assumption that just because one event followed another, the first event must have caused the second. This reasoning is the basis for many superstitions. The ancient Chinese once believed that they could make the sun reappear after an eclipse by striking a large gong because they knew that the sun had reappeared on one such occasion after a large gong had been struck. Most effects, however, are usually the result of a complex web of causes. Don't be satisfied with easy before-and-after claims; they are rarely correct.

- **Making hasty generalizations.** If someone selected one green marble from a barrel containing one hundred marbles, you wouldn't assume that the next marble would be green. After all, ninety-nine marbles are still in the barrel, and you know nothing about the colors of those marbles. Given fifty draws from the barrel, however, each of which produced a green marble after the barrel had been

YOUR TURN

....

Write and Reflect

Have you ever used any of these fallacies to justify decisions you have made? Why was it wrong to do so? Discuss your experiences in a journal entry.

shaken thoroughly, you would be more willing to conclude that the next marble drawn would be green, too. Reaching a conclusion based on the opinion of one source is like figuring that all the marbles in the barrel are green after pulling out only one.

Such fallacies can slip into even the most careful reasoning. One false claim can derail an entire argument, so look out for weak logic in what you read and write. Remember that accurate reasoning is a key factor for success in college and in life.

Bloom's Taxonomy

Benjamin Bloom, a professor of education at the University of Chicago during the second half of the twentieth century, worked with a group of other researchers to design a system of classifying goals for the learning process. His efforts to develop this system were based on his work as "university examiner." In this role he designed tests that would determine whether a student at the university should or should not receive a bachelor's degree. This system is known as Bloom's taxonomy, and it is now used at all levels of education to define and describe the process that students use to understand and think critically about what they are learning.

BLOOM'S SIX LEVELS OF LEARNING

Bloom identified six levels of learning as represented in Figure 5.2. The higher the level, the more critical thinking it requires.

- **Evaluation,** Bloom's highest level, is defined as using your ability to judge the value of ideas and information you are learning according to internal or external criteria. Evaluation includes appraising, arguing, defending, and supporting.
- **Synthesis** is defined as bringing ideas together to form a new plan, proposal, or concept. Synthesis includes collecting, organizing, creating, and composing.

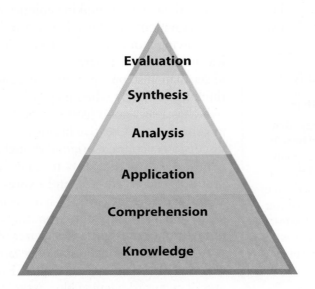

FIGURE 5.2

The Six Levels of Learning of Bloom's Taxonomy

- **Analysis** is defined as breaking down material into its parts so that you can understand its structure. Analysis includes categorizing, comparing, contrasting, and questioning.
- **Application** is defined as using what you have learned, such as rules and methods, in new situations. Application includes choosing, illustrating, practicing, and interpreting.
- **Comprehension** is defined as understanding the meaning of material. Comprehension includes classifying, describing, explaining, and translating.
- **Knowledge,** the bottom level, is defined as remembering previously learned material. Knowledge includes arranging, defining, memorizing, and recognizing.

BLOOM'S TAXONOMY AND YOUR FIRST YEAR OF COLLEGE

As you begin your first year of college, you will recognize material you've learned before and will practice your skills of defining and remembering. But you'll soon find that Bloom's bottom level isn't going to get you very far. To remember new information, you'll need to move to level 2 by understanding the information clearly enough so that you can describe the concepts to someone else. Many of your classes will require you to apply what you learn to new situations (level 3), and you'll also need to use levels 4 and 5 to analyze (break apart) and synthesize (bring together) new concepts. Finally, you'll reach level 6 as you begin trusting your own judgments in evaluating what you are learning. As you progress through your first year, be aware of how you use each of these levels to build your critical-thinking skills.

Collaboration and Critical Thinking

Researchers who study critical thinking in elementary school, high school, and college find that critical thinking and collaboration go hand in hand. Students at all levels are more likely to exercise their critical-thinking abilities when they are confronted by the experiences and opinions of others than when they are not.

> ### YOUR TURN
> #### Work Together
> Make a list of the ways that you think you could benefit from joining a study group. Make another list of the reasons you might decide not to join one. Compare what you wrote with several classmates' lists and see which of your reasons are the same or different.

Having more than one student involved in the learning process generates a greater number of ideas than just one person can generate. People think more clearly when they talk as well as listen (which is a very good reason to participate actively in your classes). Creative brainstorming and group discussion encourage original thought. These habits also teach participants to consider alternative points of view carefully and express and defend their own ideas clearly. As a group negotiates ideas and learns to agree on the most reliable thoughts, it moves closer to a surer solution.

Collaboration occurs not only face to face, but also over the Internet. Christopher P. Sessums, creator of an award-winning blog, writes the following:

Jonathan Stark

Get a Second Opinion

One way to become a better critical thinker is to practice with other people. By getting feedback from another person, you can see the possible flaws in your own position. You will also learn that there are few black-and-white answers to any question.

Web logs offer several key features that I believe can support a constructive, collaborative, reflective environment. For one, it's convenient. The medium supports self-expression and "voice." Collaboration and connectivity can be conducted efficiently, especially in terms of participants' time or place. Publishing your thoughts online forces you to concretize your thoughts.

"Collaborative Web logs," Sessums concludes, "promote the idea of learners as creators of knowledge, not merely consumers of information."[2] So do online discussion groups, wikis (which allow users to add, update, and otherwise improve material that others have posted), and, of course, face-to-face collaboration.

Whether in person or through electronic communication, teamwork improves your ability to think critically. As you leave college and enter the world of work, you will find that collaboration is essential in almost any career you pursue, not only with people in your work setting, but also with others around the globe.

Thinking Critically about Arguments

What does the word *argument* mean to you? If you're like most people, the first image it conjures up might be an ugly fight you had with a friend, a yelling match you witnessed on the street, or a heated disagreement between family members. True, such unpleasant confrontations are arguments, but the word also refers to a calm, reasoned effort to persuade someone of the value of an idea.

[2]Christopher Sessums, *Eduspaces*. Web log. 9 Nov. 2005. <http://eduspaces.net/csessums/weblog /archive/2005/11>.

When you think of it this way, you'll quickly recognize that arguments are central to academic study, work, and life in general. Scholarly articles, business memos, and requests for spending money all have something in common: The effective ones make a general claim, provide reasons to support it, and back up those reasons with evidence. That's what argument is.

As we have already seen, it's important to consider multiple points of view, or arguments, in tackling new ideas and complex questions, but arguments are not all equally valid. Good critical thinking involves thinking creatively about the assumptions that might have been left out and scrutinizing the quality of the evidence that is used to support a claim. Whether examining an argument or communicating one, a good critical thinker is careful to ensure that ideas are presented in an understandable, logical way.

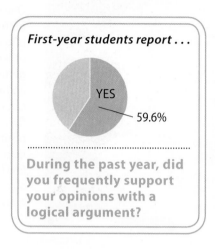

First-year students report . . .

YES

59.6%

During the past year, did you frequently support your opinions with a logical argument?

Critical Thinking in College and Life

Being a college graduate and a citizen will lead to many future opportunities to think critically about matters that affect the quality of life for you and your family. Answers are often not clear-cut but rather can be loaded with ambiguity and contention. Taking a position on behalf of you and your family will require careful, critical thinking.

For instance, what should we do about the growing problem of childhood and adult obesity? Should we tackle this problem as a society because reducing the rates of obesity would benefit society as a whole? How could you approach this public health crisis in your community?

Let's assume that you and some neighbors decide to petition the school board to place on its next agenda a decision to ban soft drinks in the public schools. In response to your request, you are granted permission to speak at the next school board meeting. Your team collaborates to identify the questions that you need to explore:

1. What is the current obesity rate of adults in this community?
2. What is the current obesity rate of school-age children in this community, and how does it compare with the rate twenty years ago?
3. What health interventions are currently in place in schools to offset the potential for obesity?
4. When were soft-drink machines placed in the schools?
5. How much profit does each school realize from the sale of such beverages?
6. How do the schools use these profits?
7. Have there been any studies on the student population in the community correlating obesity levels with other health problems such as diabetes?

Who's Thirsty?
Companies that sell sugary drinks know that students are a prime market.

© Robert Sciarrino/Star Ledger/Corbis

You collect data using resources at your town library, and in your search for evidence to support your position, you discover that according to the local health department, obesity rates for adults and children in your community exceed the national average and have gone up dramatically in the past twenty years. Rates of diabetes among young adults are also increasing every year. You also learn that soft-drink machines first appeared in schools in your district fifteen years ago. Other than regular physical education classes, the schools don't have programs in place to encourage healthy eating. Schools receive money from the soft-drink companies, but you cannot get a clear answer about how much money they receive or how it is being used.

The data about the health of the community and the schoolchildren is powerful. You carefully cite all your sources, and your team believes that it is ready to make its case. You assume that the school board will make an immediate decision to remove soft-drink machines from school grounds based on what you have discovered. You cannot imagine another side to this issue, and you wonder how anyone could possibly object to removing from school a substance that, in your view, clearly harms children.

Little did you know that your position would meet stiff opposition during the board meeting. You were shocked to hear arguments such as the following:

1. Students don't have to buy these drinks. Nobody makes them.
2. Students will be unhappy if their soft drinks are taken away, which will negatively affect their academic performance.
3. The United States is all about freedom of choice. It is morally wrong for any agency of government to interfere with people's freedom of choice, no matter what a person's age.
4. If we allow the school board to tell children what they can and cannot drink, pretty soon they will be telling children what to think or not think.
5. This proposed restriction interferes with what is best for our country and therefore our children: protecting the free enterprise system.

Weighing All the Issues

Committees made up of community members often have to make hard decisions for the common good.

AP Photo/John Milburn

6. This proposed policy will lead to significant revenue loss for our school, which will result in higher taxes to make up the shortfall.

7. There is no evidence that it is the consumption of soft drinks that actually causes obesity. Other sugary foods might be the problem.

8. If students don't have these drinks to purchase in school, they will sneak them in from home.

UNDERSTANDING YOUR AND YOUR OPPOSITION'S ASSUMPTIONS

To some extent, it's unavoidable to have beliefs based on gut feelings or blind acceptance of something we've heard or read. Some assumptions should be examined more thoughtfully, especially if they will influence an important decision or serve as the foundation for an argument. What are the assumptions behind the opposition's arguments? What assumptions lay behind the arguments *you* made?

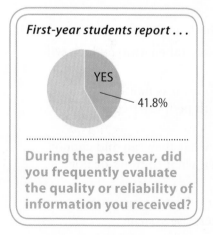

First-year students report . . .

YES

41.8%

During the past year, did you frequently evaluate the quality or reliability of information you received?

How could you and your neighbors use critical thinking to strengthen your own arguments and respond to those of the opposition? What factual bases support the assumptions and arguments on both sides? Are there exaggerations on both sides? Do you detect the use of any logical fallacies on either side? How can you evaluate the facts? If your goal is to ban soft drinks from schools in your community and to address the issue at hand—childhood obesity—what additional evidence do you need to gather and what next steps should you take?

As this scenario suggests, well-meaning people will often disagree. It's important to listen to both sides of an argument before making up your mind. If you hang on to the guidelines in this chapter, we can't promise that your classes will be easier or you'll solve community problems, but you will be better equipped to handle them. You have the skills to use critical thinking to figure things out instead of depending purely on how you feel or what you've heard. As you listen to a lecture, political debate, or argument about what is in the public's best interest, try to predict where it is heading and why. Ask yourself whether you have enough information to justify what you have said.

EXAMINE THE EVIDENCE

Critical thinkers are careful to check that the evidence supporting an argument—whether someone else's or their own—is of the highest possible quality. To do that, simply ask a few questions about the arguments as you consider them:

> What general idea am I being asked to accept?
>
> Are good and sufficient reasons given to support the overall claim?
>
> Are those reasons backed up with evidence in the form of facts, statistics, and quotations?
>
> Does the evidence support the conclusions?
>
> Is the argument based on logical reasoning, or does it appeal mainly to the emotions?
>
> Do I recognize any questionable assumptions?
>
> Can I think of any counterarguments? What facts can I muster as proof?
>
> What do I know about the person or organization making the argument?

Roz Chast, The New Yorker Collection/www.cartoonbank.com

What's for Breakfast?

Do you believe everything you read? Outlandish claims are out there. Use your critical-thinking abilities to practice healthy skepticism about what you see in print and online that seems far-fetched. Use credible sources to check it out. What examples can you think of in which a claim seemed too good to be true?

TECH TIP RESEARCH WISELY

Don't assume that any information you find on the Internet is accurate or unbiased. Thanks to the First Amendment, people can publish whatever they want online. It's up to you to filter out what's valuable, objective, and up-to-date.

the WHITE HOUSE

The White House Blog

Our Top Stories

50 Years of American Heroes

www.whitehouse.gov

 THE PROBLEM

You're not sure how to evaluate the types of information found on the Web.

 THE FIX

Get some context.

3 HOW TO DO IT

- **Portals:** One-stop shops that serve up a full range of cyber services. Expect to find search engines; news, weather, and news updates; stock quotes; reference tools; and even movie reviews. (Bonus: Most services are free.) Prime examples: **Google .com** and **Yahoo.com**.

- **News:** Sites that offer news and analysis of current events, politics, business trends, sports, entertainment, and so on. They're often sponsored by magazines, newspapers, and radio stations and include special online extras. Prime examples: **NYTimes.com**, Harvard Business Review (**hbr .org**), and **CNN.com**.

- **Corporate and marketing:** Promotional sites for businesses. Some company Web sites let you order their products or services online; others even list job openings. Prime examples: **Ford.com** and **BenJerry.com**.

- **Informational:** Fact-based sites, often created by government agencies. Click to these sites for information on everything from passports to city bus schedules to census data. Prime examples: **NYCsubway.org** and **Travel.State.gov**.

- **Blogs:** Web sites where people can air their views and opinions. Some businesses create blogs to connect with their customers; other blogs are strictly personal, designed to share with family and friends. Prime examples: **Gawker.com** and **http://thelawsonspilltheirguts.blogspot.com/**. Consider the goals for the White House blog shown here. What would you expect to find at this blog?

- **Wikis:** Informational Web sites that allow for open editing by registered users or in some cases by the general public. Prime examples: **Wikipedia.com** and **TechCrunch.com**.

Keep in mind that there's a big difference between the *Journal of the American Medical Association* and a journal written by Fred from Pomona. And no, you can't use an ad for Shake Weight as a source for a fitness article: It's an ad. Be discerning. Use your critical-thinking skills. To make sure that the research you use is unbiased and current, look for tip-offs. Most reputable Web sites are easy to navigate, contain little advertising, and list author names and credentials. In Chapter 10 you will read more about electronic sources and research.

PERSONAL BEST

Should you trust the information on a wiki? Possibly. One of the best things about the Internet is that people can be both consumers and creators of content. You have the power to publish your thoughts, creative writing, or artwork. On the flip side—so can everyone else. Using wikis, like Wikipedia, is tricky because the author of the source is almost impossible to identify. Find out about your instructors' rules about Wikipedia and follow them. Your library will have many professor-friendly alternatives.

If you're still not certain of its quality after you have evaluated the evidence used in support of a claim, it's best to keep looking. Drawing on questionable evidence for an argument has a tendency to backfire. In most cases a little persistence will help you find something better. (You can find tips on how to find and evaluate sources in Chapter 10, Information Literacy and Communication.)

CHECKLIST FOR SUCCESS

CRITICAL THINKING

☐ **Make sure that you understand what** *critical thinking* **means.** If you are not clear about this term, discuss it with another student, the instructor of this course, or a staff member in the learning center.

☐ **Find ways to express your imagination and curiosity, and practice asking questions.** If you have the impulse to raise a question, don't stifle yourself. College is for self-expression and exploration.

☐ **Challenge your own and others' assumptions that are not supported by evidence.** Practice asking politely, calmly, and not in a rejecting manner for additional information to help you better understand the position the individual may be taking.

☐ **During class lectures, presentations, and discussions, practice thinking about the subjects being discussed from multiple points of view.** Start with the view that you would most naturally take toward the matter at hand. Then force yourself to imagine what questions might be raised by someone who doesn't see the issue the same way you do.

☐ **Draw your own conclusions and explain to others what evidence you considered that led you to these positions.** Don't assume that anyone automatically understands why you reached your conclusions.

☐ **Join study groups or class project teams and work as a team member with other students.** When you are a member of a team, volunteer for roles that stretch you. That is how you will really experience significant gains in learning and development.

☐ **Learn to identify false claims in commercials and political arguments.** Then look for the same faulty reasoning in people's comments you hear each day.

☐ **Practice critical thinking not only in your academic work but also in your everyday interactions with friends and family.** Your environment both in and out of college will give you lots of opportunities to become a better critical thinker.

BUILD YOUR EXPERIENCE 1 2 3 4

1 STAY ON TRACK

Successful college students stay focused. They "stay on track." They know what they have to do to be successful, they set goals, and they monitor their progress toward their goals.

Reflect on what you have learned about college success in this chapter and how you are going to apply the chapter information or strategies in college and in your career. List your ideas.

1. _____

_____

_____

2. _____

_____

_____

3. _____

_____

_____

2 ONE-MINUTE PAPER

One major shift from being a high school student to being a college student involves the level of critical thinking your college instructors expect of you. After reading this chapter, how would you describe critical thinking to a high school student?

3 APPLYING WHAT YOU HAVE LEARNED

Now that you have read and discussed this chapter, consider how you can apply what you have learned to your academic and personal life. The following prompts will help you reflect on chapter material and its relevance to you both now and in the future.

1. After reading this chapter, think of professions (for example, physicians, engineers, marketing professionals) for whom problem solving and thinking "outside the box" are necessary. Choose one career and describe why you think critical thinking is a necessary and valuable skill.

2. In your opinion, is it harder to think critically than to base your arguments on how you feel about a topic? Why or why not? What are the advantages of finding answers based on your feelings? Based on critical thinking? How might you use both approaches in seeking answers?

4 BUILDING YOUR PORTFOLIO

My Influences   Our past experiences have shaped the way in which we think and perceive the world around us. Sometimes it is easy to interpret things without stopping to think about why we feel the way we do. How have other people shaped the way you see the world today?

1. In your personal portfolio, create a Word document and

   Describe at least three people (such as family, friends, celebrities, national leaders) who you feel have most influenced the way you think.

   Describe how these individuals' values, actions, expectations, and words have shaped the way you think about yourself and the world.

2. Describe an experience you have had since coming to college that has challenged you to think about an issue in a new and different way.

3. Save your work in your portfolio or in the Cloud.

For more on this topic watch
French Fries Are Not Vegetables and Other College Lessons

WHERE TO GO FOR HELP . . .

ON CAMPUS

> **Logic Courses** Check out the introductory course in logic offered by your college's philosophy department. It might be the single best course designed to teach you critical-thinking skills. Nearly every college offers such a course.

> **Argument Courses and Critical-Thinking Courses** Does your institution offer either an argument or a critical-thinking course? Check your campus catalog to see what you can find. Such courses will help you develop the ability to formulate logical arguments and avoid such pitfalls as logical fallacies.

> **Debating Skills** Some of the very best critical thinkers developed debating skills during college. Go to either your student activities office or your department of speech and drama to find out whether your campus has a debate club or team. Debating can be fun, and chances are you will meet some interesting student thinkers that way.

LITERATURE

> *12 Angry Men* **by Reginald Rose (New York: Penguin Classics, 2006)** This reprint of the original teleplay, which was written in 1954, was made into a film in 1958. It is also available on DVD. The stirring courtroom drama pits twelve jurors against one another as they argue the outcome of a murder trial in which the defendant is a teenage boy. Although critical thinking is needed to arrive at the truth, all the jurors except one use noncritical arguments to arrive at a guilty verdict. The analysis of that one holdout, however, produces a remarkable change in their attitudes.

ONLINE

> How to Understand and Use Bloom's Taxonomy **http://online.fiu.edu/faculty/resources /bloomstaxonomy**.

> A Guide to Critical Thinking about What You See on the Web **http://www.icyousee.org/think /think.html**.

MY INSTITUTION'S RESOURCES

_____

_____

_____

_____

_____

_____

_____

_____

6 Reading to Learn

> **While my habits have worked well for me, students should get to know their own learning habits and find a reading method that works best for them.**

Keira Sharma, 18
Communications major
Sam Houston State University

Keira Sharma was born in Texas and then spent most of her childhood in Baton Rouge, Louisiana, where she learned study habits that have helped throughout her education. Just before high school, her family moved back to Texas. She decided to go to Sam Houston State University after visiting the campus and speaking with faculty and current students in the Communications program. In addition, she thought that the campus was beautiful, and she liked the community. Last, it put her only an hour away from her family.

As someone who loves to learn, Keira came to college with some strategies in place. "There is definitely a lot more reading involved in college than in high school," she says. "However, the good thing is that professors give out syllabi that detail when readings will be due, so you can plan accordingly." Like many first-year students, she also had to learn to balance the amount of reading required. "I had to get used to measuring how long it took to read and then manage my time accordingly."

Many of the other strategies Keira employs revolve around good time management and organization.

Keira Sharma ▶

Intellistudies/Shutterstock

"Learning how to juggle all other coursework, meals, a social life, and sleep can be difficult, but it is possible. I mostly organize my time in order of priorities, usually based on due dates and how much time it takes to do [the assignment]," she says. Keira explains that once she starts reading, "I usually write down headings within the chapter as I go to keep me guided in the right direction and so that I know what the main point of upcoming sections will be. I then read through and write down any important dates, names, words, or anything that better explains the concept or explains it in a different way. This way I have multiple views on the subject that further enhance my understanding. It also doesn't hurt to reread sections and go over notes." She adds an important note: "While my habits have worked well for me, students should get to know their own learning habits and find a reading method that works best for them."

Keira also has some simple advice for other first-year students: "As much work as college is and as overwhelming as it can feel sometimes, *don't stress too much*. College is one of the best times of life. Enjoy it!"

———————

As Keira mentioned, reading college textbooks is more challenging than reading high school texts or reading for pleasure. College texts are loaded with concepts, terms, and complex information that you are expected to learn on your own in a short period of time. To accomplish it all, you will find it helpful to learn and use the active reading strategies in this chapter. They are intended to help you get the most out of your college reading. This chapter will also explore the different strategies to use when reading textbooks across the academic disciplines. These strategies include building your overall vocabulary and increasing your familiarity with terms that are unique to your particular field of study.

Depending on how much reading you did before coming to college—reading for pleasure, for your classes, or for work—you might find that reading is your favorite or least favorite way to learn. When you completed the VARK learning styles inventory in Chapter 4, you determined your preferences about reading and writing as a learning strategy. But even if reading isn't your favorite thing to do, it is absolutely essential to doing well in college, no matter what your major is.

A Plan for Active Reading

When you read actively, you use strategies that help you stay focused. Active reading is different from reading novels or magazines for pleasure. Pleasure reading doesn't require you to annotate, highlight, or take notes. As you read college textbooks, though, you'll use all these strategies and more. This plan will increase your focus and concentration, promote greater understanding of what you read, and prepare you to study for tests and exams. Here are the four steps in active reading designed to help you read college textbooks:

1. Previewing
2. Strategies for Marking Your Textbook
3. Reading with Concentration
4. Reviewing

◢ ASSESSING YOUR STRENGTHS ▮

Are you a good reader? Do you make it a practice to do all the assigned reading for each of your classes? As you read this chapter, list specific examples of your strengths in the area of reading college textbooks and supplementary academic material.

_____

_____

_____

_____

◢ SETTING GOALS ▮

What are your most important objectives in learning the material in this chapter? How can you improve your reading abilities and strategies? List three goals that relate to improving your reading of college texts (for instance, I will go back to all my course syllabi to make sure I'm up-to-date with my assigned reading; if not, I will catch up this week).

1. _____

_____

2. _____

_____

3. _____

_____

PREVIEWING

The purpose of previewing is to get the big picture, that is, to understand how what you are about to read connects with what you already know and to the material the instructor covers in class. Begin by reading the title of the chapter. Ask yourself: What do I already know about this subject? Next, quickly read through the introductory paragraphs. Then read the summary at the beginning or end of the chapter if there is one. Finally, take a few minutes to skim the chapter, looking at the headings and subheadings. Note any study exercises at the end of the chapter.

As part of your preview, note how many pages the chapter contains. It's a good idea to decide in advance how many pages you can reasonably expect to cover in your first study period. This can help build your concentration as you work toward your goal of reading a specific number of pages. Before long, you'll know how many pages are practical for you.

> ### YOUR TURN
> **Work Together**
>
> Working with a group of your classmates, discuss which of these four steps you always, sometimes, or never do. Which steps do your classmates think are necessary, if any, and why?

Keep in mind that different types of textbooks can require more or less time to read. For example, depending on your interests and previous knowledge, you might be able to read a psychology text more quickly than a logic text that presents a whole new symbol system.

mapping A preview strategy of drawing a wheel or branching structure to show relationships between main ideas and secondary ideas and how different concepts and terms fit together and help you make connections to what you already know about the subject.

Mapping.   The process of **mapping** the chapter as you preview it provides a visual guide for how different chapter ideas fit together. Because many students identify themselves as visual learners, visual mapping is an excellent learning tool for test preparation as well as reading (see Chapter 4, How You Learn). To map a chapter, use either a wheel structure or a branching structure as you preview the chapter (see Figure 6.1). In the wheel map, place the central idea of the chapter in the circle. The central idea should be in the introduction to the chapter and might be apparent in the chapter title. Place secondary ideas on the spokes emanating from the circle and place offshoots of those ideas on the lines attached to the spokes. In the branching map the main idea goes at the top, followed by supporting ideas on the second tier and so forth. Fill in the title first. Then, as you skim the chapter, use the headings and subheadings to fill in the key ideas.

Alternatives to Mapping.   Perhaps you prefer a more linear visual image. If so, consider making an outline of the headings and subheadings in the chapter. You can fill in the outline after you read. Alternatively, make a list. A list can be particularly effective when you are dealing with a text that introduces many new terms and their definitions. Set up the list with the terms in the left

FIGURE 6.1
Wheel and Branching Maps

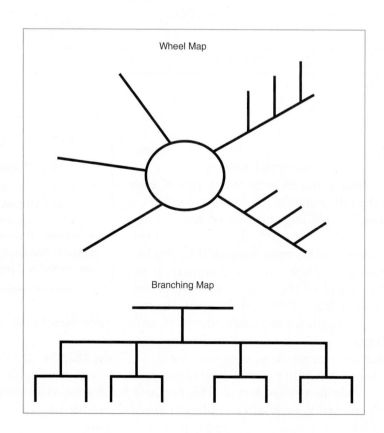

Wheel Map

Branching Map

column and fill in definitions, descriptions, and examples on the right after you read. Divide the terms on your list into groups of five, seven, or nine, and leave white space between the clusters so that you can visualize each group in your mind. This practice is known as **chunking**. Research indicates that we learn material best when it is in chunks of five, seven, or nine.

If you are an interactive learner, make lists or create a flash card for each heading and subheading (see Figure 6.2). Then fill in the back of each card after reading each section in the text. Use the lists or flash cards to review with a partner or recite the material to yourself.

Previewing, combined with mapping, outlining, or flash cards, might require more time up front, but it will save you time later because you will have created an excellent review tool for quizzes and tests. You will be using your visual learning skills as you create advanced organizers to help you associate details of the chapter with the larger ideas. Such associations will come in handy later on. As you preview the text material, look for connections between the text and the related lecture material. Call to mind the related terms and concepts that you recorded in the lecture. Use these

chunking A previewing method that involves making a list of terms and definitions from the reading and then dividing the terms into smaller clusters of five, seven, or nine to learn the material more effectively.

FIGURE 6.2

Using Flash Cards

Flash cards are a great way to retain information and are especially good tools for visual and kinesthetic learners. If you were to use the first section of this chapter to create flash cards, you would put the chapter heading on the FRONT of the first card and subheadings on the BACK (see the top card). Then you would create a separate vocabulary card for each subheading (see bottom card). The front of each vocabulary card would provide the term to define, and the back would include a three-part definition: (1) the heading the term falls under, (2) the actual definition, and (3) a cue or detail to help you remember the term. When you have finished making flash cards for the entire chapter, stack them in order by placing vocabulary cards under each corresponding heading card. This strategy is one way to learn the information in small chunks and create a strong mental file folder in your memory. Many test questions come from headings and subheadings.

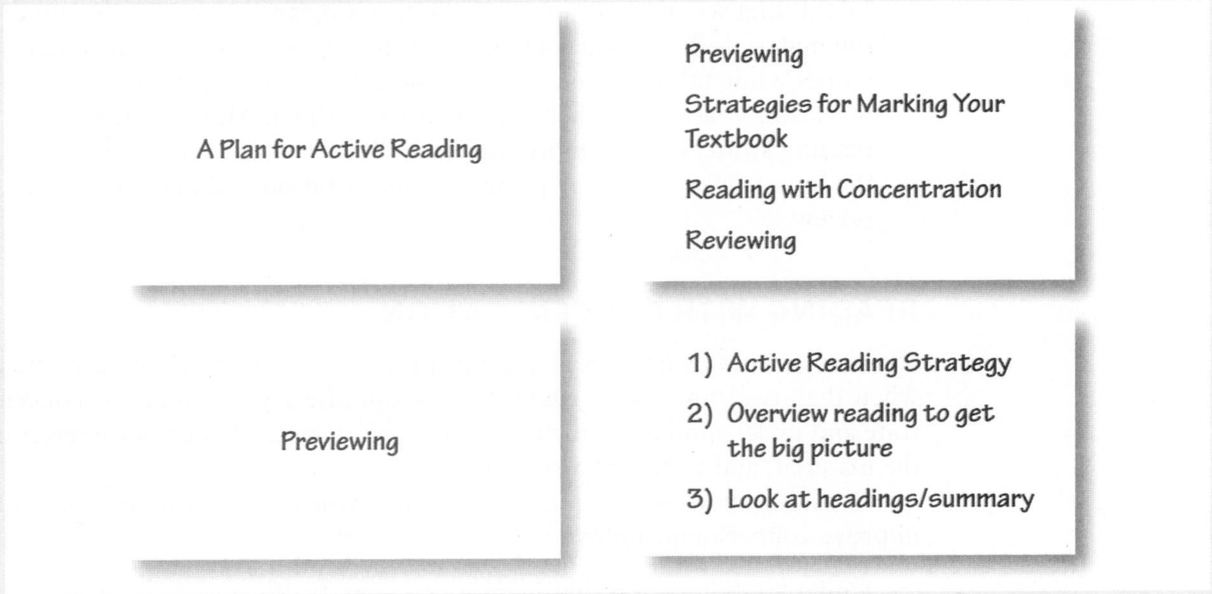

A Plan for Active Reading

Previewing

Strategies for Marking Your Textbook

Reading with Concentration

Reviewing

Previewing

1) Active Reading Strategy

2) Overview reading to get the big picture

3) Look at headings/summary

strategies to warm up. Ask yourself: Why am I reading this material? What do I want to know?

STRATEGIES FOR MARKING YOUR TEXTBOOK

After completing your preview, you are ready to read the text actively. With your map or outline to guide you, mark the sections that are most important. To avoid marking too much or marking the wrong information, first read without using your pencil or highlighter.

marking An active reading strategy of making marks in the text by underlining, highlighting, or writing margin notes or annotations.

Marking can be an active reading strategy that helps you focus and concentrate as you read. You may prefer to underline, highlight, or use margin notes or annotations. Figure 6.3 provides an example of each method. No matter what method you prefer, remember these two important guidelines:

1. **Read before you mark.** Finish reading a section before you decide which are the most important ideas and concepts.

2. **Think before you mark.** When you read a text for the first time, everything can seem important. After you complete a section, reflect on it to identify the key ideas. Ask yourself: What are the most important ideas? What will I see on the test? This step can help you avoid marking too much material.

Two other considerations might affect your decisions about textbook marking:

1. **If you just make notes or underline in your textbook, you will have to read all the pages again.** Instead, consider taking notes, creating flash cards, making lists, or outlining textbook chapters. These methods are also more practical if you intend to review with a friend or study group.

2. **Highlighting or underlining can give you a false sense of security.** Just noting what's most important doesn't mean that you understand the material. When you force yourself to put something in your own words while taking notes, you are not only predicting exam questions but also assessing whether you can answer them. Although these active reading strategies take more time initially, they can save you time in the long run because they promote concentration and make it easy to review.

READING WITH CONCENTRATION

Students commonly have trouble concentrating or understanding the content when they read textbooks. Many factors can affect your ability to concentrate and understand texts: the time of day, your energy level, your interest in the material, and your study location.

Consider these suggestions and decide which ones would help you improve your reading ability:

- Find a study location that is removed from traffic and distracting noises, such as the campus library. Turn off your cell phone's ringer

CULTURE AND HUMAN BEHAVIOR

The Stress of Adapting to a New Culture

differences affecting cultural stress

Refugees, immigrants, and even international students are often unprepared for the dramatically different values, language, food, customs, and climate that await them in their new land. The process of changing one's values and customs as a result of contact with another culture is referred to as *acculturation*. **Acculturative stress** is the stress that results from the pressure of adapting to a new culture (Sam & Berry, 2010).

acceptance of new culture reduces stress
also speaking new language, education, & social support

Many factors can influence the degree of acculturative stress that a person experiences. For example, when the new society accepts ethnic and cultural diversity, acculturative stress is reduced (Mana & others, 2009). The transition is also eased when the person has some familiarity with the new language and customs, advanced education, and social support from friends, family members, and cultural associations (Schwartz & others, 2010). Acculturative stress is also lower if the new culture is similar to the culture of origin.

how attitudes affect stress

Cross-cultural psychologist John Berry (2003, 2006) has found that a person's attitudes are important in determining how much acculturative stress is experienced (Sam & Berry, 2010). When people encounter a new cultural environment, they are faced with two questions: (1) Should I seek positive relations with the dominant society? (2) Is my original cultural identity of value to me, and should I try to maintain it?

4 patterns of acculturation

The answers produce one of four possible patterns of acculturation: integration, assimilation, separation, or marginalization (see the diagram). Each pattern represents a different way of coping with the stress of adapting to a new culture (Berry, 1994, 2003).

1 * *Integrated* individuals continue to value their original cultural customs but also seek to become part of the dominant society. They embrace a *bicultural* identity (Hunyh & others, 2011). Biculturalism is associated with higher self-esteem and lower levels of depression, anxiety, and stress, suggesting that the bicultural identity may be the most adaptive acculturation pattern (Schwartz & others, 2010). The successfully integrated individual's level of acculturative stress will be low (Lee, 2010).

2 * *Assimilated* individuals give up their old cultural identity and try to become part of the new society. They adopt the customs and social values of the new environment, and abandon their original cultural traditions.

possible rejection by both cultures

Assimilation usually involves a moderate level of stress, partly because it involves a psychological loss—one's previous cultural identity. People who follow this pattern also face the possibility of being rejected either by members of the majority culture or by members of their original culture (Schwartz & others, 2010). The

Joe Raedle/Getty Images

Acculturative Stress Acculturative stress can be reduced when immigrants learn the language and customs of their newly adopted home. Here, two friends, one from China, one from Cuba, help each other in an English class in Miami, Florida.

process of learning new behaviors and suppressing old behaviors can also be moderately stressful.

3 * Individuals who follow the pattern of *separation* maintain their cultural identity and avoid contact with the new culture. They may refuse to learn the new language, live in a neighborhood that is primarily populated by others of the same ethnic background, and socialize only with members of their own ethnic group.

separation may be self-imposed or discriminating

In some cases, separation is not voluntary, but is due to the dominant society's unwillingness to accept the new immigrants. Thus, it can be the result of discrimination. Whether voluntary or involuntary, the level of acculturative stress associated with separation tends to be high.

higher stress with separation

4 * Finally, the *marginalized* person lacks cultural and psychological contact with *both* his traditional cultural group and the culture of his new society. By taking the path of marginalization, he lost the important features of his traditional culture but has not replaced them with a new cultural identity.

marginalized = higher level of stress

Although rare, the path of marginalization is associated with the greatest degree of acculturative stress. Marginalized individuals are stuck in an unresolved conflict between their traditional culture and the new society, and may feel as if they don't really belong anywhere. Fortunately, only a small percentage of immigrants fall into this category (Schwartz & others, 2010).

Question 1:
Should I seek positive relations with the dominant society?

Question 2: Is my original cultural identity of value to me, and should I try to maintain it?		Yes	No
	Yes	Integration	Separation
	No	Assimilation	Marginalization

Patterns of Adapting to a New Culture
According to cross-cultural psychologist John Berry, there are four basic patterns of adapting to a new culture (Sam & Berry, 2010). Which pattern is followed depends on how the person responds to the two key questions shown.

FIGURE 6.3

Examples of Marking

Using a combination of highlighting, lines, and marginal notes, the reader has boiled down the content of this page for easy review. Without reading the text, note the highlighted words and phrases and the marginal notes, and see how much information you can gather from them. Then read the text itself. Does the markup serve as a study aid? Does it cover the essential points? Would you have marked this page any differently? Why or why not?

Source: "The Stress of Adapting to a New Culture," from *Psychology,* 6th ed., p. 534, by D. H. Hockenbury and S. E. Hockenbury. Copyright © 2013 by Worth Publishers. Used with permission of the publisher. Photo: Joe Readle/Getty Images.

> ## YOUR TURN
> ....
> ### Write and Reflect
>
> The next time you are reading a textbook, monitor your ability to concentrate. Check your watch when you begin and check it again when your mind begins to wander. How many minutes did you concentrate on your reading? List some strategies to keep your mind from wandering. Write down in a journal entry ideas you've heard that you think will work well for you.

and store the phone in your purse or book bag (someplace where you can't easily feel it vibrating). If you are reading an electronic document on your computer, download the information you need and disconnect from the network to keep you from easily going online and chatting, e-mailing, or checking Facebook or Twitter.

- Read in blocks of time, with short breaks in between. Some students can read for 50 minutes; others find that a 50-minute reading period is too long. By reading for small blocks of time throughout the day instead of cramming in all your reading at the end of the day, you should be able to process material more easily.

- Set goals for your study period, such as "I will read twenty pages of my psychology text in the next 50 minutes." Reward yourself with a 10-minute break after each 50-minute study period.

- If you have trouble concentrating or staying awake, take a quick walk around the library or down the hall. Stretch or take some deep breaths and think positively about your study goals. Then resume studying.

- Jot study questions in the margins, take notes, or recite key ideas. Reread confusing parts of the text and make a note to ask your instructor for clarification.

- Focus on the important portions of the text. Pay attention to the first and last sentences of paragraphs and to words in italics or bold print.

- Use the glossary in the text or a dictionary to define unfamiliar terms.

REVIEWING

The final step in active textbook reading is reviewing. Many students expect to read through their text material once and be able to remember the ideas four, six, or even twelve weeks later at test time. More realistically, you will need to include regular reviews in your study process. Here is where your notes, study questions, annotations, flash cards, visual maps, or outlines will be most useful. Your study goal should be to review the material from each chapter every week.

Consider ways to use your many senses to review. Recite aloud. Tick off each item in a list

> ### Is This You?
>
> Are you the first person in your family to go to college? If so, you are in good company. Many, many "first-generation" students attend colleges and universities today. Make sure that you understand the rules and regulations and unique higher education terminology at your institution. If you or your family members feel lost or confused, talk to your college success instructor and ask about available services for first-generation students. Also remember that some of our nation's most successful individuals were the first in their families to attend college and graduate.

on each of your fingertips. Post diagrams, maps, or outlines around your living space so that you will see them often and will likely be able to visualize them while taking the test.

Strategies for Reading Textbooks

As you begin to read, be sure to learn more about the textbook and its author by reading the frontmatter in the book, such as the preface, foreword, introduction, and author's biographical sketch. The preface is usually written by the author or authors and will tell you why they wrote the book and what material it covers. It will also explain the book's organization and give insight into the author's perspective. The preface will likely help you see the relationships among the facts presented and comprehend the ideas presented across the book. Textbooks often have a preface written to the instructor and a separate preface for the students. The foreword is often an endorsement of the book written by someone other than the author. Some books have an additional introduction that reviews the book's overall organization and its contents chapter by chapter.

Some textbooks include study questions at the end of each chapter. Take time to read and respond to these questions, whether or not your instructor requires you to do so.

Textbooks must try to cover a lot of material in a fairly limited space, and they won't necessarily provide all the things you want to know about a topic. If you find yourself fascinated by a particular topic, go to the **primary sources**, the original research or document. You'll find them referenced in almost all textbooks, either at the end of the chapters or in the back of the book. You can read more information about primary and supplementary sources on page 129.

> **primary sources** The original research or documentation on a topic, usually referenced either at the end of a chapter or at the back of the book.

You might also go to other related sources that make the text more interesting and informative. Because some textbooks are sold with test banks, your instructors might draw their examinations directly from the text, or they might use the textbook only to supplement the lectures. Ask your instructors what the tests will cover and the types of questions that will be used. Some instructors expect you to read the textbook carefully, while others are much more concerned that you be able to understand broad concepts that come primarily from lectures.

Finally, not all textbooks are equal. Some are better designed and written than others. If your textbook seems disorganized or hard to understand, let your instructor know your opinion. Others likely share your opinion. Your instructor might spend some class time explaining the text, and he or she can meet with you during office hours to help you with the material. Instructors also use student feedback on textbooks to help them choose which ones to select for future classes.

MATH TEXTS

Although the previous suggestions about textbook reading apply across the board, mathematics textbooks present some special challenges because they

All Textbooks Are Not Created Equal

Math and science texts are filled with graphs and figures that you will need to understand to grasp the content and the classroom presentations. If you have trouble reading and understanding any of your textbooks, get help from your instructor or your learning center.

Jonathan Stark

tend to have lots of symbols and very few words. Each statement and every line in the solution of a problem must be considered and digested slowly. Typically, the author presents the material through definitions, theorems, and sample problems. As you read, pay special attention to definitions. Learning all the terms that relate to a new topic is the first step toward understanding.

Math texts usually include derivations of formulas and proofs of theorems. You must understand and be able to apply the formulas and theorems, but unless your course has a particularly theoretical emphasis, you are less likely to be responsible for all the proofs. So, if you get lost in the proof of a theorem, go on to the next item in the section. When you come to a sample problem, it's time to get busy. Pick up pencil and paper, work through the problem in the book, and then cover the solution and think through the problem on your own. Of course, the exercises that follow each text section form the heart of any math book. A large portion of the time you devote to the course will be spent completing assigned textbook exercises. It is absolutely vital that you do this homework in a timely manner, whether or not your instructor collects it. Success in mathematics requires regular practice, and students who keep up with math homework, either alone or in groups, perform better than students who don't.

After you complete the assignment, skim through the other exercises in the problem set. Reading the unassigned problems will deepen your understanding of the topic and its scope. Finally, talk the material through to yourself. Be sure your focus is on understanding the problem and its solution, not on memorization. Memorizing something might help you remember how to work through one problem, but it does not help you understand the steps involved so that you can employ them for other problems.

SCIENCE TEXTS

Your approach to your science textbook will depend somewhat on whether you are studying a math-based science, such as physics, or a text-based science, such as biology. In either case, you need to become acquainted with the overall format of the book. Review the table of contents and the glossary. Also check the material in the appendices. There, you will find lists of physical constants, unit conversions, and various charts and tables. Many physics and chemistry books also include a minireview of the math you will need in science courses.

Notice the organization of each chapter. Pay special attention to graphs, charts, and boxes. The amount of technical detail might seem overwhelming, but—believe it or not—the authors have sincerely tried to present the material in an easy-to-follow format. Each chapter might begin with chapter objectives and conclude with a short summary, sections that can be useful to study both before and after reading the chapter. You will usually find answers to selected problems in the back of the book. Use the answer key or the student solutions manual to promote your mastery of each chapter.

As you begin an assigned section in a science text, skim the material quickly to gain a general idea of the topic. Begin to absorb the new vocabulary and technical symbols. Then skim the end-of-chapter problems so that

Jonathan Milavec

On Your Mark!

Adding margin notes in your textbook and taking notes while you read are great ways to improve your concentration and your comprehension of the text material.

you'll know what to look for in your detailed reading of the chapter. State a specific goal: "I'm going to learn about recent developments in plate tectonics," "I'm going to distinguish between mitosis and meiosis," or "Tonight I'm going to focus on the topics in this chapter that were stressed in class."

Should you underline and highlight, or should you outline the material in your science textbooks? You might decide to underline and highlight for a subject such as anatomy, which involves a lot of memorization. Use restraint with a highlighter, however; it should pull your eye only to important terms and facts. If highlighting is actually a form of procrastination for you (you are reading through the material but are planning to learn it at a later date) or if you are highlighting nearly everything you read, your highlighting might be doing you more harm than good. You won't be able to identify important concepts quickly if they're lost in a sea of color. Ask yourself whether the frequency of your highlighting is helping you be more active in your learning process. If not, you might want to highlight less or try a different technique such as margin notes or annotations.

In most sciences it is best to outline the text chapters. You can usually identify main topics, subtopics, and specific terms under each subtopic in your text by the size of the print. For instance, in each chapter of this textbook, the main topics (or level-1 headings) are in large orange letters with a rule below. Following each major topic heading, you will find subtopics (or level-2 headings) printed in smaller, blue capital letters. The level-3 headings, which tell more about the subtopics, are in bold, black letters, but are much smaller than the level-1 headings.

To save time when you are outlining, don't write full sentences, but do include clear explanations of new technical terms and symbols. Pay special attention to topics that the instructor covered in class. If you aren't sure whether your outlines contain too much or too little detail, compare them with the outlines that members of your study group have made. You could also consult with your instructor during office hours. In preparing for a test, it's a good idea to make condensed versions of your chapter outlines so that you can see how everything fits together.

SOCIAL SCIENCE AND HUMANITIES TEXTS

Many of the suggestions that apply to science textbooks also apply to reading in the social sciences (sociology, psychology, anthropology, economics, political science, and history). Social science texts are filled with special terms or jargon that is unique to the particular field of study. These texts also describe research and theory building and contain references to many primary sources. Your social science texts might also describe differences in opinions or perspectives. Social scientists do not all agree on any one issue, and you might be introduced to a number of ongoing debates about particular issues. In fact, your reading can become more interesting if you seek out different opinions about a common

> ### YOUR TURN
> #### Discuss
> In a small group, discuss how important you think textbooks are in your courses and other ways to access the information you want and need in order to learn.

issue. You might have to go beyond your particular textbook, but your library will be a good source of various viewpoints about ongoing controversies.

Textbooks in the **humanities** (philosophy, religion, literature, music, and art) provide facts, examples, opinions, and original material, such as stories or essays. You will often be asked to react to your reading by identifying central themes or characters.

Some instructors believe that the way in which colleges and universities structure courses and majors artificially divides human knowledge and experience. For instance, they argue that subjects such as history, political science, and philosophy are closely linked and that studying each subject separately results in only partial understanding. By stressing the links between courses, these instructors encourage students to think in an **interdisciplinary** manner. You might be asked to consider how the book or story you're reading or the music you're studying reflects the political atmosphere or the culture of the period. Your art history instructor might direct you to think about how a particular painting gives you a window on the painter's psychological makeup or religious beliefs.

> **humanities** Branches of knowledge that investigate human beings, their culture, and their self-expression. They include the study of philosophy, religion, literature, music, and art.

> **interdisciplinary** Linking two or more academic fields of study, such as history and religion. Encouraging an interdisciplinary approach to teaching can offer a better understanding of modern society.

SUPPLEMENTARY MATERIAL

Whether your instructor requires you to read material in addition to the textbook, your understanding will be enriched if you go to some of the primary and supplementary sources that are referenced in each chapter of your text. These sources can take the form of journal articles, research papers, dissertations (the major research papers that students write to earn a doctoral degree), or original essays, and they can be found online or in your library. Reading source material will give you a depth of detail that few textbooks accomplish. In addition, it is a strategy discussed in Chapter 8 to help you understand and remember.

Many sources were originally written for other instructors or researchers. They often use language and refer to concepts that are familiar to other scholars but not necessarily to first-year college students. If you are reading a journal article that describes a theory or research study, one technique for easier understanding is to read from the end to the beginning. Read the article's conclusion and discussion sections. Then go back to see how the author performed the experiment or formulated the ideas. If you aren't concerned about the specific method used to collect the data, you can skip over the "methodology" section. In almost all scholarly journals, articles are introduced by an **abstract**, a paragraph-length summary of the methods and major findings. Reading the abstract is a quick way to get the gist of a research article before you dive in. As you're reading research articles, always ask yourself: So what? In your opinion, was the research important to what we know about the topic, or was it unnecessary?

> ### YOUR TURN
>
> **Write and Reflect**
>
> Choose a chapter in this or another textbook. As you read it, list in your journal the words that are new to you or that you're not sure you understand. Look up a few of these words in the book's glossary or in a dictionary. Set a goal to add at least one new word a week to your personal vocabulary.

> **abstract** A paragraph-length summary of the methods and major findings of an article in a scholarly journal.

TECH TIP EMBRACE THE E-BOOK

1 ▸ THE PROBLEM

Your back hurts from carrying around heavy textbooks and you're aware that you can buy them as e-books.

2 ▸ THE FIX

Discover how reading a digital reader differs from (and can even be better than) reading traditional ink-on-paper books.

3 ▸ HOW TO DO IT

THE PROS

- Digital reading devices are eminently portable—most weigh about 1 pound—and can hold thousands of books. (They're fantastic for those long flights when you don't want to pack the entire *Hunger Games* trilogy.)
- They can handle a range of media, from books to newspapers to magazines.
- They save trees: no shipping costs and a low carbon footprint.
- They let you buy books online from anywhere; you can start reading within minutes.
- They let you shop internationally. Even if you're in a remote Chinese village, you can easily find plenty of cyberbooks in English.
- You can type notes in an e-book as well as highlight passages and copy and paste sections.
- You can print out pages simply by hooking the device up to your printer.
- Many of the books you can access are free: You can download books from the public library; you can even click to the British Library's Online Gallery to peruse some of the oldest and rarest books on record.
- Some e-books come with bonus audio, video, or animation features.
- Many digital reading devices even accept audio books and can read to you aloud.
- The backlit screen means that you can read in bed with the light off, without keeping your roommate awake.
- You can adjust the size of the text, making it easier to read.
- Some link directly to a built-in dictionary. Just highlight a word, and it will look it up. Others also will link to reference Web sites like Google or Wikipedia when a wi-fi or 3G connection is available.
- E-books are searchable and even sharable.

THE CONS

- Digital reading devices are expensive.
- Unlike books, they can break if you drop them.
- It's harder to flip through pages of an e-book than a printed book.
- You've never tried reading a textbook on a digital reading device.

Fuse/Getty Images

GOOD TO KNOW

The most popular electronic e-readers include versions of the iPad, Kindle, Nook, and Kobo Touch. Some versions are no-frills, basic models designed to replicate the experience of reading a paper book. Others offer touch color screens, Web browsers, video, music, and thousands of free and for-purchase apps.

PERSONAL BEST

Do you use an e-reader? How does using an e-book differ when reading a textbook versus reading a book for fun?

_____

_____

_____

_____

_____

_____

© Nikolai Golovanoff/Corbis

Improving Your Reading

With effort, you can improve your reading dramatically, but remember to be flexible. How you read should depend on the material. Assess the relative importance and difficulty of the assigned readings and adjust your reading style and the time you allot accordingly. Connect one important idea to another by asking yourself: Why am I reading this material? Where does it fit in? When the textbook material is virtually identical to the lecture material, you can save time by concentrating mainly on one or the other. It takes a planned approach to read textbook materials and other assigned readings with good understanding and recall.

MONITORING YOUR READING

Similar to asking yourself questions to make connections across different ideas, you can monitor your comprehension while reading textbooks by asking yourself: Do I understand this material? If not, stop and reread it. Look up words that are not clear. Try to clarify the main points and how they relate to one another.

Another way to check comprehension is to try to recite the material aloud, either to yourself or to your study partner. Using a study group to monitor your comprehension gives you immediate feedback and is highly motivating. After you have read and marked or taken notes on key ideas from the first section of the chapter, proceed to each subsequent section until you have finished the chapter.

After you have completed each section and before you move on to the next section, ask again: What are the key ideas? What will I see on the test?

VOCABULARY-BUILDING STRATEGIES

> During your overview of the chapter, notice and jot down unfamiliar terms. Consider making a flash card for each term or making a list of terms.

> When you encounter challenging words, consider the context. See whether you can predict the meaning of an unfamiliar term by using the surrounding words.

> If context by itself is not enough, try analyzing the term to discover the root, or base part, or other meaningful parts of the word. For example, *emissary* has the root "to emit," or "to send forth," so we can guess that an emissary is someone who is sent forth with a message. Similarly, note prefixes and suffixes. For example, *anti* means "against," and *pro* means "for." Use the glossary of the text, a dictionary, or the online **Merriam-Webster Dictionary** (**www.merriam-webster.com**) to locate the definition. Note any multiple definitions and search for the meaning that fits this usage.

> Take every opportunity to use these new terms in your writing and speaking. If you use a new term a few times, you'll soon know it. In addition, studying new terms on flash cards or study sheets can be handy at exam time.

At the end of each section, try to guess what information the author will present in the next section.

DEVELOPING YOUR VOCABULARY

Textbooks are full of new terminology. In fact, one could argue that learning chemistry is largely a matter of learning the language of chemists and that mastering philosophy, history, or sociology requires a mastery of the terminology of each particular **discipline**.

discipline An area of academic study, such as sociology, anthropology, or engineering.

If words are such a basic and essential component of our knowledge, what is the best way to learn them? Follow the basic vocabulary-building strategies outlined in the box on page 131.

IF ENGLISH IS NOT YOUR FIRST LANGUAGE

The English language is one of the most difficult languages to learn. Words are often spelled differently from the way they sound, and the language is full of idioms, phrases that are peculiar and cannot be understood from the individual meanings of the words. If you are learning English and are having trouble reading your texts, don't give up. Reading slowly and reading more than once can help you improve your comprehension. Make sure that you have two good dictionaries—one in English and one that links English with your primary language—and look up every word that you don't know. Be sure to practice thinking, writing, and speaking in English; also take advantage of your college's helping services. Your campus might have ESL (English as a Second Language) tutoring and workshops. Ask your adviser or your first-year seminar instructor to help you locate those services.

Listening, note taking, and reading are the essentials for success in each of your classes. Rather than perform these skills without a plan, practice some of the ideas presented in this chapter. If your skills in these areas are already strong, perhaps you picked up some ideas to strengthen them further.

CHECKLIST FOR SUCCESS

READING TO LEARN

☐ **Be sure to practice the four steps of active reading: previewing, marking your textbook, reading with concentration, and reviewing.** If you practice these steps, you will understand and retain more of what you read.

☐ **Take your course textbooks seriously.** They contain essential information you'll be expected to learn and understand. Never try to "get by" without the text.

☐ **Remember that not all textbooks are the same.** They vary by subject area and style of writing. Some may be easier to comprehend than others, but don't give up if the reading level is challenging.

☐ **Learn and practice the different techniques suggested in this chapter for reading and understanding texts on different subjects.** Which texts come easiest for you? Which are the hardest? Why?

☐ **In addition to the textbook, be sure to read all supplemental assigned reading material.** Also, try to find additional materials to take your reading beyond just what is required. The more you read, the more you will understand, and the better your performance will be.

☐ **As you read, be sure to take notes on the material.** Indicate in your notes what specific ideas you need help in understanding.

☐ **Get help with difficult material before much time elapses.** College courses use sequential material that builds on previous material. You will need to master the material as you go along.

☐ **Discuss difficult readings in study groups.** Explain to one another what you do and don't understand.

☐ **Find out what kind of assistance your campus offers to increase reading comprehension and speed.** Check out your learning and counseling centers for free workshops. Even faculty and staff sometimes take advantage of these services. Most everyone wants to improve reading speed and comprehension.

☐ **Use reading as a means to build your vocabulary.** Learning new words is a critical learning skill and outcome of college. The more words you know, the more you'll understand, and your grades will show it.

BUILD YOUR EXPERIENCE 1 2 3 4

1 STAY ON TRACK

Successful college students stay focused. They "stay on track." They know what they have to do to be successful, they set goals, and they monitor their progress toward their goals.

Reflect on what you have learned about college success in this chapter and how you are going to apply the chapter information or strategies in college and in your career. List your ideas.

1. _____

_____

_____

2. _____

_____

_____

3. _____

_____

_____

2 ONE-MINUTE PAPER

This chapter is full of suggestions for effectively reading your college textbooks. What suggestions did you find the most doable? What do you think is your biggest challenge in using these suggestions to improve your reading habits?

3 APPLYING WHAT YOU HAVE LEARNED

Now that you have read and discussed this chapter, consider how you can apply what you have learned to your academic life and your personal life. The following prompts will help you reflect on the chapter material and its relevance to you both now and in the future.

1. Choose a reading assignment for one of your upcoming classes. After previewing the material, begin reading until you reach a major heading or until you have read at least a page or two. Now stop and write down what you remember from the material. Go back and review what you read. Were you able to remember all the main ideas?

2. It is easy to say that there is not enough time in the day to get everything done, especially a long reading assignment. Your future depends on how well you do in college, however. Challenge yourself not to use that excuse. How can you modify your daily activities to make time for reading?

4 BUILDING YOUR PORTFOLIO

The Big Picture   This chapter introduces a reading strategy called **mapping** as a visual tool for getting the "big picture" of what you are preparing to read. Mapping a textbook chapter can help you quickly recognize how different concepts and terms fit together and make connections to what you already know about the subject. A number of ways of mapping, including wheel maps and branching maps, are described in this chapter. You might also use other types of maps, such as *matrixes*, to compare and contrast ideas or show cause and effect, a *spider web* to connect themes, or *sketches* to illustrate images, relationships, or descriptions.

1. Look through your course syllabi and identify a reading assignment that you need to complete in the next week.

2. Begin by previewing the first chapter of the reading assignment.

3. Practice mapping the chapter by creating your own map using the drawing toolbar in Microsoft Word.

4. Save your map in your portfolio or in the Cloud.

For an example of this exercise, go to the book's Web site at **macmillanhighered.com /collegesuccess/resources**.

Reading a textbook efficiently and effectively requires that you develop reading strategies that will help you to make the most of your study time. Mapping can help you to organize and retain what you have read, making it a good reading and study tool. Writing, reciting, and organizing the main points, supporting ideas, and key details of the chapter will help you recall the information on test day.

For more on this topic watch
French Fries Are Not Vegetables and Other College Lessons

WHERE TO GO FOR HELP . . .

ON CAMPUS

> **Learning Assistance Center** Find out about your campus's learning assistance center and any reading assistance that is available there. Most centers are staffed by full-time professionals and student tutors. Both the best students and struggling students use learning centers.

> **Fellow Students** Your best help can come from a fellow student. Look for the best students, those who appear to be the most serious and conscientious. Hire a tutor if you can or join a study group. You are much more likely to be successful.

ONLINE

> The Academic Skills Center at Dartmouth College has a guide to "Active Reading: Comprehension and Rate" at **https://www.dartmouth.edu/~acskills /success/reading.html**.

> Niagara University's Office for Academic Support offers reading resources at **www.niagara.edu /reading-resources/**.

MY INSTITUTION'S RESOURCES

_____

_____

_____

_____

_____

_____

_____

_____

7 Getting the Most Out of Class

> " Taking notes should never be a substitute for paying attention and understanding the deeper elements of lectures and verbal discourse.

Dillon Watts, 19
History major
San Bernardino Valley College

Dillon Watts grew up in Sacramento, California. He left high school after his junior year and obtained his GED. He now attends San Bernardino Valley College, where the benefits of participating in class and being engaged in learning are obvious to him. "Most of the time the questions you have are questions that will help the whole class. Everyone in the class benefits from an instructor's answer." He points out, however, that no one appreciates a student asking questions just for the participation points or to show off. "I try to be direct and simple when asking questions so that the class can get direct and simple answers," Dillon says.

This same no-nonsense attitude is also present in the way he prepares for class. He explains, "I just make sure to be there on time, every time, and to try to stay until the class is over. I'm not a meticulous note-taker. I find myself zoning out as much as the next guy. But as long as I make an

Dillon Watts ▶

Monkey Business Images/Shutterstock

effort to pay attention and write down key points and the chapter sections in books I'm supposed to read, I find it pretty easy to maintain good grades.

"In a class with lots of information, I take notes really well. It makes it harder to actually pay attention to concepts, but it certainly pays off for tests and such. In less formal classes such as speech or ethics, which are very idea heavy, I tend to not take notes that much or even at all. Taking notes should never be a substitute for paying attention and understanding the deeper elements of lectures and verbal discourse," he says.

Dillon plans to transfer to Stanford, Berkeley, or another four-year California school. In ten years he hopes to be a journalist or history teacher. He also hopes to put his class participation skills to good use. "It is my dream to take part in debates and public speeches," he says. His advice to other first-year students: "Take it easy and go with the flow. Try to get as much as you can out of your classes and try to do your best, whether or not you feel like it. It always pays off in the end."

Dillon's advice is sound when you consider that in virtually every college class you take, you'll need to master certain skills such as listening, taking notes, and being engaged in learning to earn high grades. Engagement in learning means that you take an active role in your classes by listening critically, asking questions, contributing to discussions, and providing answers. These active learning behaviors will enhance your ability to understand abstract ideas, find new possibilities, organize those ideas, and recall the material once the class is over.

Your academic success relies on practicing the habits of active engagement both in and out of class. In the classroom engagement starts with the basics: listening, taking notes, and participating in class discussions. Many of the questions on college exams will be drawn from class lectures and discussions. You therefore need to attend each class and be actively involved. In addition to taking notes you might consider recording the lecture and discussion if you have the instructor's permission. If you don't understand some points, take the time to meet with the instructor after class or during office hours. Another strategy to increase your engagement and your learning is to meet with a study group to compare your understanding of course material with that of your classmates.

This chapter reviews several note-taking methods. Choose the one that works best for you. Because writing down everything the instructor says is probably not possible and you might not be sure what is most important, ask questions in class. This will ensure that you clearly understand your notes. Reviewing your notes with a tutor, someone from your campus learning center, or a friend from class can also help you clarify your understanding of the most important points.

Most of all, be sure to speak up. When you have a question to ask or a comment to share, don't let embarrassment or shyness stop you. You will be more likely to remember what happens in class if you are an active participant than if you are silent.

> ## YOUR TURN
> ....
> ### Think about It
> Did you save any of your high school notes, or do you remember your note-taking method? If you have an old notebook, look at the way you took notes in high school and think about whether this method works for you now.

◢ ASSESSING YOUR STRENGTHS ◣

Students who are engaged in college life practice the behaviors that are reviewed in this chapter. What about you? How would you rate your level of engagement? As you begin to read this chapter, list specific examples of your strengths in the area of engagement.

_____

_____

_____

_____

◢ SETTING GOALS ◣

What are your most important objectives in learning the material in this chapter? Do you have a good method of note taking? Do you devote time and energy to academic work by attending class and studying out of class? List three goals that relate to engagement in learning (e.g., I will schedule a visit with one of my professors to show him or her my notes from the last class to make sure that I'm writing down the most important points).

1. _____

_____

2. _____

_____

3. _____

_____

Become Engaged in Learning

To really learn and remember material from your classes, it is important to engage in learning. Engaged students devote the time and energy necessary to develop a real love of learning, both in and out of class. Engaged learners who have good listening and note-taking skills are primed to get the most out of college.

You can acquire knowledge by listening to a lecture, and you can better absorb the information by considering what that knowledge means to you. Practice the techniques of "active" learning: talking with others, asking questions in class, studying in groups, and doing more than the required reading. Investigate other information

Is This You?

Are you a student athlete? If so, you might find that it's tough to balance the demands of team practice and games with being a good student. To keep up with your studies you'll need to go to every class and take advantage of all the academic help available to you through the athletic department and other campus resources. Whatever your athletic goal might be—whether it is to play on a professional team or just enjoy your sport as a college student—keep your eyes on the prize: a college degree.

sources in the library or on the Internet. Think about how the material relates to your own life or experience. For instance, a psychology class might help you recognize patterns of behavior in your own family, or an anthropology class may increase your interest in learning more about your own cultural origins. When you are actively engaged in learning, you will not only learn the material in your notes and textbooks, but you will also practice valuable skills that you can apply to college, work, and your personal life such as the following:

- **Working with others:** Learning to work with others is one of the most important skills you can develop for success in college and your career.

- **Improving your critical thinking, listening, writing, and speaking skills:** These primary skills define a college-educated person.

- **Functioning independently and teaching yourself:** Your first year of college will help you become an independent learner who doesn't always wait for an instructor to point you in the "right" direction.

- **Managing your time:** Time management sounds easy, but it is a challenge for almost all students, irrespective of their innate academic ability.

- **Gaining sensitivity to cultural differences:** The world we live in requires us all to develop our own knowledge about, and respect for, cultures that are different from our own.

Engagement in learning requires that you be a full and active participant in the learning process. Your instructors will set the stage and provide valuable information, but it's up to you to do the rest. For instance, if you disagree with what your instructor says, politely offer your opinion. Most instructors will listen. They might still disagree with you, but they might also think more of you for showing that you can think independently.

Not all instructors teach in a way that fosters active learning. Ask your friends for recommendations on instructors who encourage active learning. Another way to become an active learner is to interact with professors, staff members, and other students both in person and electronically. You may find that some research professors at your institution offer first-year students the ultimate opportunity in active learning: one-to-one or small-group collaboration with professors in research projects and service activities.

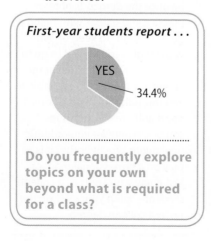

First-year students report . . .

YES

34.4%

Do you frequently explore topics on your own beyond what is required for a class?

Your college experience will be most rewarding if you take advantage of the resources your college offers, including the library, cultural events, faculty, and other students. You will also find many opportunities to become involved in campus organizations. Getting involved in out-of-class opportunities will help you develop relationships with others on campus. Use Facebook to connect with other students and with campus activities and groups. Join in discussions that are happening in those groups. All these approaches to learning have the potential to make you well rounded in all aspects of life.

PREVIEWING

> Previewing information before class is important. Previewing creates an organized mental outline for the lecture ahead of time. Take a moment to write down or type the title and headings of this chapter:

Getting the Most Out of Class
Become Engaged in Learning
Before Class
Participate in Class
Take Effective Notes

> Leave significant space between the headings for any notes, anecdotes, or ideas the professor might mention in the class lecture: The more information the instructor provides under a particular heading, the more likely that information will be emphasized on a test.

> You can use this previewing technique for all lecture classes that use a textbook as the main required reading, and *it takes only 5 minutes to set up before class.*

Before Class

Have you ever noticed how easy it is to learn the words of a song? We remember songs more easily than other kinds of information because songs follow a tune and have a beat and because they often have a personal meaning for us: We often relate songs to something in our everyday lives. We remember prose less easily unless we make an effort to relate it to what we already know. In your first-year classes you'll be listening to and reading material that might seem hard to understand. Beginning on the first day of class, you will be more likely to remember what you hear and read if you try to link it to something you have already learned or experienced.

Even if lectures don't allow for active participation, you can do a number of things to become more engaged and to make your listening and note taking more efficient. You will then learn and remember more, understand what the instructor considers important, and ultimately earn better grades.

A very important first step toward success is to prepare before class. You would not want to be unprepared to give a speech, interview for a job, plead a case in court, or compete in a sport. For each of these situations, you would prepare in some way. For the same reasons, you should begin listening, learning, and remembering before the lecture. Here are some strategies:

1. **Do the assigned reading.** Doing so allows for the lecture to have context so that it will mean a lot more to you and you will understand the terms the instructor uses. Some instructors refer to assigned readings for each class session; others might distribute a **syllabus** (course outline) and assume that you are keeping up with the assigned readings. Completing assigned reading on time will help you listen better and pick out the most important information when taking notes in class.

syllabus A formal statement of course requirements and procedures or a course outline provided by instructors to all students on the first day of class.

annotate To add critical or explanatory margin notes on a page as you read.

As you read, take good notes (there's more on good note-taking below). In books that you own, **annotate** (add critical or explanatory margin notes), highlight, or underline the text. In books that you do not own, such as library books, make a photocopy of the pages and then annotate or highlight the copy.

2. **Pay careful attention to your course syllabus.** Syllabi are formal statements of course expectations, requirements, and procedures. Instructors assume that students will understand and follow course requirements with few or no reminders once they have received a syllabus. You might find that this practice is a key difference between college and high school.

3. **Make use of additional materials provided by the instructors.** Many instructors post lecture outlines or notes online before class. Download and print these materials for easy reference during class. They often provide hints about the topics that the instructor considers most important; they also can create an organizational structure for taking notes.

4. **Warm up for class** by reviewing chapter introductions and summaries, referring to related sections in your text, and scanning your notes from the previous class period. This prepares you to pay attention, understand, and remember.

5. **Get organized.** Decide what type of notebook will work best for you. Many study-skills experts suggest using three-ring binders because you can punch holes in syllabi and other course handouts and keep them with class notes. You might want to buy notebook paper with a larger left-hand than right-hand margin (sometimes called "legal-ruled"), which will help you annotate your lecture notes easily. If you take notes on a laptop or tablet, keep your files organized in separate folders for each of your classes and make sure that the file name of each document reflects the date and topic of the class. See the Tech Tip on page 154 for more information on effective note taking using these devices.

Participate in Class

Learning is not a spectator sport. To truly learn, you must listen critically, talk about what you are learning, write about it, relate it to past experiences, and make what you learn part of yourself. Participation is the heart of **active learning.** When we say something in class, we are more likely to remember it than we are when someone else says something. When a teacher tosses a question your way or you have a question to ask, remembering the day's lesson actually becomes easier.

active learning Learning by participation, such as listening critically, discussing what you are learning, and writing about it.

LISTEN CRITICALLY AND WITH AN OPEN MIND

Listening in class is different from listening to a TV show, listening to a friend, or even listening during a meeting because you might not be required to remember or use the information you hear. Knowing how to listen in class can help you get more out of what you hear, understand better what you have heard, and save time. Here are some suggestions:

1. **Be ready for the message.** Prepare yourself to hear, listen, and receive the message. If you have done the assigned reading, you will already know details from the text, so you can focus your notes on key concepts during the lecture. You will also notice information that the text does not cover and will be prepared to pay closer attention when the instructor presents unfamiliar material.

2. **Listen to the main concepts and central ideas, not just to fragmented facts and figures.** Although facts are important, they will be easier to remember and will make more sense when you can place them in a context of concepts, themes, and ideas.

3. **Listen for new ideas.** Even if you are an expert on a topic, you can still learn something new. Do not assume that college instructors will present the same information you learned in a similar course in high school. Even if you're listening to the lecture again (perhaps because you recorded your lectures), you will pick out and learn new information. As a critical thinker, make a note of questions that arise in your mind as you listen, but save the judgments for later.

4. **Repeat mentally.** Words can go in one ear and out the other unless you make an effort to retain them. Think about what you hear and restate it silently in your own words. If you cannot translate the information into your own words, ask the instructor for further clarification.

5. **Decide whether what you have heard is not important, somewhat important, or very important.** Although most of what your instructors say and do in class is important, they may occasionally make comments or tell stories that are only loosely related to the class material or may not be related at all. If an instructor's comment is really unrelated to the focus of the class, you don't need to write it down. If it's very important, make it a major point in your notes by highlighting or underscoring it, or use it as a major topic in your outline if that's the method you use for taking notes. If it's somewhat important, try to relate it to a very important topic by writing it down as a subset of that topic.

6. **Keep an open mind.** Every class holds the promise of letting you discover new ideas and uncover different perspectives. Some instructors might intentionally present information that challenges your value system. College is supposed to teach you to think in new and different ways and train you to provide support for your own beliefs. Instructors want you to think for yourself; they don't necessarily expect you to agree with everything they or your classmates say. If you want people to respect your values and ideas, however, you must show respect for theirs as well by listening to what they have to say with an open mind.

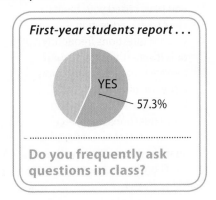

First-year students report . . .

YES
57.3%

Do you frequently ask questions in class?

7. **Ask questions.** Early in the term, determine whether the instructor is open to responding

to questions during the lecture. Some teachers prefer to save questions for the end of class or want students to ask questions during separate discussion sections or office hours. To some extent, it might depend on the nature and size of the class, such as a large lecture versus a small seminar. If your teacher answers questions as they arise, speak up if you did not hear or understand what was said. Get clarification immediately, if possible, and remember that other students are likely to have the same questions. If you can't hear another student's question or response, ask that it be repeated.

8. **Sort, organize, and categorize.** When you listen, try to match what you are hearing with what you already know. Take an active role in deciding how best to recall what you are learning.

SPEAK UP

Naturally, you will be more likely to participate in a class in which the instructor emphasizes interactive discussion, calls on students by name, shows signs of approval and interest, and avoids criticizing students for an incorrect answer. Often, answers that you and others offer that are not quite correct can lead to new perspectives on a topic.

In large classes instructors often use the lecture method, and large classes can be intimidating. You might feel very nervous asking a question in a class of a hundred students or more, fearing that you will make a fool of yourself and convinced that everyone else already knows the answer. What is highly likely is that when you ask a question in class, others also had the same question, were too timid to ask, and are silently thanking you! Many instructors devote time to answering questions in class. To take full advantage of these opportunities, try using the following techniques:

1. **Take a seat as close to the front as possible.** Visit your instructor during office hours and request to be moved up front if seating arrangements have you in the back of the room.

2. **Keep your eyes trained on the instructor.** Sitting up front will make it easier to do than sitting in the back.

3. **Focus on the lecture.** Avoid distractions. Sit away from friends who can distract you and turn off all electronic devices that you are not using solely for class.

4. **Raise your hand when you don't understand something.** The instructor might answer you immediately, ask you to wait until later in the class, or throw your question out to the rest of the class. In each case, you benefit in several ways. The instructor will get to know you, other students will get to know you, and you will learn from both the instructor and your classmates. Don't overdo it, however, or you'll risk disrupting class. Office hours

YOUR TURN

Work Together

Think about the number of times during the past week you have raised your hand in class to ask a question. Do you ask questions frequently, or is it something you avoid? Make a list of the reasons you either do or don't ask questions in class. Would asking more questions help you earn better grades? Be prepared to share your reflections with a small group.

provide the perfect opportunity for following up.

5. **Speak up in class.** Ask a question or volunteer to answer a question or make a comment. It becomes easier every time you do it.

6. **Never think that you're asking a stupid question.** If you don't understand something, you have a right to ask for an explanation.

7. **When the instructor calls on you to answer a question, don't bluff.** If you know the answer, give it. If you're not certain, begin with, "I think . . . , but I'm not sure if I have it all correct." If you don't know, just say so.

8. **If you have recently read a book or article that is relevant to the class topic, bring it in.** Use it either to ask questions about the topic or to provide information that was not covered in class.

Jonathan Stark

Hands Up

Participating in class not only helps you learn but also shows your instructor that you're interested and engaged. Like anything else, the first time you raise your hand might make you anxious. But after that first time, you'll likely find that contributing to class raises your interest and enjoyment.

Take Effective Notes

What are "effective notes"? They are notes that cover all the important points of the lecture or reading material without being too detailed or too limited. Most important, effective notes prepare you to do well on quizzes or exams. Becoming an effective note-taker takes time and practice, but this skill will help you improve your learning and your grades in the first year and beyond.

NOTE-TAKING FORMATS

You can make class time more productive by using your listening skills to take effective lecture notes, but first you have to decide on a system. Any system can work as long as you use it consistently.

Cornell Format.   Using the Cornell format, one of the best-known methods for organizing notes, you create a "recall" column on each page of your notebook by drawing a vertical line about two to three inches from the left border (see Figure 7.1). As you take notes during a lecture—whether writing down ideas, making lists, or using an outline or paragraph format—write only in the wider column on the right; leave the recall column on the left blank. (If you have large handwriting and this method seems unwieldy, consider using the back of the previous notebook page for your recall column.)

Psychology 101, 1/29/15
Theories of Personality

Personality trait: define	Personality trait = "durable disposition to behave in a particular way in a variety of situations"
Big 5: Name + describe them	Big 5-McCrae + Costa- (1)extroversion, (or positive emotionality)=outgoing, sociable, friendly, upbeat, assertive; (2) neuroticism=anxious, hostile, self-conscious, insecure, vulnerable; (3)openness to experience=curiosity, flexibility, imaginative; (4) agreeableness=sympathetic, trusting, cooperative, modest; (5)conscientiousness=diligent, disciplined, well organized, punctual, dependable
Psychodynamic Theories: Who?	Psychodynamic Theories-focus on unconscious forces Freud-psychoanalysis-3 components of personality-(1)id=primitive, instinctive, operates according to pleasure principle (immediate gratification);
3 components of personality: name and describe	(2)ego=decision-making component, operates according to reality principle (delay gratification until appropriate); (3)superego=moral component, social standards, right + wrong
3 levels of awareness: name and describe	3 levels of awareness-(1) conscious=what one is aware of at a particular moment; (2)preconscious=material just below surface, easily retrieved; (3)unconscious=thoughts, memories, + desires well below surface, but have great influence on behavior

FIGURE 7.1

Note Taking in the Cornell Format

YOUR TURN

Write and Reflect

In the next week, use each of the four note-taking methods (Cornell, outline, paragraph, list) in your other classes. In a journal entry explain which system works best for you and why.

The recall column is the place where you write down the main ideas and important details for tests and examinations as you sift through your notes as soon after class as is feasible, preferably within an hour or two. Many students have found the recall column to be a critical part of effective note taking, one that becomes an important study device for tests and exams.

Outline Format. Some students find that an outline is the best way for them to organize their notes (see Figure 7.2). You may know what a formal outline looks like, with

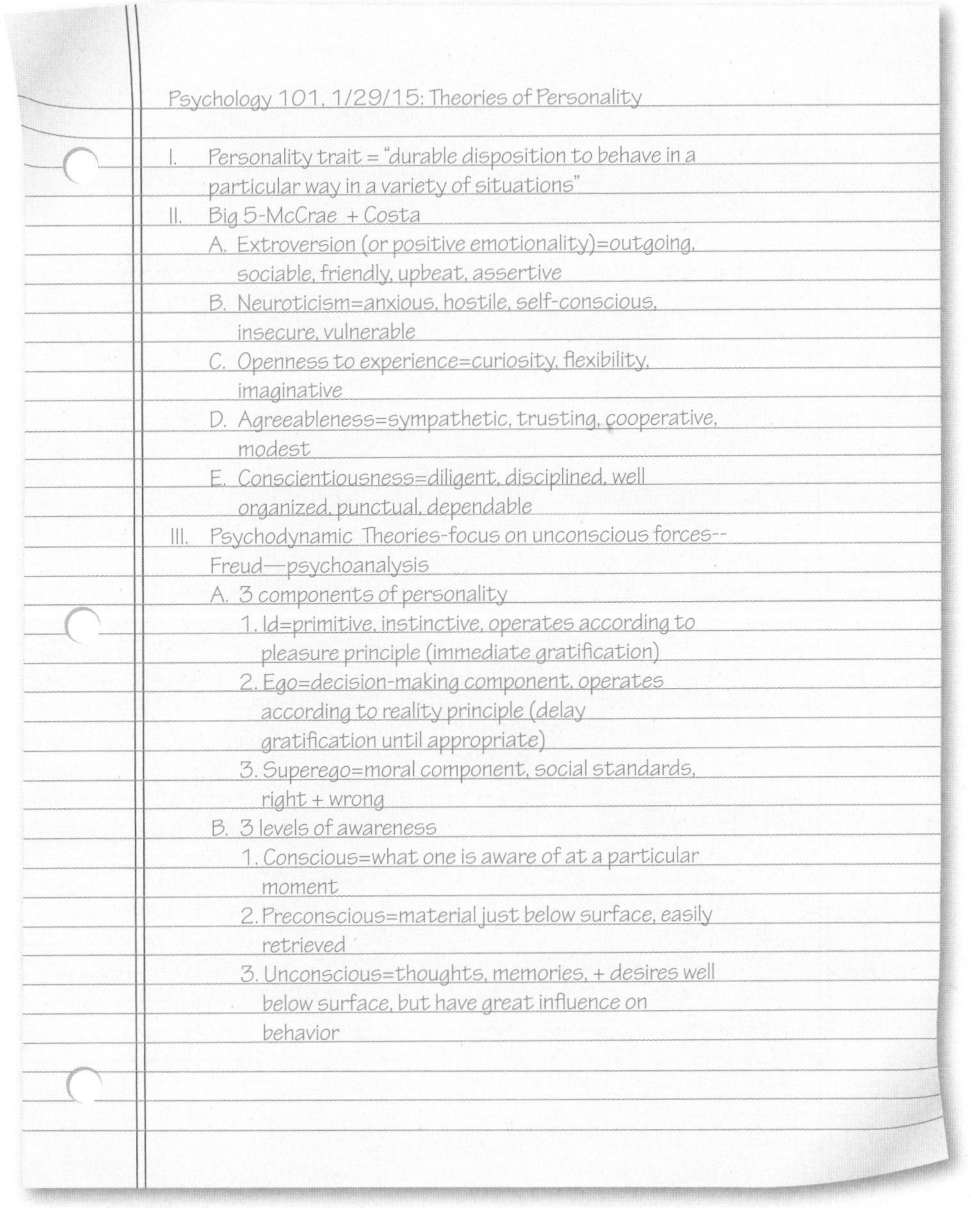

Psychology 101, 1/29/15: Theories of Personality

I. Personality trait = "durable disposition to behave in a
   particular way in a variety of situations"
II. Big 5-McCrae + Costa
    A. Extroversion (or positive emotionality)=outgoing,
       sociable, friendly, upbeat, assertive
    B. Neuroticism=anxious, hostile, self-conscious,
       insecure, vulnerable
    C. Openness to experience=curiosity, flexibility,
       imaginative
    D. Agreeableness=sympathetic, trusting, cooperative,
       modest
    E. Conscientiousness=diligent, disciplined, well
       organized, punctual, dependable
III. Psychodynamic Theories-focus on unconscious forces--
     Freud—psychoanalysis
     A. 3 components of personality
        1. Id=primitive, instinctive, operates according to
           pleasure principle (immediate gratification)
        2. Ego=decision-making component, operates
           according to reality principle (delay
           gratification until appropriate)
        3. Superego=moral component, social standards,
           right + wrong
     B. 3 levels of awareness
        1. Conscious=what one is aware of at a particular
           moment
        2. Preconscious=material just below surface, easily
           retrieved
        3. Unconscious=thoughts, memories, + desires well
           below surface, but have great influence on
           behavior

FIGURE 7.2
Note Taking in the Outline Format

key ideas represented by Roman numerals and other ideas relating to each key idea represented in order by uppercase letters, then numbers, and then lowercase letters. If you use this approach, try to determine the instructor's outline and re-create it in your notes. Add details, definitions, examples, applications, and explanations. You can combine the outline and Cornell formats (see Figure 7.5).

Paragraph Format.   You might decide to write summary paragraphs when you are taking notes on what you are reading (see Figure 7.3). This method might not work as well for class notes, however, because it's difficult to summarize a topic until your instructor has covered it

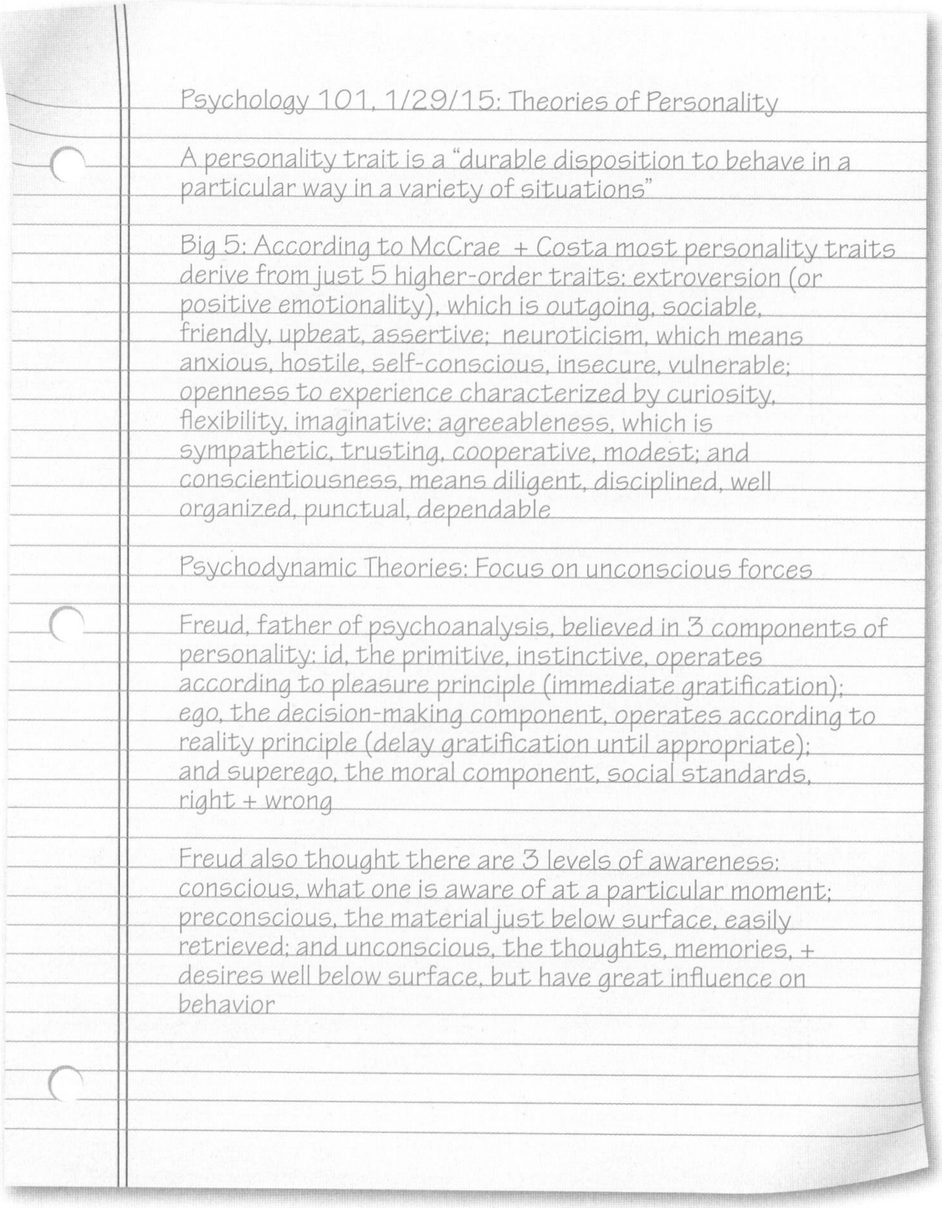

Psychology 101, 1/29/15: Theories of Personality

A personality trait is a "durable disposition to behave in a particular way in a variety of situations"

Big 5: According to McCrae + Costa most personality traits derive from just 5 higher-order traits: extroversion (or positive emotionality), which is outgoing, sociable, friendly, upbeat, assertive; neuroticism, which means anxious, hostile, self-conscious, insecure, vulnerable; openness to experience characterized by curiosity, flexibility, imaginative; agreeableness, which is sympathetic, trusting, cooperative, modest; and conscientiousness, means diligent, disciplined, well organized, punctual, dependable

Psychodynamic Theories: Focus on unconscious forces

Freud, father of psychoanalysis, believed in 3 components of personality: id, the primitive, instinctive, operates according to pleasure principle (immediate gratification); ego, the decision-making component, operates according to reality principle (delay gratification until appropriate); and superego, the moral component, social standards, right + wrong

Freud also thought there are 3 levels of awareness: conscious, what one is aware of at a particular moment; preconscious, the material just below surface, easily retrieved; and unconscious, the thoughts, memories, + desires well below surface, but have great influence on behavior

FIGURE 7.3
Note Taking in the Paragraph Format

completely. By the end of the lecture, you might have forgotten critical information.

List Format. The list format can be effective in taking notes on lists of terms and definitions, facts, or sequences, such as the body's pulmonary system (see Figure 7.4). It is easy to use lists in combination with the Cornell format, with key terms on the left and their definitions and explanations on the right.

Once you have decided on a format for taking notes, you might also want to develop your own system of abbreviations. For example, you might

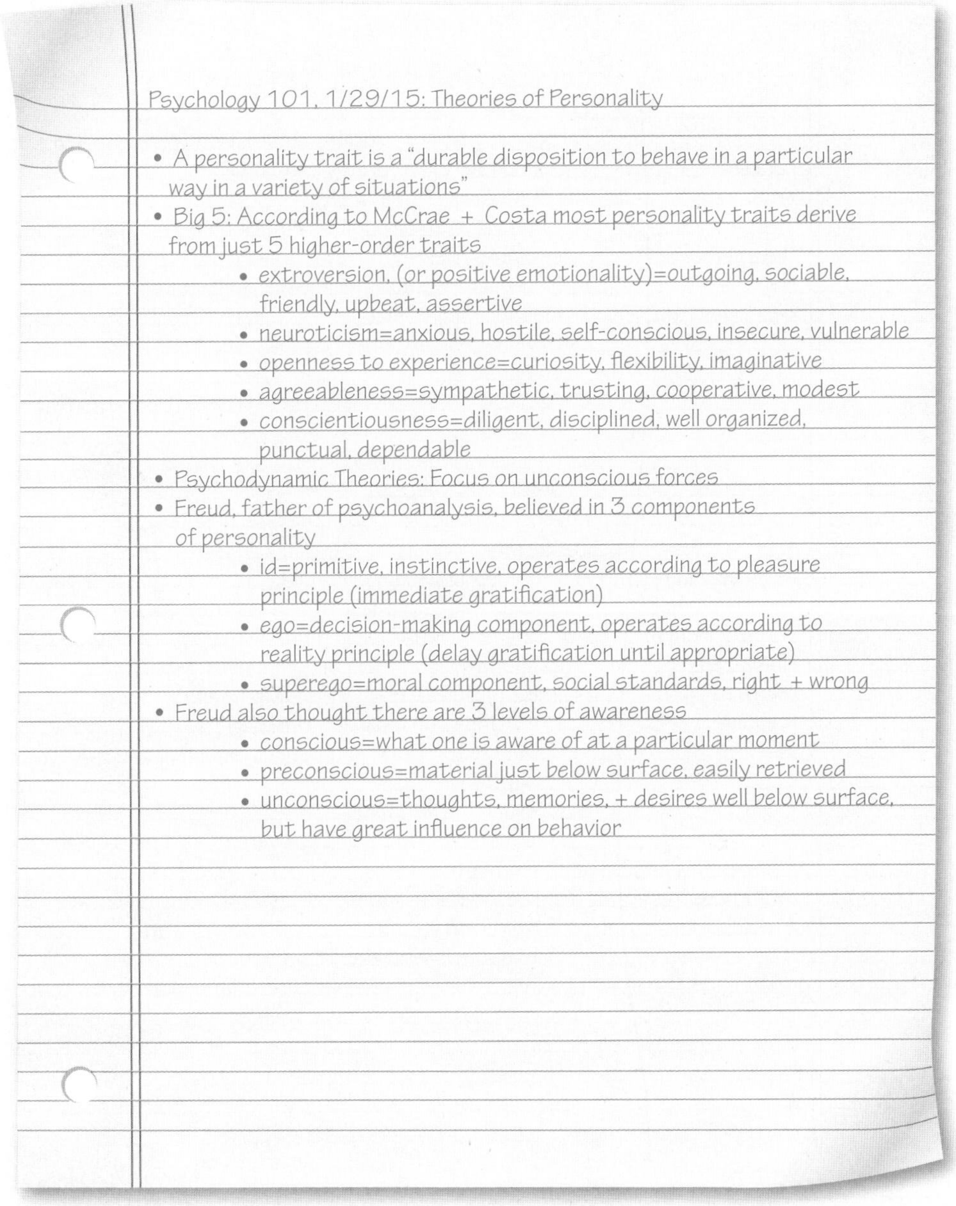

Psychology 101, 1/29/15: Theories of Personality

- A personality trait is a "durable disposition to behave in a particular way in a variety of situations"
- Big 5: According to McCrae + Costa most personality traits derive from just 5 higher-order traits
    - extroversion, (or positive emotionality)=outgoing, sociable, friendly, upbeat, assertive
    - neuroticism=anxious, hostile, self-conscious, insecure, vulnerable
    - openness to experience=curiosity, flexibility, imaginative
    - agreeableness=sympathetic, trusting, cooperative, modest
    - conscientiousness=diligent, disciplined, well organized, punctual, dependable
- Psychodynamic Theories: Focus on unconscious forces
- Freud, father of psychoanalysis, believed in 3 components of personality
    - id=primitive, instinctive, operates according to pleasure principle (immediate gratification)
    - ego=decision-making component, operates according to reality principle (delay gratification until appropriate)
    - superego=moral component, social standards, right + wrong
- Freud also thought there are 3 levels of awareness
    - conscious=what one is aware of at a particular moment
    - preconscious=material just below surface, easily retrieved
    - unconscious=thoughts, memories, + desires well below surface, but have great influence on behavior

FIGURE 7.4
Note Taking in the List Format

write "inst" instead of "institution" or "eval" instead of "evaluation." Just make sure that you will be able to understand your abbreviations when it's time to review.

NOTE-TAKING TECHNIQUES

Whatever note-taking system you choose, follow these important steps:

1. **Identify the main ideas.** Well-organized lectures always contain key points. The first principle of effective note taking is to identify and write down the most important ideas around which the lecture is built.

Personality trait	I. Personality trait = "durable disposition to behave in a particular way in a variety of situations"
	II. Big 5-McCrae + Costa
Big 5: Who? Name + describe them	A. Extroversion (or positive emotionality)=outgoing, sociable, friendly, upbeat, assertive
	B. Neuroticism=anxious, hostile, self-conscious, insecure, vulnerable
	C. Openness to experience=curiosity, flexibility, imaginative
	D. Agreeableness=sympathetic, trusting, cooperative, modest
	E. Conscientiousness=diligent, disciplined, well organized, punctual, dependable
	III. Psychodynamic Theories-focus on unconscious forces--Freud-psychoanalysis
Psychodynamic Theories: Who? 3 components. Name, define, relate each to a principle	A. 3 components of personality
	1. Id=primitive, instinctive, operates according to pleasure principle (immediate gratification)
	2. Ego=decision-making component, operates according to reality principle (delay gratification until appropriate)
	3. Superego=moral component, social standards, right + wrong
	B. 3 levels of awareness
3 levels of awareness: name and describe	1. conscious=what one is aware of at a particular moment
	2. preconscious=material just below surface, easily retrieved
	3. unconscious=thoughts, memories, + desires well below surface, but have great influence on behavior

FIGURE 7.5

Cornell Format Combined with the Outline Format

Although supporting details are also important, focus your note taking on the main ideas. Such ideas can be buried in details, statistics, anecdotes, or problems, but you will need to identify and record them for further study.

Some instructors announce the purpose of a lecture or offer an outline, thus providing you with the skeleton of main ideas followed by the details. Other instructors develop PowerPoint presentations. If they make these materials available on a class Web site before the lecture, you can print them and take notes on the teacher's outline or next to the PowerPoint slides.

Some lecturers change their tone of voice or repeat themselves for each key idea. Some ask questions or promote discussion. If a lecturer says something more than once, chances are that it is important. Ask yourself: What does my instructor want me to know at the end of today's class?

2. **Don't try to write down everything.** Some first-year students try to do just that. They stop being thinkers and become stenographers. As you take notes, leave spaces so that you can fill in additional details that you might have missed during class but remember later. Take the time to review and complete your notes as soon after class as possible.

3. **Don't be thrown by a disorganized lecturer.** When a lecture is disorganized, it's your job to try to organize what is said into general and specific frameworks. When the order is not apparent, you will need to indicate in your notes where the gaps are. After the lecture, consult the reading material or classmates to fill in these gaps or ask your instructor. Most instructors have regular office hours for student appointments, yet it is amazing how few students use these opportunities for one-on-one instruction. Asking questions can help your instructor find out which parts of the lecture need more attention and clarification.

4. **Keep your notes and supplementary materials for each course in a separate three-ring binder.** Label the binder with the course number and name. If the binders are too bulky to carry in your backpack, create a separate folder for each class stocked with loose-leaf notebook paper. Before class, label and date the paper you will be using for taking notes. Then, as soon after class as possible, move your notes from the folder to the binder.

5. **Download any notes, outlines, or diagrams, charts, graphs, and other visuals** from the instructor's Web site before class and bring them with you. You might be able to save yourself considerable time during the lecture if you do not have to try to copy complicated graphs and diagrams while the instructor is talking. Instead, you can focus on the ideas being presented while adding your own labels and notes to the visual images.

6. **Organize your notes chronologically in your binder.** Then create separate tabbed sections for homework, lab assignments, returned tests, and other materials.

7. **If handouts are distributed in class, label them and place them in your binder** near the notes for that day. Buy a portable three-ring hole punch that can be kept in your binder. Do not let handouts accumulate in your folders; add any handouts to your binders as you review your notes each day.

Taking Notes in Nonlecture Courses.   Always be ready to adapt your note-taking methods to match the situation. Group discussion is becoming a popular way to teach in college because it engages students in active participation. On your campus you might also have **Supplemental Instruction (SI)** classes that provide further opportunity to discuss the information presented in lectures. How do you keep a record of what's happening in nonlecture

Supplemental Instruction (SI) Classes that provide further opportunity to discuss the information presented in lectures.

classes? Assume that you are taking notes in a problem-solving group assignment. You would begin your notes by asking yourself: What is the problem? Then you would write down the answer. As the discussion progresses, you would list the solutions that are offered. These solutions would be your main ideas. The important details might include the positive and negative aspects of each view or solution. The important things to remember when taking notes in nonlecture courses are that you need to record the information presented by your classmates as well as by the instructor and that you need to consider all reasonable ideas, even though they might differ from your own.

When a course has separate lecture and discussion sessions, you will need to understand how the discussion sessions or SI classes relate to and augment the lectures. If different material is covered in lecture or discussion, you might need to ask for guidance in organizing your notes. When similar topics are covered, you can combine your notes so that you have comprehensive, unified coverage of each topic.

How to organize the notes you take in a class discussion depends on the purpose or form of the discussion. It usually makes good sense to begin with the list of issues or topics that the discussion leader announces. Another approach is to list the questions that participants raise for discussion. If the discussion explores reasons for and against a particular argument, divide your notes into columns or sections for pros and cons. When conflicting views are presented in discussion, record different perspectives and the rationales behind them. Your teacher might ask you to defend your own opinions in comparison to those of other students.

Taking Notes in Science and Mathematics Courses. Many mathematics and science courses build on each other from term to term and from year to year. When you take notes in these courses, you will likely need to refer to them in the future. For example, when taking organic chemistry, you might need to refer to notes taken in earlier chemistry courses. This practice can be particularly important when time has passed since your last related course, such as after a summer break. Taking notes in math and science courses can be different from taking notes in other types of classes. The box on page 153 offers tips to keep in mind specifically when taking notes in math and science classes.

Using Technology to Take Notes. Although some students use laptops for note taking, others prefer taking notes by hand so that they can easily circle important items or copy complex equations or diagrams while they are being presented. If you handwrite your notes, entering them on a computer after class for review purposes might be helpful, especially if you are a kinesthetic learner. After class you can also cut and paste diagrams and other visual representations into your notes and print a copy that might be easier to read than notes you wrote by hand.

Some students, especially aural learners, find it advantageous to record lectures, but if you do so, resist the temptation to become passive in class instead of actively listening. Students with specific types of disabilities might be urged to record lectures or use the services of note-takers who type on a laptop while the student views the notes on a separate screen.

TIPS FOR NOTE TAKING IN MATH AND SCIENCE CLASSES

> Write down any equations, formulas, diagrams, charts, graphs, and definitions that the instructor puts on the board or screen.

> Quote the instructor's words as precisely as possible. Technical terms often have exact meanings and cannot be paraphrased.

> Use standard symbols, abbreviations, and scientific notation.

> Write down all worked problems and examples, step by step. They often provide the template for exam questions. Actively engage in solving the problem yourself as it is being solved at the front of the class. Be sure that you can follow the logic and understand the sequence of steps. If you have questions that you cannot ask during the lecture, write them down in your notes so that you can ask them in discussion, in the lab, or during the instructor's office hours.

> Consider taking your notes in pencil or erasable pen. You might need to make changes if you are copying long equations while also trying to pay attention to the instructor. You want to keep your notes as neat as possible. Later, you can use colored ink to add other details.

> Listen carefully to other students' questions and the instructor's answers. Take notes on the discussion and during question-and-answer periods.

> Use asterisks, exclamation points, question marks, or symbols of your own to highlight important points in your notes or questions that you need to come back to when you review.

> Refer back to the textbook after class; the text might contain more accurate diagrams and other visual representations than you can draw while taking notes in class. If they are not provided in handouts or on the instructor's Web site, you might even want to scan or photocopy diagrams from the text and include them with your notes in your binder.

> Keep your binders for math and science courses until you graduate (or even longer if there is any chance that you will attend graduate school at some point in the future). They will serve as beneficial review materials for later classes in math and science and for preparing for standardized tests such as the Graduate Record Exam (GRE) or the Medical College Admission Test (MCAT). In some cases, these notes can also prove helpful in the workplace.

REVIEW YOUR NOTES

Most forgetting takes place within the first 24 hours of encountering the information, a phenomenon known as the "forgetting curve." So, if you do not review your notes almost immediately after class, it can be difficult to retrieve the material later. In two weeks you will have forgotten up to 70 percent of it! Forgetting can be a serious problem when you are expected to learn and remember many different facts, figures, concepts, and relationships for a number of classes. Once you understand how to improve your ability to remember, you will retain information more easily and completely. Retaining information will help your overall understanding as well as your ability to recall important details during exams. The next chapter is devoted to the topic of memory. For now, use these three strategies to work with the material immediately after class in order to remember key points from the lecture. They will pay off later, when you begin to study for your exams:

1. **Write down the main ideas.** For 5 or 10 minutes, quickly review your notes and select key words or phrases that will act as labels or tags for main ideas and key information in your notes. Fill in the details you

TECH TIP TAKE NOTES LIKE A ROCK STAR

Studies have shown that people remember only half of what they hear, which is a major reason to take lecture notes. Solid note taking will help you distill key concepts and make it easier to study for tests. So why not take your note-taking skills up a notch?

1 ▶ THE PROBLEM

You don't know how to make your digital lecture notes leap off the screen and engrave themselves on your brain.

2 ▶ THE FIX

Clue into the many ways you can use basic programs like Word, Excel, and PowerPoint to sharpen your note-taking skill set.

3 ▶ HOW TO DO IT

1. Word is great for taking notes in most classes. To highlight main ideas, you can bold or underline text. You can change the font size and color, highlight whole swaths of text, and insert text boxes or charts. You can make bullet points or properly formatted outlines and insert comment bubbles for emphasis. You can cut and paste material as you review your notes to make things more coherent. You can also create different folders for each of your classes so that you can find everything you need with one click. (Note: It's worth playing around on the toolbar until you get it all down pat.)

2. Excel is especially good for economics and accounting courses or for any class that involves making scientific calculations or financial statements. You can embed messages inside the cells of a spreadsheet to explain calculations. The notes will magically appear whenever you use your cursor to hover over that cell.

3. PowerPoint can be an invaluable tool for visual learners. Instead of keeping your notes in one giant, potentially confusing Word document, you can open up a PowerPoint slideshow and type right into it. That way, every time your instructor changes gears, you can open a new slide. It's a nice way to break up the material. Some instructors post the PowerPoint slides that they plan to use in class a few hours in advance. Print them out and take them with you as note-taking tools; you can even write notes on the slides themselves or download them and add your notes in PowerPoint.

Image Source/Jupiter Images

CLEVER TRICKS

Date your notes. Focus on writing down the main points (the material your professor emphasizes or repeats), using phrases or key words instead of long sentences. Keep all your notes in order and in one place. Back up *everything*. If you're not a tech whiz, keep a pen and paper handy for sketching graphs and diagrams. Label your notes clearly to make it easy to look things up. If you find yourself struggling to keep up, practice your listening and typing skills.

PERSONAL BEST

What concrete steps could you take to create an organized note-taking system for the semester? Start by picking a note-taking style that appeals to you. If you love a chart or spreadsheet, Excel is your kind of program. If you're an old-school type who loves nothing better than a spiral notebook and a ballpoint pen, that's OK, too.

still remember but missed writing down. You might also want to ask your instructor to glance at your notes to determine whether you have identified the major ideas.

2. **Recite your ideas out loud.** Recite a brief version of what you understand from class. If you don't have a few minutes after class when you can concentrate on reviewing your notes, find some other time during that same day to review what you have written and tell someone else what you learned in class that day. For many, the best way to learn something is to teach it to someone else. You will understand something better and remember it longer if you try to explain it. This process helps you discover your own reactions and uncover gaps in your comprehension of the material. (Asking and answering questions in class can also provide you with the feedback you need to make certain that your understanding is accurate.) Now you're ready to embed the major points from your notes in your memory.

3. **Review your notes from the previous class just before the next class session.** As you sit in class the next time it meets, waiting for the lecture to begin, use the time to quickly review your notes from the previous class session. This will put you in tune with the lecture that is about to begin and prompt you to ask questions about material from the previous lecture that might not have been clear to you.

What if you have three classes in a row and no time for studying between them? In that case, recall and recite as soon after class as possible. Review the most recent class first. Never delay recall and recitation longer than one day; if you do, it will take you longer to review, select main ideas, and recite. With practice, you can complete the review of your main ideas from your notes quickly, perhaps between classes, during lunch, or while riding the bus.

COMPARE NOTES

You might be able to improve your notes by comparing notes with another student or in a study group, SI session, or a learning community, if one is available to you. Knowing that your notes will be seen by someone else will prompt you to make them well organized, clear, and accurate. Compare your notes: Are they as clear and concise as those of other students? Do you agree on the most important points? Share with one another how you take and organize your notes. You might get new ideas for using abbreviations. Take turns testing one another on what you have learned. Doing so will help you predict exam questions and determine whether you can answer them. Comparing notes is not the same as copying another student's notes. You simply cannot learn as well from someone else's notes, no matter how good they are, if you have not attended class.

If your campus has a note-taking service, check with your instructor about making use of this for-pay service, but keep in mind that such notes are intended to supplement the ones you take, not substitute for them. Some students choose to rewrite their own notes as a means of review or because they think that their notes are messy and they will not be able to understand them later. Unless you are a tactile learner, rewriting or typing your notes might not help you learn the material. A more profitable approach might be to summarize your notes in your own words.

Finally, have a backup plan in case you need to be absent because of illness or a family emergency. Exchange phone numbers and e-mail addresses with other students so that you can contact one of them to learn what you missed and get a copy of his or her notes. Also contact your instructor to explain your absence and set up an appointment during office hours to make sure that you understand the work you missed.

CLASS NOTES AND HOMEWORK

Good class notes can help you complete homework assignments. Follow these steps:

1. **Take 10 minutes to review your notes.** Skim the notes and put a question mark next to anything you do not understand at first reading. Draw stars next to topics that warrant special emphasis. Try to place the material in context: What has been going on in the course for the past few weeks? How does today's class fit in?

2. **Do a warm-up exercise for your homework.** Before doing the assignment, look through your notes again. Use a separate sheet of paper to rework examples, problems, or exercises. If there is related assigned material in the textbook, review it. Go back to the examples. Cover the solution and attempt to answer each question or complete each problem. Look at the author's work only after you have made a serious effort to remember it. Keep in mind that it can help to go back through your course notes, reorganize them, highlight the essential items, and thus create new notes that let you connect with the material one more time. In fact, these new notes could be better than the originals.

3. **Do any assigned problems and answer any assigned questions.** When you start doing your homework, read each question or problem and ask: What am I supposed to find or find out? What is essential, and what is extraneous? Read each problem several times and state it in your own words. Work the problem without referring to your notes or the text, as though you were taking a test. In this way you will test your knowledge and know when you are prepared for exams.

4. **Persevere.** Don't give up too soon. When you encounter a problem or question that you cannot readily handle, move on only after a reasonable effort. After you have completed the entire assignment, go back to any items that stumped you. Try once more and then take a break. You might need to mull over a particularly difficult problem for several days. Let your unconscious mind have a chance. Inspiration might come when you are waiting at a stoplight or just before you fall asleep.

5. **Complete your work.** When you finish an assignment, talk to yourself about what you

---

YOUR TURN

Discuss

Now that you've read these suggestions about taking notes and studying for class, which ideas will you implement in your own note taking? Come to class ready to explain which ideas appeal to you most and why.

learned from it. Think about how the problems and questions were different from one another, which strategies were successful, and what form the answers took. Be sure to review any material you have not mastered. Seek assistance from the instructor, a classmate, a study group, the campus learning assistance center, or a tutor to learn how to answer questions that stumped you.

CHECKLIST FOR SUCCESS

GETTING THE MOST OUT OF CLASS

☐ **Practice the behaviors of engagement.** These behaviors include listening attentively, taking notes, and contributing to class discussion. Engagement also means participating in out-of-class activities without being "required" to do so.

☐ **Seek professors who practice "active" teaching.** Ask other students, your seminar instructor, and your adviser to suggest the most engaging professors.

☐ **Prepare for class before class; it is one of the simplest and most important things you can do.** Read your notes from the previous class and do the assigned readings.

☐ **Go to class.** Ninety-five percent of success is simply showing up. You have no chance of becoming engaged in learning if you're not there.

☐ **Identify the different types of note taking covered in this chapter and decide which one(s) might work best for you.** Compare your notes with those of another good student to make sure that you are covering the most important points.

☐ **As you review your notes before each class, make a list of any questions you have and ask both fellow students and your professor for help.** Don't wait until just before the exam to try to find answers to your questions.

BUILD YOUR EXPERIENCE 1 2 3 4

1 STAY ON TRACK

Successful college students stay focused. They "stay on track." They know what they have to do to be successful, they set goals, and they monitor their progress toward their goals.

Reflect on what you have learned about college success in this chapter and how you are going to apply the chapter information or strategies in college and in your career. List your ideas.

1. _____

_____

_____

2. _____

_____

_____

3. _____

_____

_____

2 ONE-MINUTE PAPER

This chapter explores multiple strategies for being an effective listener and being engaged in class. What new strategies did you learn that you had never thought about or used before? What questions about effective note taking do you still have?

3 ## APPLYING WHAT YOU HAVE LEARNED

Now that you have read and discussed this chapter, consider how you can apply what you have learned to your academic and personal life. As you try the suggestions in this chapter, consider ways in which you can encourage yourself to keep up the hard work. For example, if you have a big project, try breaking it up into several smaller pieces. As you complete each piece, reward yourself by hanging out with friends or taking time to do something you enjoy. Making an intentional effort to learn is not easy but is definitely worth it in the long run.

4 ## BUILDING YOUR PORTFOLIO

Making Meaning   This chapter includes several examples of note-taking strategies, but did you catch the emphasis on what you should do with your notes after class? Sometimes it is helpful to associate a concept with an interest you have. Preparing to teach someone else how to do something or explaining a complex idea to others can also help you understand the information more fully. Test this idea for yourself.

1. Choose a set of current class notes (it doesn't matter which class they are from) and specifically look for connections between the subject matter and your personal interests and goals (future career, social issue, sports, hobbies, etc.).

2. Next, develop a 5-minute presentation using PowerPoint that both outlines your class notes and shows the connection to your interests. Develop the presentation as though you were going to teach a group of students about the concept. Use a combination of graphics, photos, music, and video clips to help your imaginary audience connect with the material in a new and interesting way.

3. Save the PowerPoint in your portfolio or in the Cloud. Use your PowerPoint presentation as one way to study for your next exam in that course.

You probably won't create PowerPoint presentations for all your class notes, but making a habit of connecting class content to your life is an easy way to help yourself remember information. When it is time to prepare for a test, try pulling your notes into a presentation that you would feel comfortable giving to your classmates.

For more on this topic watch
French Fries Are Not Vegetables and Other College Lessons

WHERE TO GO FOR HELP . . .

ON CAMPUS

> **Learning Assistance Center**   Almost every campus has a learning assistance center, and this chapter's topic is one of their specialties. More and more, the best students—and good students who want to be better students—use learning centers as much as students who are having academic difficulties. Services at learning centers are offered by both full-time professionals and highly skilled student tutors.

> **Fellow College Students**   Often, the best help we can get comes from those who are closest to us: fellow students. Keep an eye out in your classes,

residence hall, co-curricular groups, and other places for the most serious, purposeful, and directed students. They are the ones to seek out. Find a tutor. Join a study group. Students who do these things are most likely to stay in college and be successful. It does not diminish you in any way to seek assistance from your peers.

ONLINE

> Toastmasters International offers public speaking tips at **http://www.toastmasters.org**.

> See guidelines for speaking in class at **http://www.school-for-champions.com /grades/speaking.htm**.

MY INSTITUTION'S RESOURCES

_____

_____

_____

_____

_____

_____

_____

_____

_____

_____

8 Studying

" Two of the biggest challenges transitioning from high school to college were learning to study and time management.

Joshua Mortin, 17
Mechanical Engineering major
Mass Bay Community College

Joshua Mortin didn't struggle with study skills or memory in high school. He grew up in Framingham, Massachusetts, where he is currently dual-enrolled in high school and Mass Bay Community College. "In high school," he says, "my studying habits have been slim to none. I was the type of high school student who was able to pass a test just from listening and from what I remembered from class."

Inspired by his parents, who both have Ph.D.s, Joshua decided to enroll in the local community college while still in high school. There, he quickly learned that the expectations of students in college are very different from those in high school. At Mass Bay, Joshua has had to adjust his habits when he found that he wasn't able to remember the sheer volume of content instructors threw at him. "Two of the biggest challenges transitioning from high school to college were learning to study and time management." His classes tend to go twice as fast, and instructors expect students to do a lot of work on their own. One of the first

Joshua Mortin ▶

steps Joshua took to adjust his study habits was to stop setting aside huge blocks of unstructured time. "I learned that studying for more than four hours straight is not the best for me," he says. "I need to study for an hour, take a half-hour break, and then study another hour. I realized that after an hour I had trouble remembering things." By taking breaks to eat, exercise, or watch TV, Joshua knows that he's giving his brain time to process information and move it from his short-term memory to his long-term memory, a concept you'll learn more about in this chapter. He also gives himself time to forget the material that he hasn't quite mastered so that he can go over it again and "overlearn" it.

After finishing high school this year, Joshua plans either to complete his associate's degree at Mass Bay and transfer to a four-year institution or to transfer right away. He would like to study either mechanical or aeronautical engineering. His one piece of advice to other first-year students is to remember that the first year can be the hardest because it's so different from high school. "College isn't a four-year party," he says. "The first year is going to be the hardest because it's so different. Just push through it. You'll find that it all starts making sense."

You might have learned to study effectively while you were in high school, or, like Joshua, you might find that your high school study habits no longer work. You will need to discover ways to structure your study time that work best for you. Joshua quickly learned that a four-hour study session was too long for him. But however you structure your study sessions, you will need to allocate regular times each week to review course material, do assigned reading, and keep up with your homework. Occasionally, you will also want to do additional (unassigned) reading and investigate particular topics that interest you, strategies that will help you retain knowledge.

Studying, comprehending, and remembering are essential to getting the most from your college experience. Although many students think that the only reason for studying is to do well on exams, a far more important reason is to learn and understand course information. If you study to increase your understanding, you are more likely to remember and apply what you learn not only to tests, but also to future courses and to life beyond college.

This chapter offers you a number of strategies for making the best use of your study time. It also addresses the important topic of memory. There's no getting around it: If you can't remember what you have read or heard, you won't do well on course exams.

Study to Understand and Remember

Studying will help you accomplish two goals: understanding and remembering. Although memory is a necessary tool for learning, what's most important is that you study to develop a deep understanding of course

ASSESSING YOUR STRENGTHS

What study skills have you learned and practiced, and how do you need to improve? As you read this chapter, list specific examples of your strengths in studying and remembering course material.

_____

_____

_____

_____

SETTING GOALS

What are your most important objectives in learning the material in this chapter? How do you need to improve your study skills and your memory? List three goals in this area (e.g., I will make sure that I am not distracted when I am studying; I will find a space where I can be alone, either the library or a study lounge; and I will turn off my cell phone during study time).

1. _____

_____

2. _____

_____

3. _____

_____

information. When you truly comprehend what you are learning, you will be able to place names, dates, and specific facts in context. You will also be able to exercise your critical-thinking abilities.

The human mind has discovered ingenious ways to understand and remember information. Here are some methods that might be useful to you as you're trying to nail down the causes of World War I, remember the steps in a chemistry problem, or absorb a mathematical formula:

1. **Pay attention to what you're hearing or reading.** This suggestion is perhaps the most basic and the most important. If you're sitting in class thinking about everything except what the professor is saying or if you're reading and find that your mind is wandering, you're wasting your time. Force yourself to focus. Complete the exercise in Figure 8.1 to

YOUR TURN

Write and Reflect

The next time that you are reading a textbook, monitor your ability to concentrate. Check your watch when you begin and check it again when your mind begins to wander. How many minutes did you concentrate on your reading? List some strategies to keep your mind from wandering. Write down in a journal entry ideas you have heard that you think will work well for you.

FIGURE 8.1

Concentration Is Key

Truly comprehending new material takes a lot of effort on your part. Concentration is the key to truly comprehending new material, and it isn't easy. You must focus on what you hear or read so that the information will enter your long-term memory; it won't just magically happen! If you are willing to make a few changes in behavior, you will be able to concentrate better, remember longer, and most likely need fewer hours to study because you will use your time more efficiently. What are you willing to do to make it happen? Are you willing—yes or no—to make the following tough sacrifices if doing so means that you will do better on tests and have more productive study time?

Tough Choices	Your Answer Yes or No
Are you willing to collaborate with others to form study groups or partners?	
Are you willing to find a place on campus for quiet study?	
Are you willing to turn off your cell phone for a few moments of uninterrupted reading time?	
Are you willing to turn off disruptive music or TV while you are studying?	
Are you willing to study for tests four or five days before the test date?	
Are you willing to do assigned readings before you come to class?	
Are you willing to position yourself in class so that you can see and hear better?	
Are you willing to reduce stress through exercise, sleep, or meditation?	
Are you willing to go over your notes after class to clean them up or rewrite them?	
Are you willing to take a few minutes on the weekend to organize the week ahead?	

Making these changes in behavior now will save you a lot of headaches in the future. Attending college is a huge responsibility, one that should not be taken lightly. As a mature learner, you need to be flexible and change your old patterns to create successful new habits. Making tough choices isn't easy, but it will directly impact your ability to remember and retain the information you will be required to learn in the months and years ahead.

determine how willing you are to increase your concentration when you study.

2. **"Overlearn" the material.** After you know and think that you understand the material you're studying, go over it again to make sure that you'll retain it for a long time. Test yourself or ask someone else to test you. Recite out loud, in your own words, what you're trying to remember. Explain it to another person.

3. **Check the Internet.** If you're having trouble remembering what you have learned, search a key word and try to find interesting details that will engage you in learning more, not less, about the subject. For instance, if you are taking an introductory course in psychology, you might want to investigate "controversial issues in psychology" to see where the experts disagree. Many first-year courses cover such a large

amount of material that you'll miss the more interesting details unless you seek them out for yourself. As your interest increases, so will your memory for the topic.

4. **Be sure that you have the big picture.** Whenever you begin a course, make sure that you're clear on what the course will cover. You can talk with someone who has already taken the course, or you can take a brief look at all the reading assignments. Having the big picture will help you understand and remember the details of what you're learning. For instance, the big picture in this first-year class is to give students the knowledge (e.g., ways to identify the kind of learner you are, the role of critical thinking in lifetime learning) and strategies (e.g., how to manage time, how to take effective notes) to be successful in college. Review the syllabus for this course and think about what might be missing. Are there topics related to college success that this course doesn't seem to cover?

5. **Look for connections between your life and what's going on in your courses.** College courses might seem irrelevant to you, but if you look more carefully, you'll find many connections between course material and your daily life. Seeing those connections will make your courses more interesting and will help you remember what you're learning. For example, if you're taking a music theory course and studying chord patterns, listen for those patterns in contemporary music.

6. **Get organized.** If your desk or your computer is organized, you'll spend less time trying to remember a file name or where you put a particular document. Also, as you rewrite your notes, the process of putting them in a logical order (either chronological or thematic) that makes sense to you will help you learn and remember them.

7. **Reduce stressors in your life.** Although there's no way to determine the extent to which worry or stress causes you to be unable to focus or to forget, most people will agree that stress can be a distraction. Healthy, stress-reducing behaviors such as meditation, exercise, and sleep are especially important for college students. Many campuses have counseling or health centers that can provide resources to help you deal with whatever might be causing stress in your daily life.

8. **Collaborate with others.** One of the most effective ways to study is in a group with other students. In your first year of college, gather a group of students who study together. Study groups can meet throughout the term or can review for midterm or final exams.

YOUR TURN

Work Together

Share in a small group your thoughts on whether you think that it is important to be organized. How would you describe your living space and your "electronic environment"? Today, when you return to your room, pay attention to your living or studying environment.

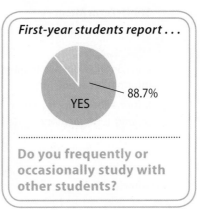

First-year students report . . .

88.7% YES

Do you frequently or occasionally study with other students?

Work Together

One way to enhance your memory is through working collaboratively with others. Each of you can share your own favorite memory strategy. You can also check specific facts and details through group consensus.

Digital Vision/Getty Images

How Memory Works

short-term memory
How many items you are able to perceive at one time. Memory that disappears in less than 30 seconds (sometimes faster) unless the items are moved to long-term memory.

Kenneth Higbee describes two different processes involved in memory (see Table 8.1). The first is **short-term memory**, defined as how many items you are able to perceive at one time. Higbee found that information stored in short-term memory is forgotten in less than 30 seconds (and sometimes much faster) unless you take action to either keep that information in short-term memory or move it to long-term memory.[1]

Although short-term memory is significantly limited, it has a number of uses. It serves as an immediate but temporary holding tank for information, some of which might not be needed for long. It helps you maintain a reasonable attention span so that you can keep track of topics mentioned in conversation, and it also enables you to stay on task with the goals you are pursuing at any moment. But even these simple functions of short-term

TABLE 8.1   Short-Term Memory and Long-Term Memory

Short-Term Memory	Long-Term Memory
Stores information for about 30 seconds	Procedural: remembering how to do something
Can contain from five to nine chunks of information at one time	Semantic: remembering facts and meanings
Information either forgotten or moved to long-term memory	Episodic: remembering the time and place of events

[1]Kenneth Higbee, *Your Memory: How It Works and How to Improve It,* 2nd ed. (New York: Marlowet, 2001).

memory fail on occasion. If the telephone rings, if someone asks you a question, or if you're interrupted in any way, you might find that your attention suffers and that you essentially have to start over in reconstructing short-term memory.

The second memory process is **long-term memory**, which is the type of memory you will need to improve so that you will remember what you're learning in college. Long-term memory can be described in three ways. *Procedural memory* is knowing how to do something, such as solving a mathematical problem or playing a musical instrument. *Semantic memory* involves facts and meanings without regard to where and when you learned those things. *Episodic memory* deals with particular events, their time, and their place.[2]

You are using your procedural memory when you get on a bicycle you haven't ridden in years, when you can recall the first piece you learned to play on the piano, when you effortlessly type a letter or class report, and when you drive a car. Your semantic memory is used continuously to recall word meanings or important dates, such as your mother's birthday. Episodic memory allows you to remember events in your life: a vacation, your first day in school, or the moment you opened your college acceptance letter. Some people can recall not only the event but also the very date and time the event happened. For others, although the event stands out, the dates and times are harder to remember immediately.

long-term memory The type of memory that is used to retain information and can be described in three ways: procedural, semantic, and episodic.

CONNECTING MEMORY TO DEEP LEARNING

It can be easy to blame a poor memory on the way we live; multitasking has become the norm for college students and instructors. Admittedly, it's hard to focus on anything for very long if your life is full of daily distractions and competing responsibilities or if you're not getting the sleep you need. Have you ever had the experience of walking into a room with a particular task in mind and immediately forgetting what that task was? You were probably interrupted either by your own thoughts or by someone or something else. Or have you ever felt the panic that comes from blanking on a test, even though you studied hard and thought that you knew the material? You might have pulled an all-nighter, and studying and exhaustion raised your stress level, causing your mind to go blank. Such experiences happen to everyone at one time or another. To do well in college, however—and in life—it's important that you improve your ability to remember what you read, hear, and experience. As one writer put it, "There is no learning without memory."[3] On the other hand, not all memory involves real learning.

Is a good memory all you need to do well in college? Most memory strategies tend to focus on helping you remember the bits and pieces of knowledge: names, dates, numbers, vocabulary, graphic materials, and

---

[2] W. F. Brewer and J. R. Pani, "The Structure of Human Memory," in G. H. Bower (Ed.), *The Psychology of Learning and Motivation: Advances in Research and Theory*, vol. 17 (New York: Academic Press, 1983), pp. 1–38.

[3] Harry Lorayne, *Super Memory, Super Student: How to Raise Your Grades in 30 Days* (Boston: Little, Brown, 1990), p. 3.

deep learning
Understanding the why and how behind the details.

formulas. However, if you know the date the Civil War began and the fort where the first shots were fired but you don't really know why the Civil War was fought, you're missing the point of a college education. College is about **deep learning**, understanding the why and how behind the details. So don't forget that although recall of specific facts is certainly necessary, it isn't sufficient. To do well in college courses, you will need to understand major themes and ideas, and you will also need to hone your ability to think critically about what you're learning. Critical thinking is discussed in depth in Chapter 5.

MYTHS ABOUT MEMORY

Although scientific knowledge about how our brains function is increasing all the time, Kenneth Higbee suggests that you might have heard some myths about memory (and maybe you even believe them). Here are five of these memory myths and what experts say about them:

1. **Myth:** Some people are stuck with bad memories.

   Reality: Although there are probably some differences among people in innate memory (the memory ability a person is born with), what really gives you the edge are memory skills that you can learn and use. Virtually anyone can improve the ability to remember and recall.

2. **Myth:** Some people have photographic memories.

   Reality: Although a few individuals have truly exceptional memories, most research has found that these abilities result more often from learned strategies, interest, and practice than from some innate ability. Even though you might not have what psychologists would classify as an exceptional memory, applying the memory strategies presented later in this chapter can help you improve it.

3. **Myth:** Memory benefits from long hours of practice.

   Reality: Practicing memorizing can help improve memory. If you have ever been a server in a restaurant, you might have been required to memorize the menu. You might even have surprised yourself at your ability to memorize not only the main entrees, but also sauces and side dishes. Experts acknowledge that practice often improves memory, but they argue that the way that you practice, such as using special creative strategies, is more important than how long you practice.

4. **Myth:** Remembering too much can clutter your mind.

   Reality: For all practical purposes, the storage capacity of your memory is unlimited. In fact, the more you learn about a particular topic, the easier it is to learn even more. How you organize the information is more important than the quantity.

5. **Myth:** People use only 10 percent of their brain power.

   Reality: No scientific research is available to accurately measure how much of our brain we actually use. Most psychologists and learning specialists, however, believe that we all have far more mental ability than we actually tap.

TECH TIP EMBRACE THE CLOUD

Abundant computer labs, laptops, tablets, and smart phones give you the opportunity to work from almost everywhere. What can you do to keep all your important files in one place so that you'll never be without them?

1 ▶ THE PROBLEM

You're at the computer lab, and you don't have the files you need. This time, you forgot your flash drive; last time, you had your tablet and not your laptop. What if your devices get run over by a truck? What then?

2 ▶ THE FIX

Save your files to a Cloud storage site and have access to them from any Internet-connected computer or tablet.

3 ▶ HOW TO DO IT

Sign up for a free account from a Cloud storage site. These sites allow you to save files to an online location. You'll have your own private storage space that can only be accessed with a password. Some sites are tailored for documents (Word files, PDFs, PowerPoint presentations), while others allow easy storage for both print files and audio/video. Cloud storage is great for collaborative projects because you can choose to share all or some of your files with your classmates and friends. Here is a list of three sites with free storage; most such sites require payment to increase your storage size.

1. Dropbox (dropbox.com) is probably the most well-known Cloud storage site. Users get 2G of free storage and are able to upgrade to up to 500 GB for a monthly fee. (Note: The abbreviation G or GB stands for gigabyte, a unit of measurement approximately equal to 1 billion bytes. The prefix *giga* comes from "gigantic." A gigabyte is used to measure memory or disk capacity.) You can also earn more storage space by referring other customers to the site. Dropbox has both a Web interface that you and others can access from any computer and a downloadable client that you can save to your computer. (In the world of computing, a client is a piece of hardware or software that accesses a service made available by a server. Think of it as a client-server relationship.) This download makes Dropbox look like any other folder on your computer; when you add files, however, it actually adds them to your online folder. Dropbox is available as a stand-alone app on iPhone, iPad, and Android devices and also works with other document-editing apps for mobile devices.

2. Google Drive (drive.google .com) allows users to store and share documents up to 5 GB. A great feature of Google Drive is that you can edit documents in real time with your friends and classmates. If you're writing a group paper, all your coauthors can sign into Google Drive and view the same document. You are able to edit it together, and there is a chat window so that you can have a conversation while editing. Google Drive allows for storage of both audio and video. Like Dropbox, Google Drive is also available as a stand-alone app, and it integrates well with iPhone, iPad, and Android apps.

Courtesy of Dropbox. *Your College Experience* is not affiliated with or otherwise sponsored by Dropbox, Inc.

3. MediaFire (mediafire.com) is newer than Dropbox and Google Drive. Its key feature is 50 GB of free storage space. Users are able to work collaboratively in the Cloud and access their files using stand-alone apps on iPhone, iPad, and Android devices.

Improving Your Memory

Throughout history, human memory has been a topic of great interest and fascination for scientists and the general public. Although severe problems with memory are extremely rare, you're in good company if you find that your memory occasionally lets you down, especially if you're nervous or stressed or when grades depend on immediate recall of what you have read, heard, or written.

So, how can you improve your ability to store information in your brain for future use? Psychologists and learning specialists have conducted research on memory and have developed a number of strategies that you can use as part of a study-skills regimen. Some of these strategies might be new to you, but others will be simple, commonsense ways to maximize your learning. You may have heard these ideas before, although perhaps not in the context of improving your memory.

The benefits of having a good memory are obvious. In college your memory will help you retain information and ace tests. After college the ability to recall names, procedures, presentations, and appointments will save you energy and time and will prevent a lot of embarrassment.

There are many ways to go about remembering. Have you ever had to memorize a speech or lines from a play? How you approach committing the lines to memory might depend on your learning style. If you're an aural learner, you might choose to record your lines as well as lines of other characters and listen to them on tape. If you're a visual learner, you might remember best by visualizing where your lines appear on the page in the script.

An Elephant (Almost) Never Forgets

Although elephants apparently do have pretty good memories, they're like the rest of us in that they occasionally forget. Work to develop your memory by using the specific strategies in this chapter. One of the most important strategies you can use is understanding the big-picture context behind bits and pieces of information.

"Is this the memory seminar?"

© Shannon Burns

If you learn best by reading, you might simply read the script over and over. If you're a kinesthetic learner, you might need to walk or move across an imaginary stage as you read the script.

Although knowing specific words will help, remembering concepts and ideas can be much more important. To embed such ideas in your mind, ask yourself these questions as you review your notes and books:

1. What is the essence of the idea?
2. Why does the idea make sense? What is the logic behind it?
3. How does this idea connect to other ideas in the material?
4. What are some possible arguments against the idea?

YOUR TURN
....
Work Together

With your instructor's help, identify other students in your class who share your learning style. Brainstorm with one another strategies for remembering material for exams using your learning style and keep track of the most helpful ideas.

MNEMONICS

Mnemonics (pronounced "ne-MON-iks") are various methods or tricks to aid the memory. Mnemonics tend to fall into four basic categories:

1. **Acronyms.** New words created from the first letters of several words can be helpful in remembering. The Great Lakes can be more easily

Photo courtesy of The Everett Collection

IN THE MEDIA

The 1997 film *Good Will Hunting*, starring Matt Damon and Ben Affleck, tells the story of a 20-year-old South Boston laborer, Will Hunting, an unrecognized genius. After Will assaults a police officer, he is "punished" by being forced to see a therapist (played by Robin Williams) and to study advanced mathematics. In one scene Will's girlfriend, Skylar (played by Minnie Driver), in trying to understand his brilliance, asks him whether he has a photographic memory.

For Reflection: Although being a genius like Will isn't realistic, what kinds of strategies can you use to improve how well you can master and retain information?

recalled by remembering the word *HOMES* for Huron, Ontario, Michigan, Erie, and Superior.

2. **Acrostics.** An acrostic is a verse in which certain letters of each word or line form a message. Many piano students were taught the notes on the treble clef lines (E, G, B, D, F) by remembering the acrostic "Every Good Boy Deserves Fudge."

3. **Rhymes or songs.** Do you remember learning "Thirty days hath September, April, June, and November. All the rest have 31, excepting February alone. It has 28 days time, but in leap years it has 29" or a similar ditty? If so, you were using a mnemonic rhyming technique to remember the number of days in each month.

4. **Visualization.** Visualization is used to associate words, concepts, or stories with visual images. The more ridiculous the image, the more likely you are to remember it. So use your imagination to create mental images when you're studying important words or concepts. For example, as you're driving to campus, choose some landmarks along the way to help you remember material for your history test. The next day, as you pass those landmarks, relate them to something from your class notes or readings. A white picket fence might remind you of the British army's eighteenth-century approach to warfare, with its official uniforms and straight lines of infantry, while a stand of trees of various shapes and sizes might remind you of the Continental army's less organized approach.

Mnemonics works because it makes information meaningful through the use of rhymes, patterns, and associations. It imposes meaning where meaning might be hard to recognize. Mnemonics provides a way of organizing material, a sort of mental filing system. It's probably not needed if what you are studying is very logical and organized, but it can be quite useful for other types of material.

Although mnemonics provides a time-tested way of remembering, the method has some limitations. The first is time. Thinking up rhymes, associations, or visual images can take longer than simply learning the words themselves through repetition. Also, it is often difficult to convert abstract concepts into concrete words or images, and you run the risk of being able to remember an image without recalling the underlying concept. Finally, memory specialists debate whether learning through mnemonics actually helps with long-term knowledge retention and whether this technique helps or interferes with deeper understanding.

USING REVIEW SHEETS, MIND MAPS, AND OTHER TOOLS

To prepare for an exam that will cover large amounts of material, you need to condense the volume of notes and text pages into manageable study units. Review your materials with these questions in mind: Is this concept one of the key ideas in the chapter or unit? Will I see it on the test? As suggested in Chapter 6, you might prefer to highlight, underline, or annotate the most important ideas or create outlines, lists, or visual maps.

Use your notes to develop review sheets. Make lists of key terms and ideas (from the recall column if you've used the Cornell method) that you need to remember. Also, don't underestimate the value of using your lecture notes to test yourself or others on information presented in class.

A **mind map** is essentially a review sheet with a visual element. Its word and visual patterns provide you with highly charged clues to jog your memory. Because they are visual, mind maps help many students recall information.

Figure 8.2 shows what a mind map might look like for a chapter on listening and learning in the classroom. Try to reconstruct the ideas in that

mind map   A review sheet with words and visual elements that jog the memory to help you recall information more easily.

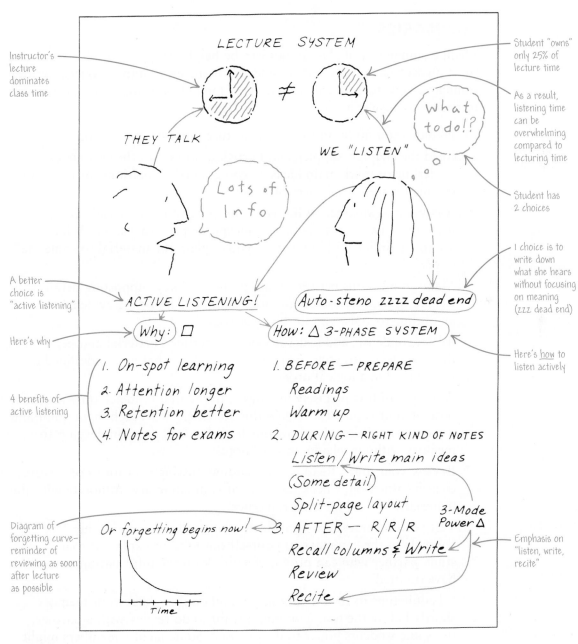

FIGURE 8.2

Sample Mind Map on Listening and Learning in the Classroom

chapter by following the connections in the map. Then make a visual mind map for the chapter and see how much more you can remember after studying it a number of times.

In addition to review sheets and mind maps, you might want to create flash cards. One advantage of flash cards is that you can keep them in a pocket of your backpack or jacket and pull them out to study anywhere, even when you might not think that you have enough time to take out your notebook to study. Also, you always know where you left off. Flash cards can help you make good use of time that might otherwise be wasted, such as time spent on the bus or waiting for a friend. See Chapter 6 for more information about creating and using flash cards.

SUMMARIES

Writing summaries of class topics can be helpful in preparing for essay and short-answer exams. By condensing the main ideas into a concise written summary, you store information in your long-term memory so that you can retrieve it to answer an essay question. Here's how:

1. Predict a test question from your lecture notes or other resources.

2. Read the chapter, supplemental articles, notes, or other resources. Underline or mark main ideas as you go, make notations, or make an outline on a separate sheet of paper.

3. Analyze and abstract. What is the purpose of the material? Does it compare two ideas, define a concept, or prove a theory? What are the main ideas? How would you explain the material to someone else?

4. Make connections between main points and key supporting details. Reread to identify each main point and the supporting evidence. Create an outline to assist you in this process.

5. Select, condense, and order. Review underlined material and begin putting the ideas into your own words. Number what you underlined or highlighted in a logical order.

6. Write your ideas precisely in a draft. In the first sentence state the purpose of your summary. Follow this statement with each main point and its supporting ideas. See how much of the draft you can develop from memory without relying on your notes.

7. Review your draft. Read it over, adding missing transitions or insufficient information. Check the logic of your summary. Annotate with the material you used for later reference.

8. Test your memory. Put your draft away and try to recite the contents of the summary to yourself out loud or explain it to a study partner who can provide feedback on the information you have omitted.

9. Schedule time to review summaries and double-check your memory shortly before the test. You might want to do review with a partner, but some students prefer to do so alone. Some faculty members might also be willing to assist you in this process and provide feedback on your summaries.

CHECKLIST FOR SUCCESS

STUDY TIME

☐ **Make studying a part of your daily routine.** Don't allow days to go by when you don't crack a book or keep up with course assignments.

☐ **Manage your study time wisely.** Create a schedule that will allow you to prepare for exams and complete course assignments on time. Be aware of "crunch times" when you might have several exams or papers due at once. Create some flexibility in your schedule to allow for unexpected distractions.

☐ **Collaborate with others.** One of the most effective ways to study is in a group with other students.

☐ **Be confident that you can improve your memory.** Remind yourself occasionally of things you have learned in the past that you didn't think you could or would remember.

☐ **Choose the memory improvement strategies that best fit your preferred learning style(s): aural, visual, reading, or kinesthetic.** Identify the courses where you can make the best use of each memory strategy.

☐ **Go beyond simply trying to memorize words and focus on trying to understand and then remember the big concepts and ideas.** Keep asking yourself: What is the main point here? Is there a big idea? Am I getting it?

☐ **Be alert for external distractions.** Choose a place to study where you can concentrate and allow yourself uninterrupted time to focus on the material you are studying.

☐ **Get a tutor.** Tutoring is not just for students who are failing. Often the best students seek assistance to ensure that they fully understand course material. Most tutors are students, and most campus tutoring services are free.

BUILD YOUR EXPERIENCE 1 2 3 4

1 STAY ON TRACK

Successful college students stay focused. They "stay on track." They know what they have to do to be successful, they set goals, and they monitor their progress toward their goals.

Reflect on what you have learned about college success in this chapter and how you are going to apply the chapter information or strategies in college and in your career. List your ideas.

1. _____

_____

_____

2. _____

_____

_____

3. _____

_____

_____

2 ONE-MINUTE PAPER

Doing well on exams is important, but being able to study, comprehend, and remember what you learn has bigger implications for your life. After reading this chapter, do you find yourself thinking about these concepts in a different way? If so, how? What kinds of questions would you ask your instructor about this chapter?

3 APPLYING WHAT YOU HAVE LEARNED

Now that you have read and discussed this chapter, consider how you can apply what you have learned to your academic life as well as your personal life. The following prompts will help you reflect on the chapter material and its relevance to you both now and in the future.

1. Give mnemonics a try. Choose a set of class notes that you need to study for an upcoming quiz or exam. As you study, pick one concept and create your own acronym, acrostic, rhyme, song, or visualization to help you remember.

2. The way in which students study in high school is often very different from the way they need to study in college. It can be difficult to adapt to new ways of doing things. Describe the way in which you studied in high school. Describe how you can improve on those habits to do well in college.

4 BUILDING YOUR PORTFOLIO

That Takes Me Back   Is there a song that reminds you, every time you hear it, of a certain time in your life or even the exact moment when something happened? Or maybe you have a photo that you look at occasionally for a trip down memory lane? Our senses often trigger memories.

1. Recall a photo, song, or object that prompts you to remember a life event or time period. Create a new document and describe just what it is about the photo, song, or object that reminds you of something else.

2. Describe that memory in as much detail as possible.

3. Describe how that memory makes you feel.

4. Describe how you might use photos or drawings, songs, or mnemonics to remember ideas or concepts in one of the classes you are currently taking.

5. Save these musings in your portfolio or in the Cloud. If possible, save the photos or music files that you described along with your document.

For more on this topic watch
French Fries Are Not Vegetables and Other College Lessons

WHERE TO GO FOR HELP . . .

ON CAMPUS

Your campus probably has a study skills center or learning assistance center that can help you develop effective memory strategies. Pay a visit to your campus learning center and ask if the staff members offer any specific workshops or one-on-one assistance with memory. Ask other students and faculty members if they have tips that they could share on how they remember course material. Ask your instructor if there is an instructor or staff member on your campus who is an expert on memory strategies. In addition, your college library will have many books on the topic of memory. Some were written by researchers for the research community, but others were written for people like you who are trying to improve their memory. Download or check out a book on memory to see what you can learn.

BOOKS

> Buzan, Tony. *Use Your Perfect Memory*, 3rd ed. New York: Penguin Books, 1991.

> Higbee, Kenneth L. *Your Memory: How It Works and How to Improve It,* 2nd ed. New York: Marlowe, 2001.

> Lorayne, Harry. *Super Memory, Super Student: How to Raise Your Grades in 30 Days.* Boston: Little, Brown, 1990.

ONLINE

> Memorization Techniques: **http://www.alamo .edu/memory**. This excellent Web site is maintained by the Alamo Community College District.

MY INSTITUTION'S RESOURCES

_____

_____

_____

_____

_____

_____

_____

9 Test Taking

> ❝ The first step to improving my test-taking abilities was changing my attitude about my 'academic self.'

Nicole Bradley, 24
Nursing major
University of Washington

Nicole Bradley grew up all over the country, moving with her parents as part of the military. "My parents were young and adventurous and willing to move wherever the military sent them," she says. At age sixteen, she landed in Bothell, Washington, near Seattle, and was able to finish high school. Soon after her graduation, Nicole gave birth to a son and found herself working to support herself and her child. For a while, college was the furthest thing from her mind, but eventually she realized that she wanted more for her son—and for herself. "Ultimately being a single mother is what motivates me, not only to provide a better life for both of us but also to set an example that was not always set for me," she explains.

Part of going to college and raising a family involves finding that ever-elusive work-life balance in areas such as preparing for tests. Nicole always thought that she just wasn't good at taking tests or learning, and so she usually finished at the middle of the pack on tests and exams. "The first step to improving my test-taking abilities," she says, "was changing my attitude about my 'academic self.'"

Nicole Bradley ▶

Victorpr/Shutterstock

Once Nicole had worked to improve her attitude, she began looking at the strategies that worked best for her. One thing she figured out was that note taking was integral to a good performance on tests. "I found that I remember things best by relating them to things that I already know," she says. Now she knows to take careful notes during class, underline key terms, and make additional marginal notes so that when she gets home she can create associations to help with memory. She also knows that her brain works best when the rest of her body is well cared for and has plenty of rest, good food, exercise, and often meditation and relaxation. "It works better than cram studying, and I get a lot more out of my courses and do better on my exams," she explains.

As with many things in life, Nicole realizes that with test taking you sometimes have to get it wrong before you get it right. Her advice to other first-year students? "Go back over the questions you got wrong on a test and try to figure out what you got wrong and why."

―――――――――――

Tests and exams are the primary ways that instructors will evaluate your learning. In general, tests are shorter than exams and will count less toward your overall course grade. A course might have only a final exam, or it might have a midterm and a final. These exams generally take two or more hours to complete and comprise a major component of your final grade in a course.

You can prepare for tests and exams in many ways. Sometimes you'll have to recall names, dates, and other specific bits of information. Many instructors, especially in courses such as literature, history, and political science, will expect you to have a good conceptual understanding of the subject matter. They often prefer essay exams that require you to use *analysis, synthesis,* and *evaluation.* They want you to provide the reasons, arguments, and assumptions behind your position. Even in math and science courses, your instructors want you not only to remember the correct theory, formula, or equation but also to understand and apply what you have learned. Knowing your preferred learning style will also help you decide on the best study methods, no matter what kind of test or exam you are facing. Review the material in Chapter 4 that helps you link your learning style to strategies for exam preparation.

Preparing for Tests and Exams

Believe it or not, you actually begin preparing for a test on the first day of the term. Your lecture notes, assigned readings, and homework are all part of that preparation. As the test day nears, you should know how much additional time you will need for review, what material the test will cover, and what format the test will take. It is very important to double-check the exam dates on the syllabus for each class, as in Figure 9.1, and to incorporate these dates into your overall plans for time management, such as in your daily and weekly to-do lists.

◤ ■ ASSESSING YOUR STRENGTHS ■

Tests and exams are an unavoidable component of college life. Good students will practice strategies to improve their exam scores. As you read this chapter, list specific examples of your strengths in preparing for and taking different kinds of exams.

_____

_____

_____

_____

◤ ■ SETTING GOALS ■

What are your most important objectives for learning the material in this chapter? Do you need to improve your abilities as a test taker, or do you need to deal with test anxiety that prevents you from doing your best? List three goals in this area (e.g., I will not wait until the last minute to study for my next exam, or, I will begin studying at least one week before the exam date).

1. _____

_____

2. _____

_____

3. _____

_____

Here are some specific suggestions to help you prepare well for any exam:

1. **Ask your instructor.** Find out the purpose, types of questions, conditions (how much time you will have to complete the exam), and content to be covered on the exam. Talk with your instructor to clarify any misunderstandings you might have about your reading or lecture notes. Some instructors might let you view copies of old exams so that you can see the types of questions they use. Never miss the last class before an exam because your instructor might summarize valuable information then.

2. **Manage your preparation time wisely.** Create a schedule that will give you time to review effectively for the exam without waiting until the night before. Make sure that your schedule has some flexibility to allow for unexpected distractions. If you are able to spread your study sessions over several days, your mind will continue to process the information between study sessions, which will help you during the test. Also, let your friends and family know when you have important exams coming up and how that will affect your time with them.

FIGURE 9.1

Exam Schedule from Sample Course Syllabus

History 111, US History to 1865
Fall 2015

Examinations
Note: In this course, most of your exams will be on Fridays, except for the Wednesday before Thanksgiving and the final. This is to give you a full week to study for the exam and permit me to grade them over the weekend and return the exams to you on Monday. I believe in using a variety of types of measurements. In addition to those scheduled below, I reserve the right to give you unannounced quizzes on daily reading assignments. Also, current events are fair game on any exam! Midterm and final exams will be cumulative (on all material since beginning of the course). Other exams cover all classroom material and all readings covered since the prior exam. The schedule is as follows:

Friday, 9/4: Objective type

Friday, 9/25: Essay type

Friday, 10/16: Midterm: essay and objective

Friday, 11/6: Objective

Wednesday, 11/25: Essay

Tuesday, 12/22: Final exam: essay and objective

3. **Focus your study.** Figure out what you can effectively review that is likely to be on the exam. Collaborate with other students to share information and try to attend all test or exam review sessions offered by your instructor.

PREPARE PHYSICALLY

Remembering these important strategies will help you prepare physically for your tests or exams.

Maintain Your Regular Sleep Routine. To do well on exams, you will need to be alert so that you can think clearly. You are more likely to be alert when you are well rested. Last-minute, late-night cramming that robs you of sufficient sleep isn't an effective study strategy.

Follow Your Regular Exercise Program. Another way to prepare physically for exams is by walking, jogging, or engaging in other kinds of physical activity. Exercise is a positive way to relieve stress and give yourself a needed break from long hours of studying.

Eat Right. Eat a light breakfast before a morning exam and avoid greasy or acidic foods that might upset your stomach. Limit the amount of caffeinated beverages you drink on exam day because caffeine can make you jittery. Choose fruits, vegetables, and other foods that are high in energy-rich complex carbohydrates. Avoid eating sweets before an exam. The immediate energy boost they create can be quickly followed by a loss of energy and alertness. Ask the instructor whether you may bring a bottle of water with you to the exam.

PREPARE EMOTIONALLY

Just as physical preparation is important, so is preparing your attitude and your emotions. You'll benefit by paying attention to these ideas.

Know Your Material. If you have given yourself adequate time to review, you will enter the classroom confident that you are in control. Study by testing yourself or quizzing others in a study group or learning community so that you will be sure to really know the material.

Practice Relaxing. Some students experience upset stomachs, sweaty palms, racing hearts, or other unpleasant physical symptoms of test anxiety. Consult your counseling center about relaxation techniques. Some campus learning assistance centers also provide workshops on reducing test anxiety. If you experience this problem, read the section on test anxiety later in this chapter and take the anxiety quiz on page 195.

> ### YOUR TURN
> ----------
> #### Discuss
> Do you sometimes predict that you'll do poorly on a test or exam, even when you've studied a lot? Discuss with your classmates why some people are hard on themselves and how a positive attitude can affect the grades you earn.

Use Positive Self-Talk. Instead of telling yourself that "I never do well on math tests" or "I'll never be able to learn all the information for my history essay exam," make positive statements such as "I have attended all the lectures, done my homework, and passed the quizzes. Now I'm ready to do well on the test!"

PREPARE FOR TEST TAKING

You can take a number of steps to learn more about upcoming tests and exams.

Find Out about the Test. Ask your instructor what format the test will have, such as essay, multiple-choice, true/false, fill-in-the-blank, or short-answer questions. Ask how long the test will last and how it will be graded. Ask whether all questions will have the same point value.

Design an Exam Plan.   Use the information about the test as you design a plan for preparing. Build that preparation into a schedule of review dates. Develop a to-do list of the major steps you need to take to be ready. Be sure that you have read and learned all the material at least one week before the exam. That way, you can use the final week to review and prepare for the exam. The week before the exam, set aside a schedule of one-hour blocks of time for review and make notes on specifically what you plan to accomplish during each hour.

Join a Study Group.   You have seen the suggestion to join or form a study group in other chapters because it is one of the most effective strategies for doing well in college, especially in preparing for exams. You can benefit from different views of your instructors' goals, objectives, and emphasis; have your study partners quiz you on facts and concepts; and gain the support and friendship of others to help sustain your motivation.

Some instructors will provide time in class for the formation of study groups. You might also choose to approach classmates on your own. Otherwise, ask your teacher, adviser, or campus tutoring or learning center to help you identify interested students and decide on guidelines for the group. Study groups can meet throughout the term, or they can just review for midterms or final exams. Group members should complete their assignments before the group meets and prepare study questions or points of discussion ahead of time. If your study group decides to meet just before exams, allow enough time to share notes and ideas.

Strength in Numbers

Study groups can meet anytime, but studying and reviewing with others in your class can be most helpful just before and just after a test or exam.

Jonathan Milavec

Get a Tutor.   Most campus tutoring centers offer their services for free. Ask your academic adviser, counselor, or campus learning center about arranging for tutoring. Many learning centers employ student tutors who have done well in the same courses you are taking. These students might have some good advice on how to prepare for tests given by particular instructors. Learning centers often have computer tutorials that can help you refresh basic skills.

First-year students report . . .

YES
33.5%

Do you think that you will seek tutoring help in specific courses?

PREPARE FOR MATH AND SCIENCE EXAMS

Math and science exams often require additional preparation techniques. Here are some suggestions for doing well on these exams:

1. Do your homework regularly, even if it is not graded, and do all the assigned problems. As you do your homework, write out your work as carefully and clearly as you will be expected to do on your tests. This practice will allow you to use your homework as a review for the test.

2. Attend each class and always be on time. Many instructors use the time at the beginning of class to review homework.

3. Create a review guide throughout the term. As you begin your homework each day, write out a random problem from each homework section in a notebook that you have set up for reviewing material for that course. As you review later, you can come back to these problems to make sure that you have a representative problem from each section you've studied.

4. Throughout the term, keep a list of definitions or important formulas (they are great to put on flash cards). Review one or two of them as part of every study session. Another technique is to post the formulas and definitions in prominent areas in your living space (e.g., on the bathroom wall, around your computer work area, or on the door of the microwave). Seeing this information frequently will help embed it in your mind.

Taking Tests and Exams

Throughout your college career you will take tests in many different formats, in many subject areas, and with many different types of questions. The box on the next page offers test-taking tips that apply to any test situation.

ESSAY QUESTIONS

Many college instructors have a strong preference for essay exams for a simple reason: Essay exams promote higher-order critical thinking, whereas other types of exams tend to be exercises in memorization. Generally, advanced

TIPS FOR SUCCESSFUL TEST TAKING

1. **Write your name on the test** (unless you are directed not to) and on the answer sheet.

2. **Analyze, ask, and stay calm.** Before you start the test, take a long, deep breath and slowly exhale. Carefully read all the directions before beginning the test so that you understand what to do. Ask the instructor or exam monitor for clarification if you don't understand something. Be confident. Don't panic. Answer one question at a time.

3. **Make the best use of your time.** Quickly survey the entire test and decide how much time you will spend on each section. Be aware of the point values of different sections of the test. If some questions are worth more points than others, they deserve more of your time.

4. **Jot down idea-starters before the test.** Before you even look at the test questions, turn the test paper over and take a moment to write down the formulas, definitions, and major ideas that you have been studying. (Check with your instructor ahead of time to make sure that this practice is OK.) It will help you go into the test with a feeling of confidence and knowledge, and it will provide quick access to the information while you are taking the test.

5. **Answer the easy questions first.** Expect that you'll be puzzled by some questions. Make a note to go back to them later. If different sections consist of different types of questions (such as multiple-choice, short-answer, and essay questions), complete the types of questions you are most comfortable with first. Be sure to leave enough time for any essays.

6. **If you feel yourself starting to panic or go blank, stop whatever you are doing.** Take a long, deep breath and slowly exhale. Remind yourself that you will be OK, that you know the material, and that you can do well on this test. Then take another deep breath. If necessary, go to another section of the test and come back later to the item that triggered your anxiety.

7. **If you finish early, don't leave.** Stay and check your work for errors. Reread the directions one last time. If you are using a machine-scored answer sheet, make sure that all bubbles are filled in accurately and completely.

courses are more likely to include essay exams than are lower-level courses. To be successful on essay exams, follow these guidelines:

1. **Budget your exam time.** Quickly survey the entire exam, and note the questions that are the easiest for you along with their point values. Take a moment to weigh their values, estimate the approximate time you should allot to each question, and write the time beside each item number. Be sure that you know whether you must answer all the questions or if you should choose among questions. Remember that writing profusely on easy questions that have low values can be a costly error because it takes up precious time you might need for more important questions. Wear a watch so that you can monitor your time, and include time at the end for a quick review.

2. **Develop a very brief outline of your answer before you begin to write.** Start working on the questions that are easiest for you, and jot down a few ideas before you begin to write. First, make sure that your outline responds to all parts of the question. Then use your first paragraph to introduce the main points and subsequent paragraphs to describe each point in more depth. If you begin to lose your concentration, you will be glad to have the outline to help you regain your focus. If you find

that you are running out of time and cannot complete an essay, provide an outline of key ideas at the very least. Instructors usually assign points on the basis of your coverage of the main topics from the material. Thus you will usually earn more points by responding briefly to all parts of the question than by addressing just one aspect of the question in detail. An outline will often earn you partial credit even if you leave the essay unfinished.

3. **Write concise, organized answers.** Many well-prepared students write good answers to questions that were not asked because they did not read a question carefully or didn't respond to all parts of the question. Other students hastily write down everything they know on a topic. Instructors will give lower grades for answers that are vague and tend to ramble or for articulate answers that don't address the actual question.

4. **Know the key task words in essay questions.** Being familiar with the key task word in an essay question will help you answer it more specifically. The key task words in Table 9.1 appear frequently on essay tests. Take time to learn them so that you can answer essay questions as accurately and precisely as possible.

© fStop/Alamy

Ace the Test

You have almost certainly taken machine-scored tests in high school. One of the simplest and most important steps you can take to do well on these tests is to make sure that you align the questions with your answer sheet. But you must also read each question carefully so that you have the best chance of selecting the right answer.

MULTIPLE-CHOICE QUESTIONS

Preparing for multiple-choice tests requires you to actively review all the material that has been covered in the course. Reciting from flash cards, summary sheets, mind maps, or the recall column in your lecture notes is a good way to review large amounts of material.

Take advantage of the many cues that multiple-choice questions contain. Careful reading of each item might uncover the correct answer. Always question choices that use absolute words such as *always, never,* and *only.* These choices are often (but not always) incorrect. Also, read carefully for terms such as *not, except,* and *but* that may be introduced before the choices. Often, the answer that is the most inclusive is correct. In general, options that do not agree grammatically with the first part of the item are incorrect. For instance, what answer could you rule out in the example in Figure 9.2?

TABLE 9.1 **Key Task Words in Essay Questions**

Analyze	Divide something into its parts to understand it better; show how the parts work together to produce the overall pattern.
Compare	Look at the characteristics or qualities of several things and identify their similarities or differences. Don't just describe the traits; define how the things are alike and how they are different.
Contrast	Identify the differences between things.
Criticize/ Critique	Analyze and judge something. Criticism can be positive, negative, or both. A criticism should generally contain your own judgments (supported by evidence) and those of authorities who can support your point.
Define	Give the meaning of a word or expression. Giving an example sometimes helps clarify a definition, but an example by itself is not a definition.
Describe	Give a general verbal sketch of something in narrative or other form.
Discuss	Examine or analyze something in a broad and detailed way. Discussion often includes identifying the important questions related to an issue and attempting to answer these questions. A good discussion explores all relevant evidence and information.
Evaluate	Discuss the strengths and weaknesses of something. Evaluation is similar to criticism, but the word *evaluate* stresses the idea of how well something meets a certain standard or fulfills some specific purpose.
Explain	Clarify something. Explanations generally focus on why or how something has come about.
Interpret	Explain the meaning of something. In science you might explain what an experiment shows and what conclusions can be drawn from it. In a literature course you might explain—or interpret— what a poem means beyond the literal meaning of the words.
Justify	Argue in support of some decision or conclusion by showing sufficient evidence or reasons in its favor. Try to support your argument with both logical and concrete examples.
Narrate	Relate a series of events in the order in which they occurred. You will also usually be asked to explain something about the events you are narrating.
Outline	Present a series of main points in an appropriate order. Some instructors want an outline with Roman numerals for main points followed by letters for supporting details. If you are in doubt, ask the instructor whether he or she wants a formal outline.
Prove	Give a convincing logical argument and evidence in support of some statement.
Review	Summarize and comment on the main parts of a problem or a series of statements. A review question usually also asks you to evaluate or criticize.
Summarize	Give information in brief form, omitting examples and details. A summary is short but covers all important points.
Trace	Narrate a course of events. Whenever possible, you should show connections from one event to the next.

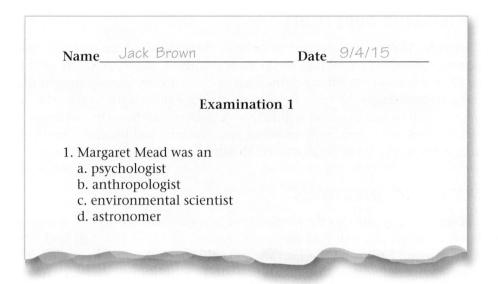

FIGURE 9.2

Example of a Multiple-Choice Question

Some students are easily confused by multiple-choice answers that sound alike. The best way to respond to a multiple-choice question is to read the first part of the item and then predict your own answer before reading the options. Choose the letter that corresponds to the option that best matches your prediction.

If you are totally confused by a question, place a check mark in the margin, leave it, and come back later, but always double-check that you are filling in the answer for the right question. Sometimes another question will provide a clue for a question that you are unsure about. If you have absolutely no idea, look for an answer that at least contains some shred of information. If there is no penalty for guessing, fill in an answer for every question, even if it is just a guess. If there is a penalty for guessing, don't just choose an answer at random; leaving the answer blank might be a wiser choice.

> ## YOUR TURN
>
> ### Discuss
>
> Many college instructors are reluctant to give essay exams in first-year courses and instead rely on multiple-choice exams. With one other classmate, discuss why you think that essay exams are less likely to be used in the first year than in later years. What kind of learning do multiple-choice exams measure, and what kind of learning do they miss? Share your reactions and ideas with the whole class.

FILL-IN-THE-BLANK QUESTIONS

In many ways preparing for fill-in-the-blank questions is similar to getting ready for multiple-choice items, but fill-in-the-blank questions can be harder because you do not have a choice of possible answers right in front of you. Not all fill-in-the-blank questions are constructed the same way. Some teachers will provide a series of blanks to give you a clue about the number of words in the answer, but if just one long blank is provided, you can't assume that the answer is only one word. If possible, ask the teacher whether the answer is supposed to be a single word per blank or whether it can be a longer phrase.

TRUE/FALSE QUESTIONS

Remember that for a statement to be true, every detail of the sentence must be true. Questions containing words such as *always, never,* and *only* tend to be false, whereas less definite terms such as *often* and *frequently* suggest that the statement might be true. Read through the entire exam to see whether information in one question will help you answer another. Do not begin to second-guess what you know or doubt your answers just because a sequence of questions appears to be all true or all false.

MATCHING QUESTIONS

The matching question is the hardest type of question to answer by guessing. In one column you will find the terms, and in the other you will find their descriptions. Before answering any question, review all the terms and descriptions. Then match the terms you are sure of. As you do so, cross out both the term and its description; then use the process of elimination to assist you in answering the remaining items. To prepare for matching questions, try using flash cards and lists that you create from the recall column in your notes.

Types of Tests

While you are in college, you will encounter many types of tests. Some tend to be used in particular disciplines; others can be used in any class you might take.

PROBLEM-SOLVING TESTS

In the physical and biological sciences, mathematics, engineering, statistics, and symbolic logic, some tests will require you to solve problems showing all the steps. Even if you know a shortcut, it is important to document how you got from step A to step B. For these tests, you must also be very careful that you have made no errors in your scientific notation. A misplaced sign, parenthesis, bracket, or exponent can make all the difference.

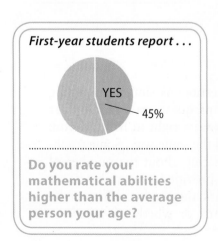

First-year students report . . .

YES

45%

Do you rate your mathematical abilities higher than the average person your age?

If you are allowed to use a calculator during the exam, it is important to check that your input is accurate. The calculator does what you tell it to, and if you miss a zero or a negative sign, the calculator will not give you the correct answer to the problem.

Be sure that you read all directions carefully, and whenever possible, after you complete the problem, work it in reverse to check your solution. Also check to make sure that your solution makes sense. You can't have negative bushels of apples, for example, or a fraction of a person, or a correlation less than negative 1 or greater than 1.

MACHINE-SCORED TESTS

It is important that you carefully follow the directions for machine-scored tests. In addition to your name, be sure to provide all the necessary information on the answer sheet. Each time you fill in an answer, make sure that the number on the answer sheet corresponds to the number of the item on the test.

Although scoring machines have become more sophisticated over time, stray marks on your answer sheet can still be misread and throw off the scoring. When a machine-scored test is returned to you, check your answer sheet against the scoring key, if one is provided, to make sure that you receive credit for all the questions that you answered correctly.

COMPUTERIZED TESTS

Your comfort with taking computerized tests might depend on your experience in taking these tests before. If your instructor provides the opportunity for practice tests, be sure to take advantage of this chance to get a better sense of how the tests will be structured. There can be significant variations depending on the kind of test, the academic subject, and whether the test was constructed by the teacher, a textbook company, or another source.

For multiple-choice and other objective forms of computerized tests, you might be allowed to scroll down and back through the entire test, but that is not always the case. Sometimes you are allowed to see only one question at a time, and after you complete that question, you might not be allowed to go back to it.

For computerized tests in math and other subjects that require you to solve each problem, be sure to check each answer before you submit it. Also, know in advance what materials you are allowed to have on hand, such as a calculator and scratch paper for working out the problems.

LABORATORY TESTS

In many science courses you will have lab tests that require you to rotate from one lab station to the next and solve problems, identify parts of models or specimens, or explain chemical reactions. At some colleges and universities lab tests are now administered at computer terminals via simulations. To prepare for lab tests always attend lab, take good notes, and be sure to study your lab notebook carefully before the test.

You might also have lab tests in foreign language courses that can include both oral and written components. Work with a partner or study group to prepare for oral exams. Ask one another questions that require using key vocabulary words. You might also have computerized lab tests that require you to identify syllables or words and indicate the order and direction of the strokes required to create them, particularly in a foreign language that uses a different symbol system, such as Chinese. The best way to prepare for these tests is to learn the meanings and parts of the symbols and regularly practice writing them.

OPEN-BOOK AND OPEN-NOTE TESTS

If you never had open-book or open-note tests in high school, you might be tempted to study less thoroughly than usual, thinking that you will have access to all the information you need during the test, but that is a common misjudgment on the part of first-year students. Open-book and open-note tests are usually harder than other exams, not easier.

Most students don't really have time to spend looking things up during an open-book exam. The best way to prepare is to begin the same way you would study for a test in which you cannot refer to your notes or text. As you do so, however, develop a list of topics and the page numbers where they are covered in your textbook or your lecture notes. Type a three-column grid (or use an Excel spreadsheet) with your list of topics in alphabetical order in the first column and corresponding pages from your textbook and lecture notebook in the second and third columns, respectively, so that you can refer to them quickly if necessary. But whatever you do, study as completely as you would for any other test and do not be fooled into thinking that you don't need to know the material thoroughly.

During the test, monitor your time carefully. Don't waste time looking up information in your text or notes if you are reasonably confident of your answers. Instead, wait until you have finished the test; then, if you have extra time, go back to look up answers and make any necessary changes.

TAKE-HOME TESTS

Like open-book and open-note tests, take-home tests are usually more difficult than in-class tests. Read the directions and questions as soon as you receive the test to help you gauge how much time you will need to complete it. Remember that your teacher will expect your essay answers to look more like assigned out-of-class papers than like the essays you would write during an in-class test.

Unfortunately, issues of academic honesty can arise for take-home tests. If you are accustomed to working with a study group or in a learning community for the course, check with the instructor in advance to determine if any type of collaboration is allowed on the test.

Overcoming Test Anxiety

Test anxiety takes many different forms. Part of combating test anxiety is understanding its sources and identifying its symptoms. Whatever the source, be assured that test anxiety is common.

Test anxiety has many sources. It can be the result of the pressure that students put on themselves to succeed. Without any pressure, students would not be motivated to study, and some stress connected with taking exams is natural and can enhance performance. When students put too much pressure on themselves or set unrealistic goals, however, the result is stress that is no longer motivating, only debilitating.

The expectations of parents, a spouse, friends, and other people who are close to you can also induce test anxiety. Sometimes, for example, students who are the first in their families to attend college bear the weight of

TECH TIP FEAR NOT THE ONLINE TEST

1 **THE PROBLEM**

You don't know how to take an online test.

2 **THE FIX**

Learn to dodge rookie errors that can trip you up.

3 **HOW TO DO IT**

Here are our top ten strategies:

© Fotosearch

1. Don't wait until the last minute to study. Whether this online test is part of a self-paced online course or a face-to-face course, start a study group (either in person or online) as far in advance as possible.

2. Get organized. An open-book quiz can take longer than a normal test if you're not sure where to locate the information you need. Having a solid grasp of the material going in is key; your notes and books should be for occasional reference only.

3. Resist the temptation to surf the Web for answers. The answer you pick might not be what your instructor is looking for. It's much better to check your notes to see what you were taught in class.

4. If your instructor doesn't forbid collaboration on tests, open up an instant message window with a fellow student. Take the test together and early.

5. Don't get distracted. When you're taking a cyberexam, it's easy to fall prey to real-life diversions like Facebook, iTunes, or a sudden urge to re-arrange your closet. Whatever you do, take the test seriously. Go somewhere quiet where you can concentrate—not Starbucks. A quiet, remote spot in the library is ideal. You get bonus points if you wear noise-canceling head-phones!

6. While taking the test, budget your time. Keep an eye on the clock so that you'll be sure to finish the entire test.

7. Tackle easy questions first. Once you get the easy questions out of the way, you can revisit the harder ones.

8. Find out in advance if there's any penalty for wrong answers. If not, bluffing is allowed, so you want to be sure to fill in all the blanks.

9. Beware: There's always the risk of losing your Internet connection midtest. To be on the safe side, type all your answers and essays into a Word document. Then leave time at the end to cut and paste them into the test itself.

10. Finish early? Take a few minutes to obsessively check your answers and spelling. (That's good advice for traditional tests, too.)

PERSONAL BEST

What additional challenges might present themselves during an online test? List three challenges and some strategies for working through them.

1. _____

_____

_____

_____

2. _____

_____

_____

_____

3. _____

_____

_____

_____

icyimage/Shutterstock

generations before them who have not had this opportunity. The pressure can be overwhelming!

Finally, some test anxiety is caused by lack of preparation, such as by not keeping up with assigned reading, homework, and other academic commitments leading up to the test. Procrastination can begin a downward spiral because if you do poorly on the first test in a course, you have even more pressure to do well on subsequent tests to pull up your course grade. This situation becomes even more dire if the units of the course build on one another, as in math and foreign languages, or if the final exam is cumulative. You have to master new material that follows the test while trying to catch up on the old material.

Some test anxiety comes from a negative prior experience. Transcending the memory of negative past experiences can be a challenge, but remember that the past is not the present. Perhaps you performed poorly in the past for good reasons. You might not have prepared for the test, you might not have read the questions carefully, or you might not have studied with other students or sought prior assistance from your professor or a tutor. If you carefully follow the strategies in this chapter, you are very likely to do well on all your tests. Remember that a little anxiety is OK. But if you find that anxiety is getting in the way of your performance on tests and exams, be sure to seek help from your campus counseling center.

YOUR TURN

Write and Reflect

Do you recall ever feeling anxious about a test or exam? Write a journal entry describing one of these experiences and how you reacted. In your journal write down some strategies you have used to stay calm.

Inhale... Exhale...

Before a test or exam, it is a good idea to take a few minutes for some positive self-talk and a few deep breaths.

Jonathan Milavec

TEST ANXIETY QUIZ

Do these statements apply to you? Check the box if the statement applies to you the day before an exam, hours before, or during the exam itself!

Mental

- ☐ Do you have trouble concentrating and find that your mind easily wanders while studying the material or during the test itself?
- ☐ During the test, does every noise, such as sounds from outside the classroom or sounds from other people, bother you?
- ☐ Do you often blank out when you see the test?
- ☐ Do you remember answers to questions only after the test is over?

Physical

- ☐ Do you get the feeling of butterflies, nausea, or pain in your stomach?
- ☐ Do you develop headaches before or during the test?
- ☐ Do you feel like your heart is racing, that you have trouble breathing, or that your pulse is erratic?
- ☐ Do you have difficulty sitting still, are you antsy, or are you unable to get comfortable?

Emotional

- ☐ Are you more sensitive and more likely than usual to lose patience with a roommate or friend before the test?
- ☐ Do you feel pressure to succeed either from yourself or from your family or friends?
- ☐ Do you toss and turn the night before the test?
- ☐ Do you fear the worst, that you will fail the class or flunk out of college because of the test?

Personal Habits

- ☐ Do you often stay up late studying the night before a test?
- ☐ Do you have a personal history of failure for taking certain types of tests (essay, math)?
- ☐ Do you drink too much caffeine or forget to eat breakfast before a test?
- ☐ Do you avoid studying until right before a test, choosing to do other activities that are less important because you "don't want to think about it"?

Test Anxiety Reflection Score. Add up the number of boxes that you checked. You may experience test anxiety if you checked . . .

13–16 Severe: You may want to see if your campus counseling center offers individual sessions to provide strategies to combat test anxiety. Your student fees have already paid for this service, so take advantage of it now before it is too late. Learn to be *proactive*!

9–12 Moderate: You may want to see if your campus will be offering a seminar on anxiety-prevention strategies. Such seminars are usually offered around midterm or just before final exams. Take the opportunity to do something valuable for yourself!

5–8 Mild: Be aware of what situations, such as certain types of classes or particular test formats, might cause anxiety and disrupt your academic success. If you discover a weakness, address it now before it is too late.

1–4 Slight: Almost everyone has some form of anxiety before tests, and it can actually be beneficial! In small doses stress can improve your performance, so consider yourself lucky.

TYPES OF TEST ANXIETY

Students who experience test anxiety under some circumstances don't necessarily feel it in all testing situations. For example, you might do fine on classroom tests but feel anxious during standardized examinations, such as the SAT and ACT. One reason standardized tests provoke anxiety is the notion that they determine your future. Believing that the stakes are so high can create unbearable pressure. One way to deal with this type of test anxiety is to ask yourself this important question: What is the worst that can happen? Remember that no matter what the result, it is not the end of the world. How you do on standardized tests might limit some of your options, but going into these tests with a negative attitude will certainly not improve your chances. Attending preparation workshops and taking practice exams not only can better prepare you for standardized tests, but also can assist you in overcoming your anxiety. Also remember that many standardized tests can be taken again at a later time, giving you the opportunity to prepare better and pull up your score.

Some students are anxious only about some types of classroom tests. Practice always helps in overcoming test anxiety; if you fear essay exams, try predicting exam questions and writing sample essays as a means of reducing your anxiety.

Some students have difficulty taking tests at a computer terminal. Some of this anxiety might be related to lack of computer experience. On the other hand, not all computerized tests are user-friendly. For example, you might be allowed to see only one item at a time. Often, you do not have the option of going back and checking over all your answers before submitting them. In preparation for computerized tests, ask the instructor questions about how the test will be structured. Also make sure that you take any opportunities to take practice tests at a learning center or lab.

Test anxiety can often be subject-specific. For example, some students have math test anxiety. It is important to distinguish between anxiety that arises from the subject matter itself and more generalized test anxiety. Perhaps subject-specific test anxiety relates to old beliefs about yourself, such as "I'm no good at math" or "I can't write well." Now is the time to try some positive self-talk and realize that by preparing well, you can be successful even in your hardest courses. If the problem persists, talk to someone in your campus counseling center to develop strategies to overcome irrational fears that can prevent you from doing your best.

SYMPTOMS OF TEST ANXIETY

Test anxiety can manifest itself in many ways. Some students feel it on the very first day of class. Other students begin showing symptoms of test anxiety when it's time to start studying for a test. Others do not get nervous until the night before the test or the morning of an exam day. Still other students experience symptoms only while they are actually taking a test.

Symptoms of test anxiety can include butterflies in the stomach, queasiness or nausea, severe headaches, a faster heartbeat than normal, hyperventilating, shaking, sweating, or muscle cramps. During the exam itself, students who are overcome with test anxiety can experience the sensation of blanking out and being unable to remember what they actually know. At this point, students can undermine both their emotional and academic preparation for the test and convince themselves that they cannot succeed.

Test anxiety can impede the success of any college student, no matter how intelligent, motivated, and prepared. That is why it is critical to seek help from your institution's counseling service or another professional if you think that you have significant test anxiety. If you are not sure where to go for help, ask your adviser, but seek help promptly! If your symptoms are so severe that you become physically ill (with migraine headaches, hyperventilating, or vomiting), you should also consult your physician or campus health service.

STRATEGIES FOR COMBATING TEST ANXIETY

In addition to studying, eating right, and getting plenty of sleep, a number of simple strategies can help you overcome the physical and emotional effects of test anxiety:

- If at any point during a test you begin to feel nervous or you cannot think clearly, take a long, deep breath and slowly exhale to restore your breathing to a normal level.
- Before you go into the test room, especially before a long final exam, stretch your muscles—legs, arms, shoulders, and neck—just as you would when preparing to exercise.
- Pay attention to the way you are sitting. As you take the test, sit with your shoulders back and relaxed rather than hunched forward. Resist the temptation to clutch your pencil or pen tightly in your fist; take a break and stretch your fingers now and then.
- Explore anxiety-reducing techniques that might be available through your campus counseling center. These methods include systematic desensitization, progressive muscle relaxation, and visualization.
- Pay attention to the mental messages that you send yourself. If you are overly negative, turn those messages around. Use **cognitive restructuring** to give yourself encouraging rather than stress-provoking messages.
- Do not allow others, including classmates, your spouse, parents, or friends, to undermine your confidence. If you belong to a study group, discuss the need to stay positive.

GETTING THE TEST BACK

Students react differently when they receive their test grades and papers. For some students the

> ### YOUR TURN
>
> #### Discuss
>
> What do you do when an instructor returns an exam to you? Do you just look at the grade, or do you review the items you answered correctly and incorrectly? List some reasons why it's important to review an exam. Share your list with another classmate.

cognitive restructuring
A technique of applying positive thinking and giving oneself encouraging messages rather than self-defeating, negative ones.

thought of seeing the actual graded test produces high levels of anxiety. Unless you look at the instructor's comments and your answers (the correct and incorrect ones), however, you will have no way to evaluate your own knowledge and test-taking strengths. You might also find that the instructor made an error in the grade that might have cost you a point or two, in which case you should let the instructor know.

Review your graded test because doing so will help you do better next time. You might find that your mistakes were caused by failing to follow directions, being careless with words or numbers, or overanalyzing a multiple-choice question. If you have any questions about your grade, be sure to talk to the instructor. Going over your grade is an excellent reason to visit your instructor during his or her office hours. You might successfully negotiate a few points in your favor, and in any case, your concern will reflect that you want to succeed.

Cheating

Imagine what our world would be like if researchers reported fraudulent results that were then used to develop new machines or medical treatments or to build bridges, airplanes, or subway systems. Integrity is a cornerstone of higher education, and activities that compromise that integrity damage everyone: your country, your community, your college or university, your classmates, and yourself.

Is This You?

You're dangerously close to failing your general psychology course, and during your midterm exam, you realize that you can clearly see how the person sitting directly in front of you is marking her answer sheet. The instructor seems to have stepped out of the classroom. Have you ever been this tempted to cheat? Review the section on the consequences of cheating and the Guidelines for Academic Honesty box.

WHAT IS CHEATING?

Institutions vary widely in how they define broad terms such as *lying* or *cheating*. One university defines cheating as "intentionally using or attempting to use unauthorized materials, information, notes, study aids, or other devices . . . [including] unauthorized communication of information during an academic exercise." This definition would apply to looking over a classmate's shoulder for an answer, using a calculator when it is not authorized, obtaining or discussing an exam (or individual questions from an exam) without permission, copying someone else's lab notes, purchasing term papers over the Internet, and duplicating computer files.

On most tests, you don't have to credit specific sources. (Some instructors do require it, though, so when in doubt, ask!) If your instructor expects you to credit your sources when taking a test or exam, failure to do so could be considered plagiarism. Chapter 10 gives more detail about plagiarism and how to avoid it.

Many schools prohibit certain activities in addition to lying or cheating. Some examples of prohibited behaviors are intentionally inventing information or results, earning credit more than once for the same piece of academic work without permission, giving your work or exam answers to another student to copy during the actual exam or before that exam is given to another section, and bribing in exchange for any kind of academic advantage. Most schools also outlaw helping or attempting to help another student commit a dishonest act.

WHY STUDENTS CHEAT AND THE CONSEQUENCES OF CHEATING

Some students develop a habit of cheating in high school and believe that they cannot do well without cheating. Other students simply don't know the rules. In a survey at the University of South Carolina, 20 percent of students incorrectly thought that buying a term paper wasn't cheating. Forty percent thought that using a test file (a collection of actual tests from previous terms) was fair behavior. Sixty percent thought that it was acceptable to get answers from someone who had taken the exam earlier in the same or in a prior term. What do you think?

Stop! Thief!

When students are seated close to each other while taking a test, they may be tempted to let their eyes wander to someone else's answers, but don't let this happen to you. Cheating is equivalent to stealing. Also, don't make it easy for other students to copy your work. Reduce that temptation by covering your answer sheet.

Jonathan Stark

Cultural and campus differences may cause some students to cheat. In other countries and on some U.S. campuses, students are encouraged to review past exams as practice exercises. Some student government associations maintain test files for use by students. Some campuses permit sharing answers and information for homework and other assignments with friends. Make sure that you know the policy on your specific campus.

Pressures from others—family, peers, and instructors—might cause some students to consider cheating. And there is no doubt that we live in a very competitive society. In truth, however, grades are nothing if you cheat to earn them. Even if your grades help you get a job, it is what you have actually learned that will help you keep the job and be promoted. If you haven't learned what you need to know, you won't be ready to work in your chosen field.

Sometimes, lack of preparation will cause students to cheat. Perhaps they tell themselves that they aren't really dishonest and that cheating just "one time" won't matter. But if you cheat one time, you're more likely to do it again.

Cheating in college is not uncommon, and researchers have found that first-year students are more likely to cheat than students in their sophomore, junior, or senior years. Although you might see some students who seem to be getting away with cheating, the consequences of such behaviors can be severe and life-changing. Recent cases of cheating on examinations have caused some college students to be suspended or expelled and even to have their college degrees revoked. The box below outlines some steps you can take to reduce the likelihood of problems.

GUIDELINES FOR ACADEMIC HONESTY

1. **Know the rules.** Learn the academic code for your college by going to its Web site. Also learn about any department guidelines on cheating. Study course syllabi. If an instructor does not clarify standards and expectations, ask exactly what they are.

2. **Set clear boundaries.** Refuse when others ask you to help them cheat. It might be hard to do, but you must say "no." In test settings keep your answers covered and your eyes down. Put all extraneous materials away, including cell phones. Because cell phones enable text messaging, instructors are rightfully suspicious when they see students looking at them during an exam.

3. **Improve time management.** Be well prepared for all quizzes, exams, projects, and papers, which might mean unlearning habits such as procrastination (see Chapter 2, Time Management).

4. **Seek help.** Find out where you can obtain assistance with study skills, time management, and test taking. If your methods are in good shape but the content of the course is too difficult, consult your instructor, join a study group, or visit your campus learning center or tutorial service.

5. **Withdraw from the course.** Your institution has a policy about dropping courses and a deadline to drop without penalty. You might decide to drop only the course that's giving you trouble. Some students choose to withdraw from all classes and take time off before returning to school if they find themselves in over their heads or if a long illness, a family crisis, or some other unexpected occurrence has caused them to fall behind. Before withdrawing, you should ask about campus policies as well as ramifications in terms of federal financial aid and other scholarship programs. See your adviser or counselor.

6. **Reexamine goals.** Stick to your own realistic goals instead of giving in to pressure from family members or friends to achieve impossibly high standards. You might also feel pressure to enter a particular career or profession that is of little or no interest to you. If that happens, sit down with counseling or career services professionals or your academic adviser and explore alternatives.

CHECKLIST FOR SUCCESS

TEST TAKING

☐ **Learn as much as you can about the type of test you will be taking.** You will study differently for an essay exam than you will for a multiple-choice test.

☐ **Start preparing for test taking the very first day of the course.** Classes early in the term are the most important ones *not* to miss.

☐ **Prepare yourself physically through proper sleep, diet, and exercise.** These behaviors are as important as studying the actual material. You may not control what is on the exams, but you can control your physical readiness to do your best.

☐ **Prepare yourself emotionally by being relaxed and confident.** Confidence comes from the knowledge that you have prepared well and know the material.

☐ **If you experience severe test anxiety, seek help from your counseling center.** Professionals can help you deal with this problem.

☐ **Develop a systematic plan of preparation for every test.** Be specific about when you are going to study, for how long, and what material you will cover.

☐ **Join a study group and participate conscientiously and regularly.** Students who join study groups perform better on tests. It's a habit you should practice.

☐ **Never cheat or plagiarize.** Experience the satisfaction that comes from learning and doing your own work and from knowing that you don't have to worry about getting caught or using material that may be incorrect.

☐ **Make sure that you understand what constitutes cheating and plagiarism on your campus so that you don't inadvertently do either.** If you are not clear about policies, ask your instructors or the professionals in your campus learning center or writing center.

BUILD YOUR EXPERIENCE 1 2 3 4

1 STAY ON TRACK

Successful college students stay focused. They "stay on track." They know what they have to do to be successful, they set goals, and they monitor their progress toward their goals.

Reflect on what you have learned about college success in this chapter and how you are going to apply the chapter information or strategies in college and in your career. List your ideas.

1. _____

_____

_____

2. _____

_____

_____

3. _____

_____

_____

2 ONE-MINUTE PAPER

As you were reading the tips for improving your performance on exams and tests, were you surprised to see different tips for different subjects, such as math and science, and for different kinds of tests, such as multiple-choice and essay? What did you find to be the most useful information in this chapter? What material was unclear to you?

3 APPLYING WHAT YOU HAVE LEARNED

Now that you have read and discussed this chapter, consider how you can apply what you have learned to your academic and personal life. The following prompts will help you reflect on the chapter material and its relevance to you both now and in the future.

1. Identify your next upcoming test or exam. What time of day is it scheduled, and what type of test will it be? What strategies have you read that will help you prepare for and take this test?

2. Is there one course that you find most difficult? If you are anxious about taking tests in that class, adopt a positive self-message to help you stay focused. It could be a favorite quote or even something as simple as "I know I can do it!"

4 BUILDING YOUR PORTFOLIO

A High Price to Pay   Academic integrity is a supreme value on college and university campuses. Faculty members, staff, and students are held to a strict code of academic integrity, and the consequences of breaking that code can be severe and life-changing. Create a Word document to record your responses to the following activity.

1. Imagine that your college or university has hired you to conduct a month-long academic integrity awareness campaign so that students will learn about and take seriously your campus's guidelines for academic integrity. To prepare for your "new job":

   a. Visit your institution's Web site and use the search feature to find the academic integrity code or policy. Take the time to read through the code, violations, and sanctions.

   b. Visit the judicial affairs office on your campus to learn more about the way your institution deals with violations of academic integrity policies.

   c. Research online resources from other campuses, such as information from the Center for Academic Integrity hosted by Clemson University (**www.academicintegrity.org/**).

   d. Check out several other college and university academic integrity policies or honor codes. How do they compare with your institution's code or policy?

2. Outline your month-long awareness campaign. Here are a few ideas to get you started:

   ■ Plan a new theme every week. Don't forget Internet-related violations.

   ■ Develop eye-catching posters to display around campus. (Check out the posters designed by students at Elizabethtown College in Pennsylvania found at **www.rubberpaw.com/integrity**.)

   ■ Consider guest speakers, debates, skits, or other presentations.

   ■ Come up with catchy slogans or phrases.

   ■ Send students a postcard highlighting your institution's policies or honor code.

   ■ Consider the most effective ways to communicate your message to different groups on campus.

3. Save your work in your portfolio or in the Cloud.

For more on this topic watch
French Fries Are Not Vegetables and Other College Lessons

WHERE TO GO FOR HELP . . .

ON CAMPUS

> **Learning Assistance Support Center.** Before you take your first tests, locate your campus's learning assistance center. Almost every campus has one, and studying for tests is one of its specialties. The best students, good students who want to be the best students, and students with academic difficulties use learning centers and tutoring services. These services are offered by both full-time professionals and highly skilled student tutors, and they are usually free.

> **Counseling Services** College and university counseling centers offer a wide array of services, often including workshops and individual or group counseling for test anxiety. Sometimes these services are also offered by the campus health center. Ask your first-year seminar instructor where you can find counseling services on your campus.

> **Fellow College Students** Often the best help we can get is the closest to us. Keep an eye out in your classes, residence hall, and extracurricular activities for the best students, those who appear to be the most serious, purposeful, and directed. Find a tutor. Join a study group. Students who do these things are much more likely to be successful than those who do not.

ONLINE

> Florida Atlantic University's Center for Learning and Student Success (CLASS) offers a list of tips to help you prepare for exams: **http://www.fau.edu/CLASS/Success/KeystoSuccess/exam_prep.pdf**.

> Learning Centre of the University of New South Wales in Sydney, Australia: **https://student.unsw.edu.au/exam-preparation**. Includes the popular SQ3R method.

MY INSTITUTION'S RESOURCES

_____

_____

_____

_____

_____

_____

_____

_____

10 Information Literacy and Communication

> ❝ I've learned that academic writing is all about preparation. It is just like anything else that we do in life.

Aaron Jacobs, 33
Business Management major
Capella University

Aaron Jacobs found himself at a crossroads when he graduated from high school. He received a full scholarship to play hockey at the University of Minnesota. At the same time, his father passed away suddenly. Although Aaron doesn't regret his decision to postpone college and start working to support his mother and younger siblings, the lack of a college education always lingered at the back of his mind. Now Aaron coaches high school hockey as well as runs a small coffee shop, and he thought that the timing was perfect to head back to college. An online degree fit his needs and lifestyle perfectly. "I work a lot and my schedule can be unpredictable, and it would be difficult for me to attend college in the traditional fashion," he explains.

Now that Aaron is in college, he's found that applying the same level of commitment to his academic work as he does to his professional work helps him succeed. "I've learned that academic writing is all about

Aaron Jacobs ▶

Phase4Studios/Shutterstock

preparation. It is just like anything else that we do in life," he says. Aaron knows that his writing process begins with careful research and note taking. Next he creates an outline to help him organize his thoughts, followed by a rough draft. The most important step, though, comes with rewriting and editing, and making sure that he has the time to work these essential steps into his overall process. "It takes a while to check everything, from spelling and grammar to the flow and rhythm of the writing; all of them are pivotal in keeping the interest of the reader," he notes.

Like many adult students, Aaron has skills that translate easily to an academic setting and that give him an advantage in his classes. His communication skills had already been honed by his years of work. "I was running my business prior to entering college and had to be very professional in communicating with customers on the phone and in person," he explains. "I got a crash course on marketing, budgeting, and HR (human resources) as well, and that taught me the importance of professionalism and making a good first impression." Presenting in online classes, however, offered him the opportunity to develop some new skills. "I have made a few different Power-Point presentations in my classes. The first one I did I had to learn as I went. I had no idea how the PowerPoint process worked, but to my surprise it was easy, and I like the format," he says.

Now, as Aaron works toward finishing his degree, he advises other students, "Be prepared, not only in doing the research and properly constructing a paper, but also in making sure that you have ample time to get the job done the right way without having to cut corners."

As Aaron's story illustrates, the ability to write and speak well makes a tremendous difference in how the rest of the world perceives you and how well you will be able to communicate throughout your life. But you will find that you often need to communicate differently depending on your audience. It's generally OK to use informal writing with your friends, family, and other students, for example, but your instructors and potential employers will expect more formality. Our purpose in this chapter is not to teach you grammar and punctuation (we'll save that for your English classes), but to get you to think of writing and speaking as some of the most important skills you will develop or improve in college.

In addition, to be successful at communicating, you must know how to manage information. Developing the skills to locate, analyze, and use information will significantly enhance your ability to keep up with what is going on in the world; to participate in activities that interest you; and to succeed in college, career, and community. The research skills you learn and use as a student will serve you well as a successful professional. That holds true for whatever career path you choose. Whether you're studying biology, engineering, business, or public relations, your task in college is to manage information for projects and presentations. In a few years, as a lab technician, a project coordinator, a loss-prevention specialist, or a campaign manager, your task will be the same: to find, manage, and present information for your employers and clients. All colleges and many companies provide libraries for this purpose, but finding and using information involves more than operating a computer or browsing the library bookshelves. To make sense of the vast amount of information at your fingertips in a reasonable amount of time, you'll need to develop a few key research and information literacy skills.

ASSESSING YOUR STRENGTHS

Information literacy, writing, and speaking are among the most important skills you will learn in college. Success in your career will also depend on your ability to communicate clearly and think critically about information. As you read this chapter, list your experiences in communicating and working with information successfully.

_____

_____

_____

_____

SETTING GOALS

What are your most important objectives in learning the material in this chapter? How can you improve your information literacy and communication skills? List three goals in this area (e.g., I will visit the library and learn about resources that relate to my classes; I will visit the writing center to get feedback on my paper).

1. _____

_____

2. _____

_____

3. _____

_____

Information Literacy

What is information literacy? Simply put, it's the ability to find, interpret, and use information to meet your needs. Information literacy has many facets, among them the following:

- **Computer literacy:** Facility with electronic tools, both for conducting searches and for presenting to others what you have found and analyzed.

- **Media literacy:** The ability to think critically about material distributed to a wide audience through television, film, advertising, radio, magazines, books, and the Internet.

- **Cultural literacy:** Knowing what has gone on and is going on around you. You have to understand the difference between the Civil War and the Revolutionary War, U2 and YouTube, Eminem and M&Ms, or you will not understand everyday conversation.

YOUR TURN

Work Together

Brainstorm with a group of classmates about the components of "information literacy" and make a list. How many separate components did your group identify? The chapter asserts that information literacy is the premier survival skill for the modern world. Does your group agree? Why or why not? Share your group's ideas with others in the class.

Information matters. It helps empower people to make good choices. The choices people make often determine their success in business, their happiness as friends and family members, and their well-being as citizens on this planet.

LEARNING TO BE INFORMATION LITERATE

People marvel at the information explosion, paper inflation, and the Internet. Many confuse mounds of information with knowledge and conclude that because they found links using a search engine, they are informed or can easily become informed. But most of us are unprepared for the number of available sources and the unsorted, unevaluated mass of information that pours over us at the press of a button. What, then, is the antidote for information overload? To become an informed and successful user of information, keep three basic goals in mind:

1. **Know how to find the information you need.** If you are sick, you need to know whose help to seek. If you lose your scholarship, you need to know where to get financial assistance. If you want to win a lawsuit, you need to know how to find the outcomes of similar cases. Once you have determined where to look for information, you'll need to ask good questions and make educated searches of information systems, such as the Internet, libraries, and **databases**. You'll also want to cultivate relationships with information professionals, such as librarians, who can help you frame questions, broaden and narrow searches, and retrieve the information you need.

2. **Learn how to interpret the information that you find.** It is very important to retrieve information. It is even more important to make sense of that information. What does the information mean? Have you selected a source that you can understand? Is the information accurate? Is the source reliable?

3. **Have a purpose.** Even the best information won't do much good if you don't know what to do with it. It's true that sometimes you'll hunt down a fact simply to satisfy your own curiosity, but more often you'll communicate what you've learned to someone else. You should know not only what form that communication will take—a research paper for a class, a proposal for your boss, a presentation at a hearing—but also what you want to accomplish. Will you use the information to make a decision, develop a new solution to a problem, influence a course of action, prove a point, or something else? In this chapter we'll explore ways to pursue each of these goals.

database A database is an organized and searchable set of information. Like a special search engine, a database is often classified by a certain subject area, such as chemistry or U.S. history.

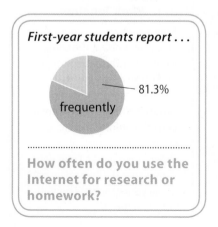

First-year students report . . .

81.3% frequently

How often do you use the Internet for research or homework?

WHAT'S RESEARCH—AND WHAT'S NOT?

To discover good information that you can use for a given purpose, you'll have to conduct research. You might be working on a college research paper right now or you might be anxious about one that's ahead of you. As you contemplate these projects, be sure that you understand what research involves.

In the past you might have completed assignments that asked you to demonstrate how to use a library's online catalog, databases, government documents collection, map depository, and interlibrary loan service. Or you might have been given a subject, such as ethics, or an assignment to find a definition or a related book, journal article, or Web page. If so, what you accomplished was retrieval, and although that is an essential element of research, it's just one step, not the end of the road.

Nor is research a matter of copying passages or finding a handful of sources and patching together bits and pieces of information without commentary. In fact, such behavior could easily slip into the category of plagiarism, a serious misstep that could result in a failing grade or worse (see pages 225–226 for more on plagiarism). At the very least, repeating information or ideas without interpreting them puts you at risk of careless use of sources that might be new or old, useful or dangerously in error, reliable or shaky, research-based or anecdotal, or objective or biased beyond credibility.

Good research, by contrast, is information literacy in action. Let's take up the ethics topic again. If you were assigned to select and report on an ethics issue, you might pick ethics in politics, accumulate a dozen sources, evaluate them, interpret them, select a few and discard a few, organize the keepers into a coherent arrangement, extract portions that hang together, write a paper or presentation that cites your sources, compose an introduction that explains what you have done, draw some conclusions of your own, and submit the results. That's research. If you learn to do it well, you'll experience the rush that comes with discovery and the pleasure that accompanies making a statement or taking a stand. The conclusion that you compose on the basis of your research is new information!

EMPLOYING INFORMATION LITERACY SKILLS

By the time you graduate, you should have a level of information literacy that will carry you through your professional life. The Association of College and Research Libraries has developed the following best practices for the information-literate student. If you learn how to apply them, you'll do well no matter where your educational and career paths take you.

- **Determine the nature and extent of the information needed.** In general, this step involves first defining and articulating what information you need and then identifying a variety of potential sources.
- **Access information effectively and efficiently.** Select the most appropriate research methods, use well-designed search strategies, refine those strategies along the way, and keep organized notes on what you find and where you find it.

- **Evaluate information and its sources critically.** As an information-literate person, you'll be able to apply criteria for judging the usefulness and reliability of both information and its sources. You'll also become skilled at summarizing the main ideas presented by others and comparing new information with what you already know.

- **Incorporate information into what you already know and believe.** To do this, you'll determine what information is new, unique, or contradictory and consider whether it has an impact on what's important to you. You'll also validate, understand, or interpret the information through talking with other people. Finally, you'll combine elements of different ideas to construct new concepts of your own making.

- **Use information effectively to accomplish a specific purpose.** You'll apply information to planning and creating a particular product or performance, revising the development process as necessary, and communicating the results to others.

- **Access and use information ethically and legally.** There are economic, legal, and social issues surrounding the retrieval and use of information. You'll need to understand and follow laws, regulations, institutional policies, and etiquette related to copyright and intellectual property. Most important, you should acknowledge the use of information from sources in everything you write, record, or broadcast.[1]

Choosing, Narrowing, and Researching a Topic

Assignments that require the use of library materials can take many forms and will be a part of many of your classes. There are numerous ways to search for information to complete an assignment, and we'll consider some of them later in the chapter. Before you start searching, however, you need to have an idea of what you're looking for.

Choosing a topic is often the most difficult part of a research project. Even if an instructor assigns a general topic, you'll need to narrow it down to a particular aspect that interests you enough to make worthwhile the time and energy you'll spend pursuing it. Imagine, for example, that you have been assigned to write a research paper on the topic of political ethics. What steps should you take?

Your first job is to get an overview of your topic. You can begin by looking at general and specific dictionaries and encyclopedias. To learn something about political ethics, for example, you might consult a political dictionary and the *Encyclopedia of American Political History*. Similar broad sources are available for just about any subject area, from marketing to sports psychology to colonial American literature. Check your library's reference area or consult with a librarian for leads.

---

[1]Adapted from *Information Literacy Competency Standards for Higher Education* (2000), http://www.ala.org/acrl/standards/informationliteracycompetency.

Once you've acquired some basic information to guide you toward an understanding of the nature of your topic, you have a decision to make: What aspects of the subject will you pursue? Even if you launch the most general of inquiries, you will discover very quickly that your topic is vast and includes many related subtopics. Reviewing your search results will give you more information and introduce you to new aspects of your topic. You can use this new information to create more keywords. **Keywords** are words or phrases that are central to finding the resources you need. You've already used keywords. When you use a search engine such as Google, you can type in an entire sentence (e.g., How does global warming affect the polar ice caps?), but when using library resources, you need to pull the main ideas, or keywords, out of the sentence and use those terms to search. The keywords in that sentence are "global warming" and "polar ice caps." (You'll read more on developing keywords for effective searches on page 214.)

You want to find a dozen or so focused and highly relevant hits on an aspect of the topic that you can fashion into a coherent, well-organized essay. Begin by assessing what you already know and asking what you would like to learn more about. Perhaps you know a little about the efforts of lobbyists and political action committees to influence legislation, and you're curious about recent efforts to limit what gifts politicians may accept; in that case you might decide on a three-pronged topic: gifts to politicians, political corruption, and lobbyists.

You can follow these steps to focus any topic. By simply consulting a few general sources, you'll find that you can narrow a broad topic to something that interests you and is manageable in size. From reference works and a quick search of a library catalog, periodical databases, or the Internet you will find definitions, introductory materials, some current and historical examples of your topic in action, and related information. You are now ready to launch a purposeful search.

Jonathan Stark

Get Thee to a Library

How often do you go to your campus library? Beyond having a library tour, have you explored this important academic resource? Although information is available from many sources, the most reliable resource will be a professional librarian, who can guide you to relevant books, articles, and online information.

keyword A term used to tell a search engine what you're looking for. Keywords are synonyms, related terms, or subtopics of your search topic.

Using the Library

Whenever you have research to do—whether for a class, your job, or your personal life—visit a library. We can't stress this advice enough. Although the Internet is loaded with billions of pages of information, don't be fooled into thinking that it will serve all your needs. For one thing, you'll have to sort through a lot of junk to find your way to good-quality sources online. More important is that if you limit yourself to the Web, you'll miss out on some of the best materials. Although we often think that everything is electronic and can be found through a computer, a great deal of valuable information is still stored in traditional formats and is most easily accessed through a library.

Every library has books and journals as well as a great number of items in electronic databases that aren't available on public Web sites. Librarians work with your professors to determine which sources and materials are required to support teaching and research at your institution. Librarians carefully select well-respected and credible resources with you and your research in mind. Most libraries also have several other types of collections, such as government documents, microfilm, rare books, manuscripts, dissertations, fine art, photographs, historical documents, maps, music, and films, including archival and documentary productions.

> ### YOUR TURN
>
> **Discuss**
>
> Have a discussion with a group of your classmates to answer this question: Is the library a necessary resource for learning in college? Did all members of the group agree or disagree? Share your group's ideas with others in the class.

TAKE ADVANTAGE OF EVERYTHING YOUR LIBRARY HAS TO OFFER

stacks The areas in libraries containing shelves that are full of books available for checkout.

Books and periodicals are essential, but a college or university library is far more than a document warehouse. For starters, most campus libraries have Web sites that offer lots of help for students. Some provide guidelines on writing research papers, conducting online searches, or navigating the **stacks**. They all provide invaluable services to students and faculty members, including virtual spaces for accessing library holdings and the Web, physical spaces where you can study in quiet or meet with other students, and perhaps even social and entertainment programs.

Of course, no one library can possibly own everything you might need or enough copies of each item, so groups of libraries share their materials with each other. If your library does not have a journal or book that looks promising for your project or if the item you need is checked out, you can use interlibrary loan, a service that allows you to request an item from another library at a different college or university. The request process is often very simple, and the librarians can help you get started. Some materials, such as digitized articles, can come via e-mail, while others, such as books, have to be sent through the mail. In most cases, you can expect to receive the materials in as little as a few days, but just in case the material is in high demand, it's always a good idea to identify and request what you might need from other libraries as far in advance as possible.

Are you a commuter or distance education student who cannot easily visit your college library in person? Most libraries provide off-campus access to their electronic materials to students who log in with a school-provided username and password. Usually, the library's home page serves as an electronic gateway to its services, which may include the following:

- A searchable catalog of the books and journals the library owns in print
- Electronic databases, some of which let you access the full text of newspaper, magazine, and journal articles from your computer

Where Do You Work Out?

Look for ways to balance your life so that you give your body a workout in the gym and your brain a workout in the library.

- Interlibrary loan requests
- Course reserve readings
- E-books
- Indexes of Web sites that have been carefully screened for reliability and relevance to particular subject areas
- Online chats with librarians who can help you in real time

To learn more, poke around your library's Web site or e-mail or call the reference desk.

Libraries also have a wide variety of physical spaces for students, staff, and faculty members to use. From individual study tables to private group rooms to comfortable chairs tucked in quiet corners, you should be able to find a study area that suits you and your needs. You might also discover places to eat, socialize, take in a movie or an art exhibit, check your e-mail, keep up with your social networks, search the Web, type your papers, make photocopies, edit videos, give presentations, hold meetings, or take a much-needed nap.

Be sure to use the handouts and guides that are available at the reference desk or online. You will also find tutorials and virtual tours that will help you to become familiar with the collections, services, and spaces available at your library.

ASK A LIBRARIAN

Of all the resources available in a library, the most useful—and often the least used—are the people who staff it. Librarians thrive on helping you. If you're not sure how to start a search, if you're not successful in your first attempts at retrieving information, or if you just need some ideas about what you might try as you pursue a research project, ask a librarian. Librarians are information experts who are trained to assist and guide you to the resources you need. The librarians who work in the reference area or supervise the computer stations might look busy, but they are busy helping people with projects much like yours, and you are *not* interrupting when you ask for assistance. Remember the 20-minute rule: If you have been working diligently on a research project for 20 minutes and haven't found what you need, stop and ask a librarian for help. Let the librarian know what searches you've tried, and he or she will be able to help you figure out new strategies to get to the information you need.

You can contact a reference librarian in several ways. If you query by e-mail, you are likely to receive a quick reply. You can also call the reference desk to ask a question, such as "Do you have a copy of the report *Problems with the Presidential Gifts System*?" You can have a "live chat" online with a library staffer in real time, and you can always visit the reference desk in person or make an appointment for a tutorial or consultation. (Hint: You will be most successful if you bring a copy of your assignment and any written instructions you have to your meeting. Tell the librarian what, if anything, you have tried.) Remember that there are no silly questions. A good librarian will treat your inquiries with respect.

The information professionals at your library are authorities on how to find information. They not only know where to find it, but they also have the wonderful ability to help you use information to meet your needs, solve problems, provide explanations, open up new possibilities, and ultimately create new knowledge.

Figure Out What You Need and Find It

Your library has myriad resources to help you with your research. Books, journal articles, newspapers, magazines, encyclopedias, and Internet sources can all be part of your research. However, different topics require different types of sources. A key component of being information literate is determining the kinds of sources you need to satisfy your research questions.

KEYWORDS

Before you start your research, take a few minutes to generate keywords related to your topic. As defined above, a keyword is a word or phrase that tells a search engine what you're looking for. You will create a list of keywords by brainstorming similar terms and subtopics that will help you find resources for your topic. For example, if you are writing a paper on global warming, keywords may include climate change, greenhouse effect, ozone layer, smog, and pollution. These are just a few examples; there are dozens more. Research is essentially trying different combinations of keywords and analyzing the results. You will use keywords whether you're looking for books, articles, or blogs.

If you are having trouble coming up with keywords, consult an encyclopedia. Encyclopedias provide general overviews of topics and can help you understand the basics of a concept or event, but you will need resources beyond encyclopedias for most college-level research projects. An encyclopedia is a great place to start but not a good place to end your research. You have probably used an encyclopedia recently and may use one all the time without thinking about it. One of the most popular encyclopedias is Wikipedia. The "wiki" part of Wikipedia refers to a type of Web site that allows many different people to edit its content. Information on wikis is constantly evolving. Wikipedia is controversial in college settings. Many people believe that the information on Wikipedia cannot be guaranteed to be reliable because anyone can change it. Some instructors prefer that students use encyclopedias that have gone through a formal editing and reviewing process like those available in print or online through your library. These instructors might forbid Wikipedia, and if any of yours do, don't use it. Using sources that you were told to avoid will jeopardize your grade. Always cite information that you take from an outside source; if you do not, you are in danger of plagiarizing. The most important thing to remember is that no matter which encyclopedia you use, encyclopedias are a helpful first step in providing general information about your topic to help you generate keywords. Librarians are another great resource to help you with keywords. Once you have your list of works started, you're on your way to finding sources.

> ### YOUR TURN
> **Work Together**
>
> Do you ever use Wikipedia as a resource? Why or why not? Think of a topic that you and other students in your class know well. Work together to write and upload an entry to Wikipedia. Check back in a month to see if anyone else has "edited" your entry.

SOURCES

What kinds of sources do you need for your research project, and where should you start? First, consider the "when" or time frame of your topic. Are you researching a historical event, such as the Dust Bowl drought of the 1930s, or a historical figure, such as social justice crusader Ida B. Wells? Is your topic a current event or issue, such as the recovery from Superstorm Sandy, or a present-day person, such as Governor Chris Christie of New Jersey? Consider also the "where" aspect of your topic. Do you need information about recent weather disasters in the United States, or do you need a global perspective?

Even with an understanding of various types of sources, it can be difficult to determine exactly what you need for your assignment. Figure 10.1 (see p. 217) provides an overview of when to use different common research sources and gives examples of what you'll find in each source. Review your assignment and use Figure 10.1 to help you find the best resources for your project.

Scholarly Articles. Many college-level research projects will require you to use **scholarly articles**, which are articles written by experts in their fields, such as researchers, librarians, or professors, and then assessed and edited by other experts in a process called peer review. Authors submit their articles to a scholarly journal that has a board of respected and highly qualified reviewers who check the articles for all the basics (e.g., spelling, grammar, quality of the writing), but also evaluate the work based on its thesis, research methods, and originality. You might find that some of your instructors use the terms *peer*

scholarly articles Articles written by experts in their fields, such as researchers, librarians, or professors, and then assessed and edited by other experts in a process called peer review.

TECH TIP CHECK YOUR ENGINE

1 ▸ THE PROBLEM

You understand the basics of online research but don't know how to apply it to an academic setting.

2 ▸ THE FIX

Learn what research passes scholarly muster: peer-reviewed academic journals (e.g., *Harvard Business Review*), government Web sites (U.S. ones usually end in .gov), or newspaper Web sites (e.g., *New York Times, Washington Post*).

3 ▸ HOW TO DO IT

Unlike the examples above, much of the information that you find online isn't objective or factual; it's a digital free-for-all out there. When digging for academic research, you need to be fanatically picky and filter out all the garbage. That's called critical thinking, and it's what college is all about.

Ask a Librarian

Your college library offers free access to a wealth of academic databases, LexisNexis, e-journals, and so on. If you have questions about how to use them (and about what kinds of materials qualify as academic research in general), make an appointment with a reference librarian. In 30 minutes you'll probably be smarter than anyone else in your class. Go online to **http://libguides.bgsu.edu /library_basics** to visit the library at Bowling Green State University and find helpful "getting started" guides to online research.

- **Hone your online research skills.** Make sure that you understand Boolean operators. The most common Boolean operators are the words *AND, OR,* and *NOT,* and how you use them affects your search results.

- **Keywords separated by the word *AND* yield results that contain both of the required words, in any order.** According to the Bowling Green Web site, "A search for rock AND roll will locate all records containing both the word *rock* and the word *roll*. It will locate items about rock and roll music. It might also locate records that contain both words in a different context."

- **Keywords separated by the word *OR* yield results that contain one word or the other.** The Bowling Green Web site notes, "A search for rock OR roll will locate all records containing either the word *rock* or the word *roll*—not necessarily both. It will retrieve items about bakery rolls, tumbling, rocks, music, gemstones, etc."

- **Keywords separated by the word *NOT* yield results that feature the first word and exclude the second.** The Bowling Green Web site states, "A search for rock NOT roll will locate records containing the word *rock* but NOT the word *roll*. It will retrieve items about rocks, gemstones, diamonds, etc."*

- **Other tips:** Frame keywords with asterisks to yield results that include the exact phrase within the asterisks. If you get too few hits, omit a search term. Add an asterisk to a keyword for a wildcard search that yields results that include any word that starts with the keyword.

GOOD TO KNOW

Learn the quirks of the databases or search engines you use often. Whether you use AltaVista, Bing, Google, or Google Scholar, learn tricks to refine your search. Some engines yield better results from Boolean operators (e.g., "politicians AND lobbyists"); others are more attuned to natural language searches (e.g., "ethics in politics" or "gifts to politicians").

PERSONAL BEST

Avoid Internet plagiarism. You cannot cut and paste whole sentences from the Internet into your essays. Instructors can easily catch you, and the penalties are stiff.

KEY TIPS

1. **Don't procrastinate.** If you leave a big paper until the last minute, you'll be more tempted to cut and paste and less scrupulous about footnotes.

2. **Avoid *unintentional* cheating.** Whenever you copy online research into your notes, be sure to add a URL in brackets at the end. While you're at it, place quotation marks around all cited materials or highlight them in a bright color. It's surprisingly easy to forget which words are your own and which words came from another author.

3. **When in doubt, footnote.** Paraphrasing anything off the Internet or from any other source and using it without attribution is cheating. Most colleges have a zero-tolerance policy on the subject.

* http://libguides.bgsu.edu/library_basics.

Information Time Line Topic: Climate Change/U.S. Politics		
Source/when to access information	**What it offers**	**Examples**
Newspapers (print and online) Daily/hourly after an event	Primary-source, firsthand discussions of current events, what happened at the time of the event; short articles	Coverage of presidential speeches, results of Supreme Court decisions, congressional votes
Magazines Weekly/monthly after event	Analysis of an event a few weeks after it occurs; longer articles than in newspapers; might include more interviews or research historical context	Articles comparing past presidents' positions on climate change; in-depth interviews with experts in the field; analyses of opposing viewpoints
Scholarly articles Months after event	In-depth analyses of issues; research-based scientific studies	Similar to magazines but with the rigor of academic research, including extensive citations; review of other articles on the topic
Books Months/years after event	Comprehensive overview of a topic with broad and in-depth analysis	Comprehensive overview of climate-related legislation spanning multiple decades

FIGURE 10.1

The information time line helps identify when and how to use each type of source. Use it for classwork and also your personal life. Where would you go to find information about a political or environmental issue affecting your neighborhood? Use the chart to determine what kind of information each source provides.

reviewed, refereed, or *academic* to refer to scholarly articles. Be sure to clarify what your instructor expects of your sources before you begin your work.

Unlike an encyclopedia, scholarly articles do not usually provide a general overview of a topic. Rather, they are often research or scientific studies with a hypothesis and rigorous testing. For example, for our topic of climate change we might find scholarly articles that compare temperature data over a certain time period, analyze a specific pollutant's effect on climate change, or explore public and political discourse on the topic.

Finding Scholarly Articles.   Scholarly articles are published in scholarly journals. You can find journals in your library in a few ways. The first and most popular way is to conduct a search using an online database, which will result in titles, descriptions, and sometimes full texts of articles within the journal. The second way is to use your library's catalog. Both methods are discussed below. The key thing to remember, however, is that online databases will let you search *inside* the journal. This is a much more effective approach given how difficult it would be to browse decades of print journals in the library stacks. You can always look for the print edition of the journal using the volume and issue number you find in an online database. When searching the library catalog, you are likely to find only the names of journals and *not* the titles of the articles within the journal.

Periodicals (Journals and Magazines).   You may have heard the word *periodical* before. Many sources that we use in both academic research and our personal lives are periodicals. A periodical is a resource that is published multiple times a year, such as a magazine. Periodicals often have issue and volume numbers, but the title of the periodical is always the same (e.g., *Rolling Stone* or *Journal of Academic Librarianship*). You might use magazines for some of your college research, and you will definitely use journals.

Be warned that not all periodicals are scholarly. As mentioned above, *Rolling Stone* is a periodical. There is a new issue every two weeks, which classifies it as a periodical, but it does not go through the rigorous peer-review process like the articles in scholarly journals. Remember, this step does *not* disqualify magazines as a viable source for your research, but they will not satisfy an assignment's scholarly article requirement. Refer to Figure 10.1 for a breakdown of when and how to use different types of sources.

Using Databases to Find Scholarly Articles.   To find scholarly articles, you will use databases. Remember that a database is an organized and searchable set of information often classified by a certain subject area. Your library will have online databases that cover a variety of topics. Although some databases are available to anyone regardless of their affiliation with a college, access to most of the databases you'll use for research in college requires paid subscriptions, and the material is available only to people who are affiliated with a school that pays for the service. For this reason, you will most likely need to log in with your college username and password to use the databases from off campus. Also remember that even though databases might look just like Web sites, they're actually carefully chosen subscriptions paid for by the library. So you can use the library resources without ever stepping foot into the building, but the librarians would be happier if you came to visit.

Librarians have insider knowledge of the databases that your school can access and are masters at database searches. Working with a librarian can help you search more effectively than working solo and leads to better results with less wasted time. Some databases are specific to one subject, such as chemistry, while others include articles from a wide variety of disciplines. Many libraries have dozens, if not hundreds, of databases. It can be difficult to figure out which ones you should use, but your librarian can help you determine which databases are best for your research. Don't be afraid to ask! It's better to ask than to waste hours searching in the wrong place. We've said this before, but remember that if you search for more than 20 minutes without finding anything, it's time to ask a librarian for help.

Scholarly articles can be a great resource. Depending on your topic, however, you might also need other types of sources.

Books.   When doing research in today's world, online resources often overshadow books. Students and faculty alike love the convenience of online resources that can be accessed immediately and from any place with Internet access. Restricting searches to only online resources, however, will severely limit the results and might also exclude some of the best information available.

In the first few years of college, books are especially useful for research projects. Often students are in introductory classes and write research papers on broad topics, such as the Civil War. Although countless scholarly articles have been written about the Civil War, they will not provide a general overview of the topic. Such articles tend to have a narrow focus on aspects like an analysis of the economic factors that contributed to the start of the war. Many students mistakenly search databases of scholarly articles looking for a broad overview when, in fact, they should be looking for books to give them this perspective. Do not be afraid of books. Libraries—with their thousands, if not millions, of books—might intimidate many new students, but librarians who are trained to help await you. Doing research without a librarian is like driving cross country without a map or GPS. Technically, you can do it, but you will get lost along the way. It might be fun to head down uncharted paths, but when you're facing a deadline, you want to get to your destination as quickly and efficiently as possible.

Using the Online Catalog.   To find books, print journals, and other materials physically located in the library, such as CDs and DVDs, you will use the library catalog, an online resource accessible on or off campus. Sometimes off-campus access requires you to log in with your school username and password. Please note that most library catalogs will not search articles inside the print journals; it will find only the journals by title (e.g., *Journal of Climate*). Searching the library catalog is a lot like searching databases. Use your keywords to find relevant materials. When you find a source that looks promising, check to see if it is currently available or if it is checked out to another student. If it's available, write down the title, author, and the call number—which is like an address for the book that tells you where it is in the library—and head into the stacks to locate your item. If it's checked out to another student or if your library doesn't own the source that you're looking for, remember to ask about interlibrary loan. One of the biggest benefits of searching for books or other sources is the ability to browse. For instance, when you find your book on the shelf, look at the other books around it. They will be on the same topic.

THE INTERNET

The Internet simultaneously makes research easier and more difficult. Internet research is easier than research done in previous decades because people can access enormous amounts of information from virtually anywhere for free after conducting a simple search on a site like Google. The Internet also makes research much more difficult and complicated, however. First is the common misconception that search engines such as Google or Bing find everything there is to know on a topic. Many of the sources you will need to use for college-level research are accessible *only* through subscription databases, not through Google. Second, more results mean more shuffling through the Web pages to find relevant and credible sources. Third, the order of the search

> **YOUR TURN**
>
> ···
>
> **Discuss**
>
> While reading this chapter, do an Internet search for the phrase "Finding Resources for Research Papers." What ideas did your search yield? Write them down and share them with your classmates.

results is determined by the search engine's secret search formulas that factor in popularity, not credibility, and are often influenced by who pays for their Web pages to be on the top of the list. Finally, search engines search a wide variety of sources, many of which are not appropriate for most college-level research. When you use a database instead, you can easily add filters to ensure that your results include scholarly articles only, and you can clearly see who the authors are. Anybody can put up a Web site, which means you can't be sure of the Web site owner's credibility and reliability. The sources found on the Web might be written by anyone: a fifth grader, a distinguished professor, a professional society, or a biased advocate.

A recent Google search on the subject "political corruption," for instance, generated more than ten million hits. The first page yielded some interesting results:

A collection of links on politics and political corruption

A Libertarian Party legislative program on political corruption

Two Amazon.com ads

A site that offers "research" on gambling and political corruption

A university site offering research on political corruption in Illinois

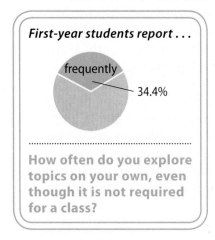

First-year students report . . .

frequently

34.4%

How often do you explore topics on your own, even though it is not required for a class?

These varied results demonstrate that you must be alert when examining Internet sources. From this example, we saw that mixed in with credible scholarship and useful links to sources on the topic of political corruption were sales promotions and arguments against gambling. It isn't always easy to evaluate the quality of Internet sources. Check pages 221–224 in this chapter for some helpful strategies that you can use to determine whether a source is credible and authentic.

TIPS FOR USING ELECTRONIC RESOURCES LIKE A PRO

To become a successful and savvy user of electronic resources, study the Tech Tip on page 216 and follow these guidelines:

- **Consult the Help or Frequently Asked Questions (FAQ) links.** The first time you use any catalog, database, or search engine, use the Help or FAQ links to learn specific searching techniques. You will get the best results if you use the tips and strategies suggested by the database provider.

- **Write out your topic or problem as a statement or question.** Writing out a statement or question, such as "Is it right for politicians to take gifts from lobbyists?" or "The influence of lobbyists or PACs has dramatically changed American political ethics," will help you identify potentially useful keywords.

- **Brainstorm keywords.** Think about synonyms, related terms, and people or historical events to use as case studies. If one search does not yield any useful hits, you'll have some backup terms on hand. It's also a good idea to search more than one database or engine; different ones might pull up dramatically different sources.

- **Know when to limit your search.** You can often limit a search by date, language, journal name, full text, or word(s) in title. If you still get too many hits, add more search terms. Think about narrowing your topic by geographic region, a specific population, or a time period. For example, instead of just using the keyword "poverty," you can use "poverty" and "United States" and "children" and "Great Depression."

- **Know when to expand your search.** If you get too few hits, omit a search term. You can also truncate (i.e., shorten) a word by using an asterisk to retrieve broader results. For instance, by truncating the word *political* to *politic** you will get results with the words *political, politics, politician,* and/or *politicize.*

- **Learn the quirks of the databases or search engines that you use often.** Some yield better results from Boolean operators (e.g., "politicians AND lobbyists"); others are more attuned to natural language searches (e.g., "ethics in politics" or "gifts to politicians"). Librarians have a lot of experience working in various databases and can definitely help you learn the ins and outs of the ones you need.

- **Check your library's electronic resources page.** Here you will see what else is available online. Most libraries have links to other commonly used electronic reference tools, including online encyclopedias, dictionaries, almanacs, style guides, biographical and statistical resources, and news sources.

- **Keep trying.** Research is an iterative process, meaning that you generate keywords, do searches, read, learn new things, and then repeat all or part of the process until you have what you need. The more you learn about a topic, the better your searches will be.

> ## YOUR TURN
> ### Write and Reflect
> Talk to a faculty member, a parent, or an older friend who went to college. Ask this person how he or she conducted research before the Internet. Write a short review of the strategies used by previous generations to access and use information. Describe your reactions.

Evaluating Sources

It's easy to assume that huge amounts of available information automatically provide knowledge. Some students might at first be excited about receiving 20,800,000 hits from a Google search on political ethics, but shock takes hold when they realize that their discovery is utterly unsorted. They might respond by using only the first several hits, irrespective of quality. A more productive approach is to think critically about the usefulness of potential sources by measuring them against three important criteria: relevance, authority, and bias.

Google-itis

Search engines such as Google have made finding immediate answers to any question easier than ever before. Be careful, though: Some Google hits may be authentic and valuable, but others may take you to advertisements or biased reports that don't give you exactly *the* answer that you were looking for.

"It's a new syndrome we're seeing more of... "Google-itis"."

www.cartoonstock.com

RELEVANCE

The first thing to consider when looking at a possible source is how well it fits your needs. That, in turn, will be affected by the nature of your research project and the kind of information you are seeking.

- **Is it introductory?** Introductory information is basic and elementary. It neither assumes nor requires prior knowledge about the topic. Introductory sources can be useful when you're first learning about a subject. They are less useful when you're drawing conclusions about a particular aspect of the subject.

- **Is it definitional?** Definitional information provides some descriptive details about a subject. It might help you introduce a topic to others or clarify the focus of your investigation.

- **Is it analytical?** Analytical information supplies and interprets data about origins, behaviors, differences, and uses. In most cases, it's the kind of information that you want.

- **Is it comprehensive?** The more detail, the better. Avoid unsubstantiated opinions and look instead for sources that consider the topic in depth and offer plenty of evidence to support their conclusions.

- **Is it current?** You should usually give preference to recent sources, although older ones can sometimes be useful (i.e., primary sources for a historical topic or if the source is still cited by others in a field).

- **Can you conclude anything from it?** Use the "So what?" test: How important is this information? Why does it matter to my project?

AUTHORITY

Once you have determined that a source is relevant to your project, check that it was created by somebody who has the qualifications to write or speak on the subject. Such checking will depend on your subject and the nature of your inquiry (a fifth grader's opinion might be exactly what you're looking for). In most cases, though, you'll want expert conclusions based on rigorous evidence.

Make sure that you can identify the author and be ready to explain why that author is a reliable source. Good qualifications might include academic degrees, institutional affiliations, an established record of researching and publishing on a topic, and personal experience with a subject. On the other hand, be wary of anonymous or commercial sources or those written by someone whose credibility is questionable.

Also understand whether your project calls for scholarly publications, popular magazines, or both. As mentioned in the previous section, you don't necessarily have to dismiss popular magazines. Many journalists and columnists are extremely well qualified, and their work might well be appropriate for your needs. Also, independent and small-press magazines offer perspectives from groups of people who are not often represented in mainstream media outlets. As a general rule, however, scholarly sources will have been vetted through a rigorous process that gives the work credibility in academic environments.

Scholarly Journals	Popular Magazines
Long articles	Shorter articles
In-depth information on topic	Broad overview of topic
Written by academic experts	Written by journalists or reporters
Graphs, tables, and charts	Photos of people and events
Articles "refereed" or reviewed by experts	Articles not rigidly evaluated
Formally credited sources	Sources credited informally

BIAS

When you are searching for sources, you should realize that all materials have an author who has personal beliefs that affect the way he or she views the world and approaches a topic. This bias is a normal part of the research process, and researchers have adopted methodologies to reduce it and improve accuracy. Many sources, however, will be heavily biased toward a specific viewpoint or ideology. Although nothing is inherently wrong with someone having a particular point of view, it is dangerous for a reader not to know that the bias exists.

Research consists of considering multiple analyses, opinions, points of views, and perspectives on a topic; analyzing the sources; and creating something new from your analysis. Some signs of bias indicate that you should question the credibility and accuracy of a source and possibly exclude it from your research. If you detect overly positive or overly harsh language, hints of a personal agenda, or a stubborn refusal to consider other points of view, think carefully about how well you can trust the information in a document.

A NOTE ON INTERNET SOURCES

Be especially careful when evaluating online resources. It is often difficult to tell where something on the Internet came from or who wrote it. The lack of this information can make it very difficult to judge the credibility of the source. Although an editorial board reviews most print matter (books, articles, etc.) for accuracy and overall quality, it's frequently difficult to confirm that the same is true for information on a Web site. There are some exceptions, however. If you are searching through an online database such as the Human Genome Database or Eldis: The Gateway to Development Information (a poverty database), it is highly likely that the documents in these collections have been reviewed. Likewise, online versions of print magazines and journals have usually been checked out by editors. And information from academic and government Web sites (those whose URLs end in .edu or .gov, respectively) is generally—but not always—trustworthy.

Making Use of What You Find

You have probably heard the saying that "knowledge is power." Although knowledge can certainly contribute to power, this saying is true only if that knowledge is put to use. When you retrieve, sort, interpret, analyze, and synthesize sources from an information center—be it the library, a computer database, or the Web—you can produce a product that has power.

But first, you have to decide what form that product will take and what kind of power you want it to hold. Who are you going to tell about your discoveries, and how? What do you hope to accomplish by sharing your conclusions? Remember that a major goal of information literacy is to use information effectively to accomplish a specific purpose (see p. 208). Make it a point to *do* something with the results of your research. Otherwise, why bother?

SYNTHESIZING INFORMATION AND IDEAS

Ultimately, the point of conducting research is that the process contributes to the development of new knowledge. As a researcher, you sought the answer to a question. Now is the time to formulate that answer and share it.

Many students satisfy themselves with a straightforward report that merely summarizes what they found. Sometimes that's enough. More often, however, you'll want to apply the information to ideas of your own. To do that, first consider all the information that you found and how your sources relate to each other. What do they have in common, and where do they disagree? What conclusions can you draw from those similarities and differences? What new ideas did they spark? How can you use the information that you have on hand to support your conclusions? (Refer to Chapter 5 for tips on drawing conclusions from different points of view and using evidence to construct an argument.)

What you're doing at this stage of any research project is processing information, an activity known as **synthesis**. By accepting some ideas, rejecting others, combining related concepts, assessing the implications, and pulling it all together, you'll create new information and ideas that other people can use.

> **synthesis** The process of combining separate information and ideas to formulate a more complete understanding.

Your final paper will include analysis and synthesis of the sources that you found through your research along with your original ideas. You must make sure that you clearly delineate which thoughts and ideas came from the sources you found.

ABOUT PLAGIARISM

Plagiarism, or taking another person's idea or work and presenting it as your own, is especially intolerable in academic culture. Just as taking someone else's property constitutes physical theft, taking credit for someone else's ideas—someone's **intellectual property**—constitutes intellectual theft. In written reports and papers, you must give credit any time you use (a) another person's actual words; (b) another person's ideas or theories, even if you don't quote them directly; or (c) any other information that is not considered common knowledge.

> **plagiarism** The act of taking another person's idea or work and presenting it as your own. This gross academic misconduct can result in suspension or expulsion, and even the revocation of the violator's college degree.

Writers and journalists whose plagiarism has been discovered—such as Jayson Blair, formerly of the *New York Times,* and Stephen Glass, formerly of the *New Republic*—have lost their jobs and their journalistic careers. Even college presidents have occasionally been found guilty of "borrowing" the words of others and using them as their own in speeches and written documents. Such discoveries result not only in embarrassment and shame, but also in lawsuits and criminal actions.

> **intellectual property** Ownership over nonphysical creative works such as slogans, artwork, and inventions. Copyright, trademarks, and patents are kinds of intellectual property.

Because plagiarism can be a problem on college campuses, faculty members are now using electronic systems such as **www.turnitin.com** to identify passages in student papers that have been plagiarized. Many instructors routinely check their students' papers to make sure that the writing is original. So even though the temptation to cheat or plagiarize might be strong, the chance of possibly getting a better grade isn't worth misrepresenting yourself or your knowledge and suffering the potential consequences. Because no universal code dictates such behaviors, ask your instructors for clarification. When a student is caught violating the academic code of a particular school or instructor, pleading ignorance of the rules is a weak defense.

It should go without saying (but we'll say it anyway) that deliberate cheating is a bad idea on many levels. Submitting a paper that you purchased from an Internet source or from an individual will cause you to miss out on the discovery and skill development that research assignments are meant to teach. Intentional plagiarism is easily detected and will almost certainly earn you a failing grade and maybe even expulsion.

Although most cases of plagiarism are the result of misunderstanding or carelessness, be aware that "I didn't know" is not a valid excuse. Although your instructors might acknowledge that plagiarism can be an honest mistake, they will still expect you to avoid errors, and they will call you on it if you don't. Luckily, plagiarism is relatively easy to avoid. Keep careful notes as you conduct your research so that later on you don't inadvertently mistake someone else's words or ideas for your own. Finally, be sure to check out your own campus's definition of what constitutes plagiarism, which you will find in the student handbook or in first-year English course materials. If you have any questions or doubts about what is and is not acceptable, ask.

CITE YOUR SOURCES AND AVOID PLAGIARISM

At some point you'll present your findings. Whether they take the form of an essay, a formal research paper, a script for a presentation or broadcast, a page for a Web site, or something else entirely, you must give credit to your sources.

Citing your sources serves many purposes. For one thing, acknowledging the information and ideas you've borrowed from other writers shows respect for their contributions. It also distinguishes between other writers' ideas and your own. Source citations demonstrate to your audience that you have based your conclusions on thoughtful consideration of good, reliable evidence. Source citations also provide a starting place for anyone who would like more information or is curious about how you reached your conclusions. Most important is that citing your sources is the simplest way to avoid plagiarism.

The particular requirements of source citation can get complicated, but it all boils down to two rules. As you write, just remember:

1. If you use somebody else's exact words, you must give that person credit.

2. If you use somebody else's ideas, **even if you use your own words to express those ideas**, you must give that person credit.

Your instructors will indicate their preferred method for citation: footnotes, references in parentheses included in the text of your paper, or endnotes. If you're not provided with guidelines or if you simply want to be sure that you do it right, consult a handbook or writing style manual, such as those prepared by the Modern Language Association (*MLA Handbook for Writers of Research Papers*), the American Psychological Association (*Publication Manual of the American Psychological Association*), the University of Chicago Press (*The Chicago Manual of Style*), or the Council of Science Editors (*Scientific Style and Format: The CSE Manual for Authors, Editors, and Publishers*).

From Research to Writing

Your writing provides tangible evidence of how well you think and how well you understand concepts related to the courses you are taking. It is your chance to show what you discovered through your research and demonstrate your ability to analyze and synthesize sources into a new product that is uniquely your own. Like research, writing takes practice, and it is always a good idea to ask for help. This section will get you started by providing guidelines for effective and efficient writing.

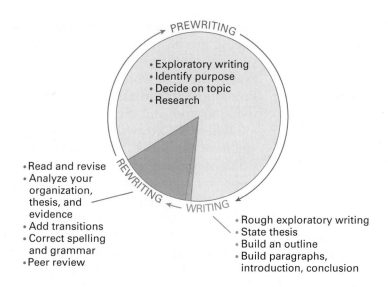

FIGURE 10.2
The Writing Process

STEPS TO GOOD WRITING

One of the more popular ways of thinking about the writing process includes the following steps (see Figure 10.2):

1. **Freewriting.** This step includes preparing to write by filling your mind (and your notebook or laptop) with information from the sources that you found through your research. It is generally considered to be the first stage of exploratory writing.

2. **Writing or drafting.** Transform your less formal exploratory writing into a draft that will eventually become your final paper.

3. **Rewriting or revision.** This step involves polishing your work until it clearly explains what you want to communicate and is ready for your audience.

> ### YOUR TURN
> ....
> **Work Together**
>
> Think about your writing process—and then share it with another student. Do you both use the same process? If not, what can you learn from each other?

STEP ONE: FREEWRITING TO DISCOVER WHAT YOU WANT TO SAY

Also known as prewriting or rehearsing, freewriting is a way to explore a topic. This preliminary step in the writing process involves preparing to write by filling your mind and the page or the screen with information from the sources that you found through your research. Writing expert Peter Elbow asserts that it's impossible to write effectively if you simultaneously try to organize, check grammar and spelling, and offer intelligent thoughts to your readers.[2]

Elbow argues that we can free up our writing and bring more energy and voice into it by writing more like we speak and trying to avoid the heavy overlay of editing in our initial efforts to write. By freewriting, Elbow simply

---

[2]Peter Elbow, *Writing without Teachers*, 2nd ed. (New York: Oxford University Press, 1998).

YOUR TURN

Discuss

Have you tried freewriting before? To see what freewriting feels like, write on this general prompt: important issues on our campus. Write for at least 10 minutes, nonstop, about that statement. Don't think about organization, grammar, punctuation, or spelling, and don't stop writing until the time is up. Discuss with your classmates your reactions to writing this way and what each of you wrote.

means writing without worrying about punctuation, grammar, spelling, and context. In this step you are writing without trying to organize, find exactly the right words, or think about structure. Freewriting is also a way to break the habit of trying to write and edit at the same time.

When you freewrite, you might notice that you have more ideas than can fit into one paper, which is very common. Fortunately, freewriting helps you choose, narrow, and research a topic (see pp. 210–211). It helps you figure out what you really want to say as you make connections between different ideas. When you freewrite, you'll see important issues emerge that you can use as keywords in developing your theme and thesis. Remember that keywords are synonyms, related terms, or subtopics that we use to find materials for our research papers.

STEP TWO: WRITING OR DRAFTING

Once you have completed your research and you and your librarian have exhausted the information sources and ideas, it's time to move to the writing, or drafting, stage. It might be a good idea to begin with a **thesis statement** and an outline so that you can put things where they logically belong. A thesis statement is a short statement that clearly defines the purpose of the paper (see Figure 10.3).

Many people find creating an outline to be a helpful exercise that creates a manageable path from your thesis to your conclusion. See Figure 10.4 for an example. Once you've set the structure for your paper, you then support the sections with analysis and synthesis of your research findings, and you're well on your way to a final draft. Now, with your workable outline and thesis, you can begin to pay attention to the flow of ideas from one sentence to the next and from one paragraph to the next, including subheadings where needed. If you have chosen the thesis

thesis statement
A short statement that clearly defines the purpose of the paper.

FIGURE 10.3

Example of a Thesis Statement

Thesis: Napoleon's dual personality can be explained by examining incidents throughout his life.
1. Explain why I am using the term "dual personality" to describe Napoleon.
2. Briefly comment on his early life and his relationship with his mother.
3. Describe Napoleon's rise to fame from soldier to emperor. Stress the contradictions in his personality and attitudes.
4. Describe the contradictions in his relationship with Josephine.
5. Summarize my thoughts about Napoleon's personality.
6. Possibly conclude by referring to opening question: "Did Napoleon actually have a dual personality?"

FIGURE 10.4

Example of an Outline

An outline is a working document; you do not need a complete outline to begin writing. Note how this outline author has a placeholder for another example; she has not yet decided which example from her research to use.

```
I.    Thesis—Napoleon's dual personality can be explained by examining
      incidents in his life
II.   Dual Personality
          a.  What is it?
          b.  How does it apply to Napoleon
III.  Napoleon's Rise to Fame
          a.  Contradictions in his personality and attitudes
              i.   Relationship with Josephine
              ii.  Example #2 (TBD)
IV.   Summary of my thoughts about Napoleon's personality
V.    Conclusion
          a.  Restate and answer thesis
              i.   Yes, he had a dual personality because:
                   1.  Josephine
                   2.  Example #2
```

carefully, it will help you check to see that each sentence relates to your main idea. When you have completed this stage, you will have the first draft of your paper in hand.

STEP THREE: REWRITING AND REVISING

Next comes the stage at which you take a good piece of writing and do your best to make it great. The essence of good writing is rewriting. You read. You correct. You add smoother transitions. You slash through wordy sentences and paragraphs, removing anything that is repetitive or adds nothing of value to your paper. You substitute stronger words for weaker ones. You double-check spelling and grammar. It also might help to share your paper with one or more of your classmates to get their feedback. You should also check to see if your college provides any writing or editing assistance. Many schools offer a writing center where students can get help during any stage of the writing process: brainstorming, creating a thesis, narrowing a topic, outlining, or polishing that draft. Once you have talked with your reviewers about their suggested changes, you can either accept or reject them. At this point, you are ready to finalize your writing and "publish" (turn in) your paper.

The Importance of Time in the Writing Process.   Many students turn in poorly written papers because they skip the first step (freewriting/prewriting/rehearsing) and last step (rewriting/revision) and make do with the middle one (writing/drafting). The result is often a poorly written assignment, because the best writing is usually done over an extended period of time, not as a last-minute task.

When planning the amount of time that you'll need to write your paper, make sure to factor in enough time for the unexpected. You'll be glad that you left enough time for the following:

- Asking your instructor for clarification on the assignment
- Seeking help from a librarian or from the writing center

- Narrowing or expanding your topic, which might require finding some new sources
- Balancing other school work and commitments
- Dealing with technology problems, knowing that a technology crisis of some degree has happened to us all

Writing for class projects might be a challenge at first. As mentioned, it is important to leave time to visit your institution's writing center both when you are starting to work on your paper and at other times during the writing process. Professional staff and trained peer consultants who work in writing centers are available to help students express their ideas clearly through writing. You can also ask your instructor for examples of papers that have received good grades, and you might show your instructor your writing in progress and explain how the writing center helped you.

KNOW YOUR AUDIENCE

Before you came to college, you probably spent much more time writing informally than writing formally. Think about all the time that you've spent writing e-mails, Facebook and blog comments, text messages, and tweets. Now think about the time that you've spent writing papers for school or work. The informal style that you use in writing an e-mail or text message can become a problem when you try to write a formal research paper. It is important to be aware of when it's OK to be sloppy or use abbreviations and when you have to be meticulous. When you write research papers in college, you should assume that your audience is composed of instructors, researchers, and other serious students, people who will make judgments about your knowledge and abilities based on your writing. It's never OK to be sloppy or casual when writing a formal paper.

Being aware of the differences between formal writing and informal writing will help you build appropriate writing skills for college work. How would you write an e-mail to friends telling them about the

© Radius Images/Corbis

Write, Revise, Repeat

Good writers spend more time editing and revising their written work than they spend writing the original version. Never turn in your first draft; spend the necessary time to reread and improve your work.

volunteer work you did this past weekend? How would you write that same e-mail to a potential employer who might hire you for your first job after college? How would you write about volunteer work in a research paper?

Consider your audience when you make a public presentation of your work. Taking your work from research to writing to delivering it while standing before a group of people is a step you will likely take in your first year of college. You will likely take a course in public speaking soon, or maybe you are already taking one. You need to understand the people that you'll be talking to. Ask yourself the following questions:

- **What do they already know about my topic?** If you're going to give a presentation on the health risks of fast food, you'll want to find out how much your listeners already know about fast food so that you don't risk boring them or wasting their time.

- **What do they want or need to know?** If your presentation will be about fast food and health, how much interest do your listeners have in nutrition? Would they be more interested in some other aspect of college life?

- **Who are my listeners?** What do the members of your audience have in common with you? How are they different from you?

- **What are their attitudes toward me, my ideas, and my topic?** How are your listeners likely to feel about the ideas you are planning to present? For instance, what are their attitudes about fast food?

The final section of this chapter will help you take your work one step further from research to writing and making a speech.

Speaking

What you have learned in this chapter about writing also applies to public speaking: Both are processes that you can learn and master, and each results in a product. The major difference, of course, is that although you write a paper and a speech, you also have to present the speech to an audience. Because many people believe that fear of public speaking ranks up there with fear of death, you might be thinking along these lines: What if I plan, organize, prepare, and rehearse, but calamity strikes anyway? What if my mind goes completely blank, I drop my note cards, or I say something totally embarrassing? Remember that people in your audience have been in your position and will understand your anxiety. Your audience wants you to succeed. Just accentuate the positive, rely on your wit, and keep speaking. Your recovery is what they are most likely to recognize; your success is what they are most likely to remember. The following guidelines can help you improve your speaking skills significantly, including losing your fear of speaking publicly.

GUIDELINES FOR SUCCESSFUL SPEAKING

Just as with writing, there is a process to developing a good speech, and some of the steps mirror those of writing a well-developed essay.

1. **Clarify your objective.** Begin by identifying what you want to accomplish. Do you want to persuade your listeners that your campus needs additional student parking? Do you want to inform your listeners about the student government's accomplishments? What do you want your listeners to know, believe, or do when you are finished?

2. **Analyze your audience.** To understand the people you'll be talking to, ask yourself the following questions (see p. 231): What do they already know about my topic? What do they want or need to know? Who are my listeners? What are their attitudes toward me, my ideas, and my topic?

3. **Organize your presentation.** Now comes the most critical part of the process: building your presentation by selecting and arranging blocks of information. One useful analogy is to think of yourself as guiding your listeners through the maze of ideas that they already have to the new knowledge, attitudes, and beliefs that you would like them to have. You can apply the suggestions from earlier in the chapter for creating an outline for writing to actually composing an outline for a speech.

4. **Choose appropriate visual aids.** You might choose to prepare a chart, show a video clip, write on the board, or distribute handouts. You might also use your computer to prepare overhead transparencies or dynamic PowerPoint presentations. As you select and use your visual aids, consider these rules of thumb:

   > Make visuals easy to follow. Use readable lettering and don't overload your audience by trying to cover too much on one slide.

   > Explain each visual clearly.

   > Allow your listeners enough time to process visuals.

   > Proofread carefully. Misspelled words hurt your credibility as a speaker.

   > Maintain eye contact with your listeners while you discuss the visuals. Don't turn around and address the screen.

   A fancy PowerPoint slideshow can't make up for inadequate preparation or poor delivery skills, but using clear, attractive visual aids can help you organize your material and help your listeners understand what they're hearing. The quality of your visual aids and your skill in using them can contribute to making your presentation effective.

5. **Prepare your notes.** If you are like most speakers, having an entire written copy of your speech in front of you may tempt you to read much of your presentation, but a speech that is read word for word will often sound canned or artificial. A better strategy is to memorize only the introduction and conclusion; then use a minimal outline, carefully prepared, from which you can speak extemporaneously, which means off-the-cuff, spontaneous, or unplanned. You will rehearse thoroughly in advance. Because you are speaking from brief notes, however, your choice of words will be slightly different each time that you give your presentation, with the result that you will sound prepared yet natural. Because you're not reading, you also will be able to maintain eye contact and build rapport with your listeners. You may wish to use note cards because they are unobtrusive. (Be sure to number them in case you accidentally drop the stack on your way to the front of the room.) After you become more experienced, you may want to let your visuals serve as notes. A handout or PowerPoint slide listing key points may also serve as your basic outline. Eventually, you may find that you no longer need notes.

6. **Practice your delivery.** Practice delivery before an audience—a friend, your dog, even the mirror—and use eye contact and smile. Talking to someone or something helps simulate the distraction that listeners cause. As you rehearse, form a mental image of success rather than failure. Practice your presentation aloud several times to harness that energy-producing anxiety. Begin a few days before your target date and continue until you're about to go on stage. Make sure to rehearse aloud, because thinking through your speech and talking through your speech have very different results. Consider making an audio or video recording of yourself to pinpoint your mistakes and reinforce your strengths. If you ask your practice audience to critique you, you'll have some idea of what changes you might make.

7. Pay attention to word choice and pronunciation. As you reread your presentation, make sure that you have used the right words to express your ideas. Get help ahead of time with words that you aren't certain how to pronounce. Try your best to avoid *um, uh, like, you know,* and other distracting fillers.

8. Dress appropriately and give your presentation. Now you're almost ready to give your presentation, but don't forget one last step: Dress appropriately. Leave the baseball cap, the T-shirt, and the tennis shoes at home. You don't have to overdress, but look professional. Experts suggest that your clothes should be a "little nicer" than what your audience is wearing. Some speakers find that when they dress professionally, they deliver a better presentation!

9. Request feedback from someone in your audience. After you have completed your speech, ask a friend or your instructor to give you some honest feedback. If you receive written evaluations from your audience, read them and pay attention to suggestions for ways you can improve.

CHECKLIST FOR SUCCESS

INFORMATION LITERACY AND COMMUNICATION

☐ **Work to learn "information literacy" skills.** These skills include the abilities to find, evaluate, and use information. They are important not only for college but also for your career because you will be working in the information economy, which uses and produces information.

☐ **Become comfortable in your campus library.** Use it as a place to read, relax, study, or just be by yourself.

☐ **Accept that research projects and papers are part of college life.** Learn how to do them well. Doing so will teach you how to "research" the information you need in life after college. After all, modern professional life is one big term paper after another!

☐ **Get to know your college librarians.** They are anxious to help you find the information you need. Ask them for help even if they look busy. If possible, get to know one as your personal "library consultant."

☐ **Take courses early in college that require you to do research and use your library skills.** Yes, these will demand more of you, especially in writing, but you will be thankful for them later. Go ahead, bite the bullet.

☐ **Learn as many new electronic sources as possible.** You must be able to do research and seek the new information you need now and after college by doing more than using Google or Wikipedia.

☐ **When you use the ideas of others, be sure to give them credit; then create your own unique synthesis and conclusions.** Someday you will create your own "intellectual property," and you will want others to give you credit for your ideas.

☐ **Take the time and effort to develop your writing and speaking skills.** Effective writing and speaking are skills for success in college and in life after college. They are skills that employers desire for all employees.

☐ **Understand the differences between formal and informal communication.** When you are in doubt about what's appropriate, use a more formal writing style.

☐ **Learn and practice the three distinct stages of writing.** Freewriting, writing, and rewriting are separate steps. Going through each step will improve the finished product. Ask for feedback on your writing. Accepting criticism and praise will make you a better writer.

☐ **Learn and practice the guidelines for effective speaking.** Clarify your objective, analyze your audience, organize your presentation, choose appropriate visual aids, prepare your notes, and practice delivery. Pay attention to word choice and pronunciation, give your presentation, and request feedback from someone in your audience.

BUILD YOUR EXPERIENCE 1 2 3 4

1 STAY ON TRACK

Successful college students stay focused. They "stay on track." They know what they have to do to be successful, they set goals, and they monitor their progress toward their goals.

Reflect on what you have learned about college success in this chapter and how you are going to apply the chapter information or strategies in college and in your career. List your ideas.

1. _____

_____

_____

2. _____

_____

_____

3. _____

_____

_____

2 ONE-MINUTE PAPER

Did the material in this chapter make you think about libraries, research, and communication in a new light? What did you find to be the most useful information in this chapter? What would you like to learn more about?

3 APPLYING WHAT YOU HAVE LEARNED

Now that you have read and discussed this chapter, consider how you can apply what you have learned to your academic life and your personal life. The following prompts will help you reflect on chapter material and its relevance to you both now and in the future.

1. It is important to get familiar with all the resources in your campus library. Think about a book that you love that was turned into a movie (e.g., *The Lord of the Rings* or the *Harry Potter* series). Search your library catalog to find the print copy. See if the library has it as an audio-book or in a language other than English. Find the DVD and soundtrack in your library's media collection. Take a moment to appreciate what is available at your campus library!

2. The importance of using information literacy skills in college is a no-brainer, but think beyond your college experience. How will improving your information literacy skills help you once you are out of college?

3. Before reading this chapter, had you considered the differences between writing an exam response and writing a blog post or responding to someone on Facebook? Think about the online communications you've had in the last week. Did you send anything that could be misinterpreted? What advice about online communications would you give to other students?

4 BUILDING YOUR PORTFOLIO

In the Know   Reviewing multiple sources of information can help you get the whole story, which is especially important when using the Internet as a research tool. Although the Internet is becoming a primary source of worldwide news, there is no overarching quality control system for information posted on the Internet. Regardless of where you are gathering your information, you need to read with a discerning eye to make sure that the source is credible.

1. Choose a national current event. Carefully read about it in two places:

   a. On your favorite news Web site (e.g., **www.cnn.com**).

   b. In a traditional print national newspaper (e.g., *New York Times, Wall Street Journal,* or *USA Today*). Your campus library will have these national newspapers.

2. In a Word document, compare and contrast the differences in the way the event was portrayed by the two sources.

   Are there clues that the authors are taking a biased stand in reporting? If so, describe these clues.

   Were the authors writing for any reader or specific readers?

   Were the facts presented the same way by both the Internet source and the print source? Explain your answer.

   Were the writers' information sources listed? If so, what were those sources?

3. Save your responses in your portfolio or in the Cloud. Use this process as a tool to make sure that you use valid resources when you do research.

For more on this topic watch
French Fries Are Not Vegetables and Other College Lessons

WHERE TO GO FOR HELP . . .

ON CAMPUS

> **Your Instructor** Talk to your instructor after class, drop by during office hours, or make a one-on-one appointment. Check with your instructors to make sure that you understand their expectations for any writing, speaking, or researching assignments.

> **Library** Go to the library! Check out the library Web site or ask about a calendar of upcoming events. Many libraries have drop-in classes or workshops to help you learn specific skills. Head over to the reference desk and talk with a librarian about an assignment that you are working on.

> **Specialized Libraries and Collections** Review your library's Web site to see how many separate libraries are on your campus. Make it a point to visit them all. If there is a library specific to your major, such as business, medicine, or music, make that one your first stop.

> **Technology Support Centers** *Everyone* faces some sort of computer crisis in their life. It seems that so many of these are just before a deadline for a major paper. Prepare yourself! Check out your school's technology support services *before* you need them. Attend an orientation, chat with help-desk staff, and review their Web site so that you know where to go when you're in crisis mode.

> **Writing Center** Most campuses have one. Frequently, it is found within the English department.

> **Discipline-Based Courses** Always keep one step ahead and have your eye on the future. Check for upper-division courses that will help you practice and hone your information literacy, research writing, and speaking skills. Review your course catalog early and often to make sure that you have all the prerequisites needed to get into these helpful classes.

ONLINE

> Research and documenting sources: **http://owl .english.purdue.edu/owl/resource/584/02**. Purdue University has an excellent resource on documenting sources, both print and electronic.

> Writing tips: **http://clas.uiowa.edu/history /teaching-and-writing-center/guides**. The University of Iowa's History Department offers help on common writing mistakes.

> **Plain Language** Have you ever been confused by government jargon? Here's a guide to writing user-friendly documents for federal employees: **http:// www.plainlanguage.gov.**

MY INSTITUTION'S RESOURCES

_____

_____

_____

_____

_____

_____

_____

_____

11 Diversity

> ❝ Diversity is like a salad of people . . . mixed well.

> Olivia Castilla, 19, Undecided major
> Simone Hisakawa, 20, Graphic Design major
> Darrell Stiehl, 25, Sociology major
> Leticia Turner, 19, Computer Science major
> Wei Zhan, 21, Marine Biology major
> Florida Atlantic University

Diversity can mean many things to many people. For the purposes of introducing this chapter, we spoke to a number of students about their personal experiences with the topic. We started at Florida Atlantic University in Boca Raton, Florida, and asked five students to tell us about themselves, where they were from, why they decided to attend college, and how diversity has played a part in their lives, both in college and elsewhere.

The students range in ages from nineteen to twenty-five and grew up in New Zealand, the state of Florida (among other places), China, New York City, and Mexico City. Most of the students chose Florida Atlantic University because of its numerous academic opportunities and diverse community. Leticia is the first person in her family to attend college, and she explains, "The reason I decided to go to college was to ensure a better

Florida Atlantic University Students ▶

Sam Edwards/Getty Images

future for myself and set a good example for my younger sister." Some of the students are adjusting to life in America for the first time, while others were born and raised here. Being an international student and living far away from his family was a tough transition for Wei, but he says that "despite the challenges, the opportunity to meet and interact with students from diverse backgrounds has been enriching for me personally and academically." Some came to Florida Atlantic straight from high school, while others are returning to college after a break. The list of differences could go on and on, but each of them brings his or her own unique experience to Florida Atlantic, and each strives to learn about the differences and similarities among them.

We asked the students to talk a bit about diversity and how it has played a part in their education. Darrell believes that it is important to seek out other people and other opinions. He says, "Your view in life is one of billions. Get to know what your peers' thoughts are!" Leticia, Olivia, and Simone emphasize getting involved on campus so that you can learn to work with many people toward a common goal. As Simone puts it, "Diversity brings language skills, new ways of thinking, and creative solutions to different problems." Leticia mentions joining a summer program called Jumpstart that had participants from all different backgrounds. She says, "We worked together to reach our common goal, and when we were successful, it was as a group." Wei adds, "I learned so much from working with [one group] that I started to appreciate my own heritage." Darrell reminds us that diversity is international, adding, "The Internet and improved transportation mean that contact between countries is increasing. Diversity is various people, various skins, various backgrounds, various beliefs, various philosophies, and various cultures. Learning about diversity equals learning people skills." Olivia sums it all up: "Diversity is like a salad of people . . . mixed well."

These Florida Atlantic students had a great deal to say about diversity as shown by all the wonderful responses you've just read.

As demonstrated by the diverse group profiled here, a college or university serves as a microcosm of the real world, a world that requires us all to work, live, and socialize with people from various ethnic and cultural groups. In few settings do members of ethnic and cultural groups interact in such close proximity to one another as they do on a college campus. Whether you are attending a four-year university or a community college, you will be exposed to new experiences and opportunities, all of which can enhance learning and understanding.

Through self-assessment, discovery, and open-mindedness, you can begin to understand your perspectives on diversity. This work, although difficult at times, will intensify your educational experiences, personal growth, and development. Thinking critically about your personal values and belief systems will allow you to have a greater sense of belonging and make a positive contribution to our multicultural society.

YOUR TURN

Discuss

Look around your classroom. What kinds of diversity do you see? What other kinds of diversity might exist but can't be seen? Discuss with a classmate reasons some college students have an interest in diversity, both seen and unseen, and why other students avoid the topic. Share your ideas with the whole class.

◢ **ASSESSING YOUR STRENGTHS** ▮▮▮▮▮▮▮▮

Your college or university campus has many opportunities for you to experience diversity. Through classes, clubs, and informal interactions, you will likely have experiences that enable you to explore diverse ideas or people who are from different countries, cultures, or religions. As you begin to read this chapter, list specific examples of the ways that you've already experienced new ideas and people who are different from you.

_____

_____

_____

_____

_____

◢ **SETTING GOALS** ▮▮▮▮▮▮▮▮

What are your most important objectives in learning the material in this chapter? Think about the challenges that you've had in the past in the area of diversity and write down three goals for the future (e.g., I will take a course that is part of the "diversity curriculum" next semester; I will ask my academic adviser for help in choosing the course).

1. _____

_____

2. _____

_____

3. _____

_____

Understanding Diversity and the Source of Our Beliefs

Diversity is the variation in social and cultural identities among people living together. **Multiculturalism** is the active process of acknowledging and respecting social groups, cultures, religions, races, ethnicities, attitudes, and opinions. As your journey through higher education unfolds, you will find yourself immersed in this mixture of identities. Regardless of the size of the institution, going to college brings together people who have differing backgrounds and experiences but similar goals and aspirations. Each person brings to campus a unique combination of life story, upbringing, value system, view of the world, and set of judgments. Familiarizing yourself with such differences can greatly enhance your experiences in the classes you will take, the organizations you will join, and the relationships you will cultivate. For many students, college is the first time they have been exposed to so much diversity. Learning experiences and challenges await you both in and

diversity Variations in social and cultural identities among people living together.

multiculturalism The active process of acknowledging and respecting the diverse social groups, cultures, religions, races, ethnicities, attitudes, and opinions within a community.

outside the classroom. College provides opportunities to learn not only about others but also about yourself.

Many of our beliefs grow out of personal experience and reinforcement. If you have had a negative experience or endured a series of incidents involving members of a particular group, you're more likely to develop **stereotypes**, or negative judgments, about people in that group than if you haven't had such experiences. Or maybe you have heard repeatedly that everyone associated with a particular group behaves in a certain way, and you might have bought into that stereotype without even thinking about it. Children who grow up in an environment in which dislike and distrust of certain types of people are openly expressed might agree with those very judgments even if they have had no direct interaction with those being judged.

In college you might encounter beliefs about diversity that run counter to your basic values. When your friendships with others are affected by differing values, tolerance is generally a good goal. Talking about diversity with someone else whose beliefs seem to conflict with your own can be very rewarding. Your goal in this kind of discussion is not to reach agreement, but to enhance your understanding of why people see diversity differently, why some seem to flee

stereotype An over-simplified set of assumptions about another person or group.

YOUR TURN

Think about It

Think back to the earliest messages you received from family members about how you should react to people who are different from you. Which messages still affect your behavior? Which messages have you revised?

Jonathan Stark

Expand Your Worldview

How has coming to college changed your experience with diversity? Are you getting to know people of different races or ethnic groups? Do your classes have both traditional-aged and older students? Colleges and universities can be a microcosm of our world. Make it a point to seek out people who are different from you and share your personal stories and worldviews with each other.

from it but others allow experiences with diversity to enrich their college experience.

Before coming to college, you might never have coexisted with most of the groups you now see on campus. Your home community might not have been very diverse, although possibly it seemed so before you reached campus. In college you have the opportunity to learn from many kinds of people. From your roommate in the residence hall to your lab partner in your biology class to the members of your sociology study group, your college experience will be enriched if you allow yourself to be open to the possibility of learning from members of all cultural groups.

When you think about diversity, you might first think of differences in race or ethnicity. Although it is true that those are two forms of diversity, you will most likely experience many other types of diversity in college and in the workplace, including age, religion, physical ability, learning ability, sexual orientation, gender, and economic status.

ETHNICITY, CULTURE, RACE, AND RELIGION

Often the words *ethnicity* and *culture* are used interchangeably, although their definitions are quite distinct. Throughout this chapter we will use these two terms together and in isolation. Before we start using them, it's a good idea to learn their definitions so that you're clear on what they actually mean.

Ethnicity refers to the identity that is assigned to a specific group of people who are historically connected by a common national origin or language. For example, let's look at one of the largest ethnic groups, Latinos. Latin America encompasses more than thirty countries within North America, Central America, and South America, all of which share the Spanish language. A notable exception is Brazil, but even though the national language is Portuguese, Brazilians are considered Latinos (both Spanish and Portuguese are languages that evolved from Latin). The countries also share many traditions and beliefs, with some variations, but we shouldn't generalize. Not every Latino who speaks Spanish is of Mexican descent, and not every Latino speaks Spanish. Acknowledging that differences exist within ethnic groups is a big step in becoming ethnically aware.

Culture is defined as those aspects of a group of people that are passed on or learned. Traditions, food, language, clothing styles, artistic expression, and beliefs are all part of culture. Certainly, ethnic groups are also cultural groups; they share a language, foods, traditions, art, and clothing, which are passed from one generation to the next. Numerous other, nonethnic cultural groups can fit this concept of culture, too. Think of the hip-hop community, in which a common style of dress, specific terminology, and distinct forms of musical and artistic expression also constitute a culture but not an ethnicity.

Although we don't use the term *race* often in this chapter, it's important to understand this word as it is commonly used in everyday language. **Race** refers to biological characteristics that are shared by groups of people, including

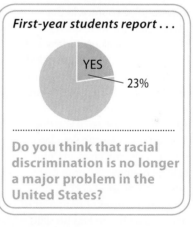

First-year students report . . .

YES

23%

Do you think that racial discrimination is no longer a major problem in the United States?

ethnicity An affiliation assigned to a specific group of people historically connected by a common national heritage or language.

culture The aspects of a group of people that are passed on or learned. Traditions, food, language, clothing styles, artistic expression, and beliefs are all part of culture.

race A term that refers to biological characteristics shared by groups of people, including skin tone, hair texture and color, and facial features.

skin tone, hair texture and color, and facial features. Making generalizations about someone's racial group affiliation is risky. Even people who share some biological features—such as similar eye shape or dark skin—might be ethnically very distinct. For instance, people of Asian descent are not necessarily ethnically and culturally alike because Asia is a vast region encompassing such disparate places as Mongolia, India, and Japan. Likewise, people of African descent come from very different backgrounds; the African continent is home to more than fifty countries and hundreds of different languages, and Africans are genetically very diverse. More and more individuals today, including President Barack Obama, describe themselves as multiracial. You might meet fellow students whose families include parents, grandparents, and great-grandparents of several different racial groups.

We come into the world with our own unique characteristics—aspects of our physical appearance and personalities that make us who we are—but people around the world have one attribute in common: We want to be respected even if we are different from others in some ways. Whatever the color of your skin or hair, whatever your life experiences or cultural background, you will want others to treat you fairly and acknowledge and value your contribution to your communities and the world. Of course, others will also want the same from you.

Diversity of religion has been central to the American experience since the country's colonial origins. In fact, many settlers of the original thirteen colonies came to North America to escape religious persecution. Religious diversity might or might not have been obvious in your hometown or neighborhood, but unless you are attending an institution that enrolls only students of one religious sect, you will find religious diversity to be part of your college experience. Religious denominations might sponsor campus centers or organizations, and students' religious affiliations might determine their dress, attitudes, or avoidance of certain behaviors. While you are in college, your openness to religious diversity will add to your understanding of the many ways in which people are different from one another.

> ### Is This You?
>
> Are you a student who has recently come to the United States from another country? Perhaps you have immigrated to the United States with family members, or perhaps you immigrated on your own. Whatever your particular situation, learning the unique language, culture, and expectations of a United States college or university can be a challenge, especially if your primary language is not English. You might find that instructors' expectations seem different from what you experienced in your home country. In the United States, instructors want students to speak up in class and work in groups. You will also find that American students will sometimes challenge their instructors in ways that might seem disrespectful to you. Even if you don't feel comfortable with your language skills, don't give up. Your college or university probably offers English as a Second Language courses or programs to help you with your English skills. Also, visit the international student office or center to investigate ways to increase your understanding of life in the United States, both on and off campus.

AGE

Although many students enter college around age eighteen, others choose to enter or return in their thirties and beyond. According to a 2009 report, more than 38 percent of American college students were twenty-five years of age or older. Age diversity in the classroom gives everyone the opportunity to learn from others who have different life experiences. All kinds of factors determine when students enter higher education for the first time or stop and then reenter. Therefore, when considering the age of a college student, there is no such thing as "normal." If you are attending a college that has a large number of students who are older (or younger) than you, view this as an advantage for learning. A campus where younger and older students learn together can be much more interesting than a campus where everyone is the same age.

> ## YOUR TURN
> ### Write and Reflect
>
> Brainstorm in a small group how you might meet some older people on campus or in your community. Plan to meet and interview an older person about his or her experiences in college or in life after college, and write a journal entry about the meeting.

LEARNING AND PHYSICAL ABILITIES

Although the majority of students have reasonably average learning and physical abilities, the number of students with physical and learning disabilities is rising on most college campuses, as are the services that are available to them. Physical disabilities can include deafness, blindness, paralysis, or a mental disorder. Also, many students have some form of learning disability (see Chapter 4) that makes college work a challenge.

People with physical and learning disabilities want to be treated just as you would treat anyone else: with respect. If a student with a disability is in your class, treat him or her as you would any student. Overzealousness to help might be seen as an expression of pity.

If you have, or think you might have, a learning disability, consult your campus learning center for a diagnosis and advice on compensating for learning problems. Most campuses have a special office to serve students with both physical and learning disabilities.

GENDER

The words *gender* and *sex* are often used interchangeably, but as you become part of an academic community, you will start to think differently about terms and ideas you've always known. Generally speaking, *sex* is used when discussing someone's biological makeup, whereas *gender* refers to the things a person says, does, or wears that help display to the world what the person's gender is. While *sex* is often thought of as either male or female, *gender* is generally understood as a continuum consisting of many different ways of identifying oneself.

> ## YOUR TURN
> ### Write and Reflect
>
> Make a list of the careers or occupations that you are considering. Would anyone try to tell you that one or more of them are "inappropriate" because you are male or female? Write a persuasive statement that you could use to argue that gender should not narrow life choices or options.

While in college, make friends with all kinds of people, avoid stereotyping what is "appropriate" for one group or another, and don't limit your own interests. Although sexism is still present in today's world, there is almost no activity or profession that isn't legally open to everyone, regardless of gender. If your school has a gender studies department, consider taking a course. Gender studies courses are generally interdisciplinary and look at subject matter from the perspective of gender. These classes aren't necessarily about women or men; rather, they consider how the concept of gender influences the way we see and shape the world around us. Such a course could open up new ways of thinking about many aspects of your world.

SEXUALITY

One's sexuality relates to the people to whom you are romantically attracted. You have probably heard the words *gay, straight, homosexual, heterosexual,* and *bisexual* before, but sexuality includes many other categories as well. In college you will likely meet students, staff members, and professors who have sexualities other than your own. Although some people are lucky enough to come from welcoming and affirming environments, for many students college is the first time that they have been able to openly express their sexual identity. The subject of sexual orientation can be difficult to talk about, and it is important that you respect all individuals. Most colleges and universities have campus codes or standards of behavior to help ensure safety and a free exchange of ideas regardless of race, ethnicity, gender, or sexual orientation. Check to see if your campus has a gender and sexuality center or a center for the gay, lesbian, bisexual, or transgendered (GLBT or LGBT) community. Go see some speakers and expand your worldview.

ECONOMIC STATUS

The United States is a country of vast differences in wealth. This considerable economic diversity can be both a positive and a negative aspect of college life. As a positive, you will be exposed to, and can learn from, students who present you with a wide range of economic differences. Assuming that you meet and become friends with students who are more or less affluent than you, you may have some special opportunities for growth, learning, sharing, and friendship that were not available in your secondary school or neighborhood. After all, college is one of the last melting pots left in the United States! On the other hand, you may feel distant from students whose financial circumstances are different from yours.

Try to avoid the natural tendency to segregate yourself into a group of people with similar economic means. We urge you to make the most of economic differences and seek them out. This experience is all part of going to college and learning how to live in a democracy that embraces all different backgrounds.

One of the best things about college is that it provides a level playing field: Everyone can excel, regardless of family background and wealth. All students can succeed if they practice the college success strategies taught in this text. What matters is what you do with the opportunities that college provides.

The bottom line is to not be distracted by an increased awareness of economic diversity. Try to avoid developing exaggerated feelings of superiority or inferiority. What matters now is not what you had or didn't have before you came to college; what matters is what you do in college. You have more in common with other students than you think. Your individual efforts, aspirations, courage, determination, and ability to stay focused will enable you to transcend the boundaries of income and social class in the United States.

Seeking Diversity on Campus

Acknowledging the importance of diversity to education, colleges and universities have begun to take the concepts of diversity and apply them to student learning opportunities. We see these steps in efforts by colleges to embrace an **inclusive curriculum**. Today you can find courses with a diversity focus, and many of them meet graduation requirements. The college setting is ideal for promoting education about diversity because it allows students and faculty of varying backgrounds to come together for the common purpose of learning and critical thinking.

inclusive curriculum
A curriculum that offers courses that introduce students to diverse people, worldviews, and approaches.

According to Gloria Ameny-Dixon, education about diversity can do the following:

- Increase problem-solving skills through different perspectives applied to reaching solutions
- Increase positive relationships through the achievement of common goals, respect, appreciation, and commitment to equality
- Decrease stereotyping and prejudice through contact and interaction with diverse individuals
- Promote the development of a more in-depth view of the world[1]

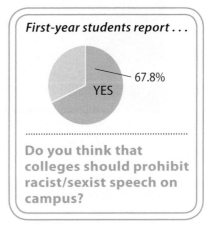

First-year students report . . .

67.8% YES

Do you think that colleges should prohibit racist/sexist speech on campus?

Be it religious affiliation, sexual orientation, gender, ethnicity, age, culture, economic status, or ability, your campus provides the opportunity to interact with and learn alongside a kaleidoscope of individuals.

THE CURRICULUM

College students have led the movement for a curriculum that reflects disenfranchised groups such as women, people of color, the elderly, the disabled, gays, lesbians, bisexuals, and the transgendered. By protesting, students have demanded the hiring of more instructors from different ethnic groups, the creation of Ethnic Studies departments, and a variety of initiatives designed to support diverse students academically and socially. Included are multicultural centers, women's resource centers, enabling services, and numerous academic support programs.

In almost all colleges and universities, you will be required to take some general education courses that will expose you to a wide range of topics and issues. We hope that you will include a course or two with a multicultural basis in your schedule. Such courses can provide you with new perspectives and an understanding of issues that affect your fellow students and community members. They can also affect you, possibly in ways you had not considered. Just as your

[1] Gloria M. Ameny-Dixon, "Why Multicultural Education Is More Important in Higher Education Now Than Ever: A Global Perspective," McNeese State University, http://www .nationalforum.com.

Commit to Coexist

In a college or university environment, students often learn that there are more commonalities than differences between themselves and others who have been on the opposite side of the fence for centuries. By learning to coexist respectfully and peacefully, students can take the first step toward building a better world.

Jamie Smith/http://futilephotographer.wordpress.com

college or university campus is diverse, so too is the workforce you will be entering. A multicultural education can improve the quality of your entire life.

STUDENT-RUN ORGANIZATIONS

Student-run organizations can provide multiple avenues to express ideas, pursue interests, and cultivate relationships. According to our definition of culture, all student-run organizations provide an outlet for the promotion and celebration of a culture. Let's take, for instance, a Muslim Student Union and an Animation Club and apply the components of culture to them. Both groups promote a belief system that is common among their members: The first is based on religious beliefs, and the second is based on animation as an art form. Both have aspects that can be taught: the teachings of the Muslim faith and the rules and techniques used in drawing. Both groups use a specific language related to the group's belief system. Most campus organizations bring like-minded students together and are open to anyone who wants to become involved.

To promote learning and discovery not only inside the classroom but outside as well, colleges and universities provide programming that highlights ethnic and cultural celebrations, such as Chinese New Year and Kwanzaa; gender-related activities, such as Take Back the Night; and a broad range of entertainment, including concerts and art exhibits. These events expose you to new and exciting ideas and viewpoints, enhancing your education and challenging your current views.

FRATERNITIES AND SORORITIES

Fraternities and sororities provide a quick connection to other individuals and a link to the social pipeline, camaraderie, and support. These organizations differ in their philosophies and commitment to philanthropy. Some are committed to community service; others are more socially oriented. Fraternities and sororities created by and for specific ethnic groups, such as Nu Alpha Kappa Fraternity and Sigma Omicron Pi Sorority, have existed for years and were developed by students of color who wanted campus groups that allowed them to connect to their communities and cultures. Such organizations have provided many students with a means to become familiar with their campus as well as gain friendships and support while promoting their cultures and ethnicities.

CAREER/MAJOR GROUPS

You can also explore diversity through your major and career interests. Groups that focus on a specific field of study can be great assets as you explore your interests. Are you interested in helping minority and majority groups interact more effectively? Consider majoring in sociology or social work. Do you want to learn more about human behavior? Study psychology. If you join a club that is affiliated with the major that interests you, not only will you find out more about the major, but you can also make contacts in the field that could lead to career options.

POLITICAL/ACTIVIST ORGANIZATIONS

Adding to the diversity mix on campuses are organizations devoted to specific political affiliations and causes, such as Campus Republicans, Young Democrats, Amnesty International, and Native Students in Social Action. These organizations contribute to the diversity of ideas and provide debating events and forums to address current issues and events.

SPECIAL-INTEREST GROUPS

Perhaps the largest subgroup of student organizations is the special-interest category, which encompasses everything from recreational interests to hobbies. On your campus you might find special-interest clubs such as the Brazilian Jujitsu Club, the Kite Flyers' Club, the Flamenco Club, and the Video Gamers' Society. Students can cultivate an interest in bird watching or indulge their curiosity about ballroom dance without ever leaving campus. If a club for your special interest is not available, create one yourself.

Discrimination, Prejudice, and Insensitivity on College Campuses

You might feel uncomfortable when asked about your views of diversity. We all have **biases** against certain groups or value systems, yet it is what we do with our individual beliefs that separates the average person from the racist, the bigot, and the extremist.

Unfortunately, some individuals opt not to seek education for the common good but instead respond negatively to groups that differ from their own. Documented acts of **discrimination** and **prejudice** on campuses span the country. You might be shocked to hear that these acts of violence, intimidation, and stupidity occur on campuses, when the assumption is that college students are "supposed to be above that."

bias The tendency to hold a certain perspective when there are valid alternatives.

discrimination The act of treating people differently because of their race, ethnicity, gender, socioeconomic class, or other identifying characteristics rather than on their merits.

prejudice A preconceived judgment or opinion of someone based not on facts or knowledge, such as prejudging someone based entirely on his or her skin color.

RAISING AWARENESS

At a midwestern university, students arrived on campus to find racial slurs and demeaning images aimed at various ethnic groups spray-painted on the walls of the multicultural center. In the wake of the terrorist attacks on the World Trade Center and the Pentagon in September 2001, many students of Middle Eastern descent were subjected to both violence and intimidation because of their ancestry.

Although such actions are deliberate and hateful, others occur out of a lack of common sense. Consider a campus party to celebrate Cinco de Mayo. Party organizers asked everyone to wear sombreros. On arrival, guests encountered a mock-up of a border patrol station on the front lawn and were required to crawl under or climb over a section of chain-link fencing. Student groups voiced their disapproval over such insensitivity, which resulted in campus probationary measures for the organization that had thrown the party. At a Halloween party at a large university, members of a campus organization decided to dress in Ku Klux Klan outfits while other members dressed as slaves and wore black shoe polish on their faces. The group then simulated slave hangings during the party. When photos of the events surfaced, the university suspended the group from campus, and the community demanded that the group be banned indefinitely.

For a number of years stereotypes that are used to identify school sports teams and their supporters have disturbed ethnic and cultural groups such as Native Americans. Mascots that incorporate a bow and arrow, a tomahawk, feathers, and war paint have raised awareness about the promotion and acceptance of stereotypes associated with the concept of the "savage Indian." Some schools have responded by altering the images while retaining the mascot. Other schools have changed their mascots altogether.

Colleges and universities are working to ensure that a welcoming and inclusive campus environment awaits all students, both current and prospective. Campus resources and centers focus on acknowledging and supporting the diverse student population. Campus administrations have established policies against any and all forms of discriminatory actions, racism, and insensitivity, and many campuses have adopted zero-tolerance policies that prohibit verbal and nonverbal harassment, intimidation, and violence. Find out what resources are available on your campus to protect you and other students from discriminatory and racist behavior and what steps your college or university takes to promote the understanding of diversity and multiculturalism. If you have been a victim of a racist, insensitive, or discriminatory act, report it to the proper authorities.

> ### YOUR TURN
>
> ·······································
>
> #### Discuss
>
> Think back on your life. Can you recall an occasion when you were harassed for any reason or when you witnessed harassment? Discuss the event with a classmate, how it made you feel, and how you reacted.

WHAT YOU CAN DO TO FIGHT HATE ON CAMPUS

Hate crimes, regardless of where they occur, should be taken very seriously. A hate crime is any prejudicial activity and can include physical assault, vandalism, and intimidation. One of the most common forms of hate crime on campus is graffiti that expresses racial, ethnic, and cultural slurs.

Whatever form these crimes might take on your campus, it is important to examine your thoughts and feelings about their occurrence. The most important question to ask yourself is: Will you do something about it, or do you think that it is someone else's problem? If you or a group to which you belong is the target of the hate crime, you might be compelled to take a stand and speak out against the incident, but what if the target is not a group you associate with? Will you feel strongly enough to express your discontent with the actions that are taken? Or will you think that it is the problem only of the targeted group?

Many students, whether or not they were directly targeted in a hate crime, find strength in unity, forming action committees and making it clear that hate crimes will not be ignored or tolerated. In most cases, instead of dividing students, hate crimes bring students together to work toward denouncing hate. It is important not to respond to prejudice and hate crimes with violence. It is more effective to unite with fellow students, faculty, staff, campus police, and administrators to address the issue and educate the greater campus community.

How can you get involved? Work with existing campus services such as campus police and the multicultural center as well as faculty and administration to plan and host educational opportunities, such as training sessions, workshops, and symposiums centered on diversity, sensitivity, and multiculturalism. Organize an antidiscrimination event on campus in which campus and community leaders address the issues and provide solutions. Join prevention programs to come up with ideas to battle hate crimes on campus or in the community. Finally, look into the antidiscrimination measures your college is employing. Do you think that they need updating or revising?

Just because you or your particular group has not been targeted in a hate crime doesn't mean that you should do nothing. Commit to becoming involved in making your campus a safe place for students with diverse views, lifestyles, languages, politics, religions, and interests to come together and learn. If nothing happens to make it clear that hate crimes on campus will not be tolerated, it's anyone's guess as to who will be the next target.

CHALLENGE YOURSELF TO EXPERIENCE DIVERSITY

Diversity enriches us all. Allowing yourself to become more culturally aware and more open to differing viewpoints will help you become a truly educated person. Understanding the value of working with others and the importance of an open mind will enhance your educational and career goals and provide gratifying

Yellow Dog Productions/Photodisc/Getty Images

The Power to Vote

Elected officials know who votes. If you want those who represent you in government to consider the issues that are important to you, communicate with them by voting. Whether it is legislation related to hate crime, credit card reform, or interest rates on student loans, voice your opinion with your vote.

TECH TIP THE CASE FOR VOLUNTEERING

Al Diaz/Miami Herald/MCT via Getty Images

1 ▶ THE PROBLEM

You need to build your résumé, explore career options, and broaden your horizons (and maybe save the world).

2 ▶ THE FIX

Roll up your sleeves and volunteer in an area that interests you.

3 ▶ HOW TO DO IT

Volunteering is about doing something you care about and gaining experience, but it's also about opening your mind. Here are a few of the pluses:

1. You'll get to go to interesting places and do important work. Opportunities to volunteer can involve traveling and experiences that you've never had.

2. You'll learn to appreciate diversity. If you're like many college students, you may have led a relatively sheltered life. Volunteer work tests you in new ways and in new situations. It puts you in touch with lots of different people from different backgrounds. It also helps you connect with your community and the rest of the world on a deeper level.

3. Some volunteer positions let you travel internationally. Volunteer abroad and you'll probably get to polish your foreign language skills.

4. You'll gain valuable experience that could help you in your career. Volunteering adds depth to your résumé. Even if you volunteer close to home, you'll learn new skills and might discover talents that you didn't know you had. You might even make some useful networking contacts.

5. Volunteering will help you become a happier, more fascinating, and less self-absorbed person. Studies show that helping others actually lowers your stress levels.

6. Need more motivation? Employers say that applicants who do volunteer work stand out from the pack. Being socially responsible tells the world that you're ambitious and a good team player.

GOOD TO KNOW

You can find rewarding volunteer opportunities in almost every field you can imagine: animal welfare, agriculture, the arts, education, the environment, fair trade, health care, human rights, politics, technology, you name it. Here is a list of national and international volunteer organizations to get you on your way:

Amigos de las Americas	amigoslink.org
AmeriCorps	americorps.gov
Directory on International Voluntary Service	avso.org
Child Family Health International	cfhi.org
Cross-Cultural Solutions	crossculturalsolutions.org
Corporation for National and Community Service	cncs.gov
Earthwatch Worldwide	earthwatch.org
Foundation for Sustainable Development	fsdinternational.org
Idealist.org: Action Without Borders	idealist.org
International Partnership for Service Learning	ipsl.org
International Volunteer Programs Association (IVPA)	volunteerinternational.org
Peace Corps	peacecorps.gov
Projects Abroad	projects-abroad.org
South American Explorers Volunteer Opportunities	saexplorers.org
Teach for America	teachforamerica.org
Volunteer Match	volunteermatch.com
Volunteers for Peace	vfp.org

PERSONAL BEST

What types of volunteer activities interest you most? List five here:

_____

_____

_____

_____

_____

_____

experiences, both on and off campus. Making the decision to become active in your multicultural education will require you to be active and sometimes step out of your comfort zone. There are many ways to become more culturally aware, including a variety of opportunities on your campus. Look into what cultural programming is being offered throughout the school year. From concerts to films, from guest speakers to information tables, you might not have to go far to gain additional insight into the value of diversity.

During his first inaugural address, President Obama reiterated the value of diversity:

> For we know that our patchwork heritage is a strength, not a weakness. We are a nation of Christians and Muslims, Jews and Hindus, and non-believers. We are shaped by every language and culture, drawn from every end of this earth; and because we have tasted the bitter swill of civil war and segregation, and emerged from that dark chapter stronger and more united, we cannot help but believe that the old hatreds shall someday pass; that the lines of tribe shall soon dissolve; that as the world grows smaller, our common humanity shall reveal itself; and that America must play its role in ushering in a new era of peace.

Challenge yourself to learn about various groups in and around your community, both at school and at home. These two settings might differ ethnically and culturally, giving you an opportunity to develop the skills you need to function in and adjust to a variety of settings. Attend events and celebrations outside of your regular groups. Whether they are in the general community or on campus, it is a good way to see and hear traditions that are specific to the groups being represented. Exposing yourself to new experiences through events and celebrations can be gratifying. You can also become active in your own learning by making time for travel. Seeing the world and its people can be an uplifting experience. Finally, when in doubt, ask. If you do so in a tactful, genuine way, most people will be happy to share information about their viewpoints, traditions, and history. It is only through allowing ourselves to grow that we really learn.

CHECKLIST FOR SUCCESS

DIVERSITY

☐ **Know that successful college students have strong skills in understanding, appreciating, and embracing diversity.** Most employers now hold these skills as an expectation, too. It is just good business.

☐ **Use college as the ideal environment to learn about people who are different from you.** Practice acknowledging and respecting other people, even if you don't agree with them.

☐ **Use college to help you improve your understanding of the dynamics of diversity.** You can and should study, in both the curriculum and the co-curriculum, diversity of people and diversity of ideas.

☐ **Be alert for examples of racism and discrimination.** College is a microcosm of our society. You may therefore see examples of discrimination, prejudice, and insensitivity on your campus. Become aware of what you can do to combat hate on campus.

☐ **Don't fear diversity.** The best students allow themselves to break out of their comfort zones and be challenged by new people and new experiences.

BUILD YOUR EXPERIENCE 1 2 3 4

1 STAY ON TRACK

Successful college students stay focused. They "stay on track." They know what they have to do to be successful, they set goals, and they monitor their progress toward their goals.

Reflect on what you have learned about college success in this chapter and how you are going to apply the chapter information or strategies in college and in your career. List your ideas.

1. _____

   _____

   _____

2. _____

   _____

   _____

3. _____

   _____

   _____

2 ONE-MINUTE PAPER

One aspect of a liberal arts education is learning about differences in cultures, races, and other groups. Were there any ideas in this chapter that influenced your personal opinions, viewpoints, or values? Was there anything that you disagreed with or found unsettling?

3 APPLYING WHAT YOU HAVE LEARNED

Now that you have read and discussed this chapter, consider how you can apply what you have learned to your academic life and your personal life. The following prompts will help you reflect on the chapter material and its relevance to you both now and in the future.

1. Use your print or online campus course catalog to identify courses that focus on topics of multiculturalism and diversity. Why do you think that academic departments have included these issues in the curriculum? How would studying diversity and multiculturalism help you prepare for different academic fields?

2. Reflecting on our personal identities and values is a step to increase self-awareness. Read and answer the following questions to the best of your ability:

   How do you identify and express yourself ethnically and culturally?

   Are there practices or beliefs in your culture to which you have difficulty subscribing? If so, what are they? Why do you have difficulty accepting these beliefs?

   What aspects of your identity do you truly enjoy?

4 BUILDING YOUR PORTFOLIO

It's a Small World after All!   The concepts of diversity, ethnicity, culture, and multiculturalism have been explored in this chapter. Reading about these controversial topics is one thing, but really stepping into someone else's shoes is another. Study-abroad and student-exchange programs are excellent ways of adding new perspectives to your college experience.
   Consider the possibilities:

1. Visit your institution's International Programs/Study Abroad office or, if you are at a college that does not have a study-abroad program, search for study-abroad opportunities on the Web. Tip: Look for the Center for Global Education (**http://globaled.us/**), the Council on International Education Exchange (**http://www.ciee.org**), or the International Partnership for Service Learning (**http://www.ipsl.org**). Using a major or career that interests you, think about how you might spend time abroad to gain experience in your major field.

2. On the basis of your research, create a PowerPoint presentation to share with your class that outlines the opportunities to study abroad or participate in an exchange program.
   - Describe the steps students need to take at your campus to include a study-abroad trip in their college plan (e.g., whom to contact, financial aid, the best time to study abroad, how to earn course credit).
   - Describe the benefits of studying abroad, and include photos of the country or countries that you would like to visit.
   - Include information about your current or intended major and career and how a study-abroad or exchange trip would fit into your plans.
   - Reference Web links that you found useful in preparing your presentation.

3. Save your presentation in your portfolio or in the Cloud.

For more on this topic watch
French Fries Are Not Vegetables and Other College Lessons

WHERE TO GO FOR HELP . . .

ON CAMPUS

> Most college and university campuses take an active role in promoting diversity. In the effort to ensure a welcoming and supportive environment for all students, institutions have established offices, centers, and resources to provide students with educational opportunities, academic guidance, and support networks. Look into the availability of the following resources on your campus, and visit one or more: Office of Student Affairs; Office of Diversity; Multicultural Centers; Women's and Men's Centers; Lesbian, Gay, Bisexual, and Transgendered Student Alliances; Centers for Students with Disabilities; and academic support programs for under-represented groups.

ONLINE

> **Diversity Resources** The Diversity Web (**http://www.diversityweb.org**) lists resources related to diversity on campus.

> The Tolerance.org Web site (**http://www.tolerance.org**), a project of the Southern Poverty Law Center, provides numerous resources for dealing with discrimination and prejudice both on and off campus.

MY INSTITUTION'S RESOURCES

_____

_____

_____

_____

_____

_____

_____

_____

12 Money

> " I have had to keep my spending to the bare minimum in college. That was a tough transition.

Juliana Henry, 19
Business major
University of Arizona

Juliana Henry was born in Bogota, Colombia, and was adopted as an infant by a family in Massachusetts, where she attended high school. During the college application process she decided that she wanted to attend a big university, one with Greek life and lots to do, and she wanted to find an institution with a highly ranked business program. The University of Arizona fit the bill, and the warm weather far from the harsh New England winters didn't hurt either.

Juliana had worked hard during high school, especially the summer before she left for college when she saved a lot of money, so she opted to try attending the university without holding an outside job. The trade-off was that she had to keep her spending low. "It was a tough transition from having lots of money while working full-time," she says, but she quickly learned how important it was to have a balanced budget. "When I first got to school I wasn't able to immediately adjust to the thought of not buying things when I wanted them. I have had to keep my spending to the bare minimum in college. That was a

Juliana Henry ▶

tough transition." Like many students, Juliana also has a credit card now, which she got to begin building a good credit score. She has to be careful with that, too, and she tries to use it only for necessities. "My parents cosigned for it," she says, "but I am still the one who has to make the monthly payments!"

After a year at the University of Arizona, Juliana has realized that she actually misses New England more than she thought she would and has decided to transfer to a college back East. "The process of applying to colleges as a transfer was exhausting but worth it in the end," she says. "I am at a point in my life where I need to make decisions that will truly benefit my future and help me set up my career." She sees herself working in hotel management in the future and hopes to get a job at one of Boston's many fine hotels. Her advice for other first-year students? "Save much more than you think you will need. That money can come in handy!"

Although your primary goal in college should be a strong academic record, money or the lack of it can make it easier or more difficult to complete your degree. Juliana made a hard choice; she had just enough money to manage expenses without working, but her strict budget didn't allow her to spend her hard-earned dollars on anything that was unnecessary. Living within a budget during the first year of college is sometimes tough, and that's why some students begin to depend on credit cards. Counting on credit cards to extend your available financial resources can be a slippery slope, however. Juliana has a credit card, but she knows that she needs to be careful to use it for necessities.

Educators recognize that not understanding personal finances can hinder a student's progress, and mandatory personal finance classes are now being added in many high schools and are available as options at some colleges. The purpose of this chapter is to provide general information and suggestions about managing your money. Learning to live on a budget during the college years is a skill that will serve you well for the rest of your life. Think of this chapter as a summary of needed financial skills; if you want more information, consider taking a personal finance class at your college or in your community.

> ## YOUR TURN
> ....
> ### Write and Reflect
> Write a "warning letter" to a younger sibling (real or imaginary) about ways that students are tempted to waste money in college and what can happen as a result. Include in your letter strategies from this chapter for carefully managing money.

Living on a Budget

Face it: College is expensive, and most students have limited financial resources. Not only is tuition a major cost, but day-to-day expenses can add up quickly. No matter what your financial situation, a budget for college is a must. Although a budget might not completely eliminate debt after graduation, it can help you become realistic about your finances so that you can have a basis for future life planning.

A budget is a spending plan that tracks all sources of income (student loan disbursements, money from parents, etc.) and expenses (rent, tuition, etc.) during a set period of time (weekly, monthly, etc.). Creating and following a

◼ ASSESSING YOUR STRENGTHS

Whether they work, receive financial aid, or receive money from their family, successful college students will learn to live on a budget. As you begin to read this chapter, make a list of areas where you think that you have had some success managing your money in the past.

_____

_____

_____

_____

◼ SETTING GOALS

What are your most important objectives in learning the material in this chapter? Think about challenges you have had in the past with money management or areas that confuse you or make you nervous. Write down three money-management goals (e.g., I will track my spending and expenses for one month and use the information to create a monthly budget).

1. _____

_____

2. _____

_____

3. _____

_____

budget will allow you to pay your bills on time, cut costs, put some money away for emergencies, and finish college with as little debt as possible.

CREATING A BUDGET

A budget will condition you to live within your means, put money into savings, and possibly invest down the road. Here are a few tips to help you get started.

Gather Income Information. To create an effective budget, you need to learn more about your income and your spending behaviors. First, determine how much money is coming in and when. Sources of income might include a job, your savings, gifts from relatives, student loans, scholarship dollars, or grants. List all your income sources, making note of how often you receive each type of income (weekly or monthly paychecks, quarterly loan disbursements, one-time gifts, etc.) and how much money you can expect each time. Knowing when your money is coming in will help you decide how to structure your budget. For example, if most of your income comes in on a monthly basis, you'll want to create a monthly budget. If you are paid every other week, a biweekly budget might work better.

Budget worksheet

College Student (18-25) Budget Worksheet

	Projected Monthly	Actual Jan	Actual Feb	Actual Mar	Actual Apr	Actual May	Actual June	Actual July	Actual Aug	Actual Sept	Actual Oct	Actual Nov	Actual Dec
Income													
Wages	$0.00												
Gifts	$0.00												
Allowance	$0.00												
Financial aid	$0.00												
Other	$0.00												
TOTAL Income	$0.00	$0.00	$0.00	$0.00	$0.00	$0.00	$0.00	$0.00	$0.00	$0.00	$0.00	$0.00	$0.00
Expenses													
School expenses													
Tuition	$0.00												
Residence Hall Room and Board	$0.00												
Organization Dues	$0.00												
Books	$0.00												
Supplies	$0.00												
TOTAL School expenses	$0.00	$0.00	$0.00	$0.00	$0.00	$0.00	$0.00	$0.00	$0.00	$0.00	$0.00	$0.00	$0.00
Food/household expenses													
Groceries	$0.00												
Household goods	$0.00												
Other	$0.00												
TOTAL Food/household expenses	$0.00	$0.00	$0.00	$0.00	$0.00	$0.00	$0.00	$0.00	$0.00	$0.00	$0.00	$0.00	$0.00
Communication													
Cell phone monthly plan	$0.00												
Internet	$0.00												
Communication devices	$0.00												
Other	$0.00												
TOTAL Communication	$0.00	$0.00	$0.00	$0.00	$0.00	$0.00	$0.00	$0.00	$0.00	$0.00	$0.00	$0.00	$0.00
Debts													
Student loan payments	$0.00												
Consumer debt payments (credit cards)	$0.00												
Other	$0.00												
TOTAL Debts	$0.00	$0.00	$0.00	$0.00	$0.00	$0.00	$0.00	$0.00	$0.00	$0.00	$0.00	$0.00	$0.00

Courtesy of College in Colorado

IN THE MEDIA

Various tools are available online to help you create a budget, such as easy-to-use spreadsheets or budget "wizards" that you can download for free. Built-in formulas do the math, making it easy to keep track of money that comes in and goes out. A quick Internet search yielded the following budgeting resources, among many others:

- www.cicmoney101.org/Calculators/Budget-Worksheets/Traditional-College-Student.aspx

- http://budget.cashcourse.org/

- www.vertex42.com/ExcelTemplates/college-budget.html

Web sites like cicmoney101.org are loaded with helpful resources in addition to budget tools and calculators (including ones for both traditional and returning college students). Resources include short courses on money management, spending, and paying for college; videos; articles; and a glossary to help you develop personal financial literacy.

For Reflection: Are you willing to commit to creating a budget? Do you already have a budget that works? Do you think that the costs at your institution are justified? Why or why not? Do you think that students who have all college costs paid by someone else are more or less motivated than those who work their way through college?

Gather Expense Information for Your College or University. Expenses will include tuition; residence hall fees if you live on campus; and the costs of books and course materials, lab fees, and membership fees for any organizations you might join. Some institutions offer a separate January or May term. Although your tuition for these one-month terms is generally covered in your overall tuition payment, you would have extra expenses if you wanted to travel to another location in the United States or abroad.

Gather Information about Living Expenses. First, get a "reality check." How do you *think* that you are spending your money? To find out for sure where your money is going and when, track your spending for a few weeks—ideally at least a full month—in a notebook or in a table or spreadsheet. The kinds of expense categories you should consider will vary depending on your situation. If you are a traditional full-time student who lives with your parents or family members, your living expenses won't be the same as students living in a campus residence hall or in an off-campus apartment. If you are a returning student who is holding down a job and has a family of your own to support, you will calculate your expenses differently. Whatever your situation, keeping track of your expenses and learning about your spending behaviors are important habits to develop. Consider which of the following expense categories are relevant to you:

- Rent
- Utilities (e.g., electricity, gas, water)
- Cell phone
- Cable/Internet
- Transportation (car payment, car insurance, car maintenance/repairs, gasoline, public transportation)
- Child care
- Groceries
- Medical expenses (prescriptions, doctor visits, hospital bills)
- Clothing
- Entertainment (dining out, hobbies, movies)
- Laundry
- Personal grooming (e.g., haircuts, toiletries)
- Miscellaneous (e.g., travel, organization dues)

Be sure to recognize which expenses are fixed and which are variable. A *fixed expense* is one that will cost you the same amount every time you pay it. For example, your rent is a fixed expense because you owe your landlord the same amount each month. A *variable expense* is one that may change. Your textbooks are a variable expense because the number and cost of them will be different each term.

Find Out How You Are Doing. Once you have a sense of how your total income compares to

> ## Is This You?
>
> Are you having serious problems managing your money? Were you counting on a source of income that isn't going to be available after all? Do you need a budget but aren't sure how to create one that will work for you? Are you using credit cards to buy things that you don't really need? To stay in college and do your best academically, you have to learn to manage your money. That might mean seeking out loans or scholarships, destroying or hiding your credit cards until they are paid off, or seeking some financial counseling at your institution or through a community resource. This chapter will help you figure out what you need to do to stay on top of your financial situation so that it doesn't derail your college plans.

your total weekly or monthly expenses, you can get a clearer picture of your current financial situation.

Make Adjustments. Although your budget might never be perfect, you can strive to improve it. In what areas did you spend much more or much less than expected? Do you need to reallocate funds to better meet the needs of your current situation? Be realistic and thoughtful in how you spend your money, and use your budget to help meet your goals, such as planning for a trip or getting a new pair of jeans.

Whatever you do, don't give up if your bottom line doesn't end up the way that you expected it would. Budgeting is a lot like dieting; you might slip up and eat a pizza (or spend too much buying one), but all is not lost. If you stay focused and flexible, your budget can lead you to financial stability and independence.

CUTTING COSTS

Once you have put together a working budget, have tried it out, and have adjusted it, you're likely to discover that your expenses still exceed your income. Don't panic. Simply begin to look for ways to reduce those expenses. Here are some tips for saving money in college:

- **Recognize the difference between your *needs* and your *wants*.** A *need* is something that you must have. For example, tuition and textbooks are considered *needs*. On the other hand, your *wants* are goods, services, or experiences that you wish to purchase but could reasonably live without. For example, concert tickets and mochas are *wants*. Your budget should always provide for your *needs* first.

- **Share expenses.** Having a roommate (or several) can be one of the easiest ways to cut costs on a regular basis. In exchange for giving up a little bit of privacy, you'll save hundreds of dollars on rent, utilities, and food. Make sure, however, that you work out a plan for sharing expenses equally and that everyone accepts his or her responsibilities. For instance, remember that if only your name is on the cable account, you (and only you) are legally responsible for that bill. You'll need to collect money from your roommates so that you can pay the bill in full and on time.

- **Consider the pros and cons of living on campus.** Depending on your school's location, off-campus housing might be less expensive than paying for a room and a meal plan on campus. Be aware, however, that although you might save some cash, you will give up a great deal of convenience by moving out of your campus residence. You almost certainly won't be able to roll out of bed 10 minutes before class, and you will have to prepare your own meals. At the same time, living on campus makes it easier to make friends and develop a sense of connection to your college or university. Before you make the decision about where to live, weigh the advantages and disadvantages of each option.

- **Use low-cost transportation.** If you live close to campus, consider whether or not you need to keep a car on campus. Take advantage of lower-cost options such as public transportation or biking to class to save money on gasoline and parking. If you live farther away, check to see whether your institution hosts a ride-sharing program for commuter students or join a carpool with someone in your area.

- **Seek out discount entertainment options.** Take advantage of discounted or free programming through your college. Most institutions use a portion of their student fees to provide affordable entertainment options such as discounted or free tickets to concerts, movie theaters, sporting events, or other special events.

- **Embrace secondhand goods.** Use online resources such as Craigslist and thrift stores such as Goodwill to expand your wardrobe, purchase extras such as games and sports equipment, or furnish and decorate your room or apartment. You'll save money, and you won't mind as much when someone spills a drink on your "new" couch.

- **Avoid unnecessary fees.** Making late payments on credit cards and other bills can lead to expensive fees and can lower your credit score (which in turn will raise your interest rates). You might want to set up online, automatic payments to avoid making this costly mistake.

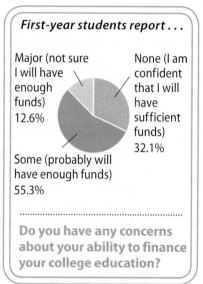

First-year students report . . .

Major (not sure I will have enough funds) 12.6%

None (I am confident that I will have sufficient funds) 32.1%

Some (probably will have enough funds) 55.3%

Do you have any concerns about your ability to finance your college education?

Getting Financial Aid

Very few students can pay the costs of college tuition, fees, books, room and board, bills, and random expenses without some kind of help. Luckily, several sources of financial aid, including some you might not know about, are available to help cover your costs. With a combination of research, diligence, and luck, some students even manage to enroll and succeed in college with little or no financial support from their families because of the financial aid they receive.

TYPES OF AID

Financial aid seems complex because it can come from so many different sources. Each source may have different rules about how to receive the money and how not to lose it. The financial aid staff at your college can help you find the way to get the largest amount of money that doesn't need to be repaid, the lowest interest rate on loans, and work possibilities that fit your academic program. Whether or not your family can help you pay for college, you should not overlook this valuable campus resource. The financial aid office and its Web site are the best places to begin looking for all types of assistance. Other organizations that can help students find the right college and money to help them attend are located across the United States. Many of these organizations are members of the National College Access Network or participate in a national effort called Know How to Go. Check their Web sites at **http://www .collegeaccess.org/accessprogramdirectory** and **http://www.knowhow2go.org**.

Very few students complete college without some type of financial assistance, and it is rare for students to cover all college expenses with only scholarships. The majority of students pay for college through a combination of various types of financial assistance: scholarships, grants, loans, and paid employment. Financial aid professionals refer to this combination as a "package."

Although scholarships and grants are unquestionably the best forms of aid because they do not have to be repaid, the federal government, states, and colleges offer many other forms of assistance, such as loans, work-study opportunities, and cooperative education. You might also be able to obtain funds from your employer, a local organization, or a private group.

- **Need-based scholarships** are based on both a talent and financial need. "Talent" can be past accomplishments in the arts or athletics, your potential for future accomplishments, or even where you are from. Some colleges and universities want to admit students from other states or countries. "Need" in this context means the cost of college minus a federal determination of what you and your family can afford to contribute toward those costs. Your institution might provide scholarships from its own resources or from individual donors. Donors themselves sometimes stipulate characteristics of scholarship recipients, such as age or academic major.

- **Merit scholarships** are based on talent as defined above but do not require you to demonstrate financial need. It can be challenging to match your talent with merit scholarships. Most of them come through colleges and are part of the admissions and financial aid processes, usually described on the college's Web site. Web-based scholarship search services are another good source to explore. Be certain that the Web site you use is free, will keep your information confidential unless you release your name, and will send you a notice (usually through e-mail) when a new scholarship that matches your qualifications is posted. Also be sure to ask your employer, your family's employers, and social, community, or religious organizations about any available scholarships.

- **Grants** are based on financial need but, like scholarships, do not have to be repaid. Grants are awarded by the federal government, state governments, and institutions themselves. Students meet academic qualifications for grants by being admitted to the college and maintaining grades that are acceptable to the grant provider.

- **Work-study jobs** are reserved for students with financial need. Students receive work-study notices as part of the overall financial aid notice and then can sign up to be interviewed for work-study jobs. Although some work-study jobs can be relatively menial, the best options provide experience related to your academic studies while allowing you to earn money for college. The salary is based on the skills required for a particular position and the hours involved. Keep in mind that you will be expected to accomplish specific tasks while on duty, although some employers might permit you to study during any downtime.

- **Cooperative (co-op) education** allows you to alternate a term of study (a semester or quarter) with a term of paid work. Engineering co-op opportunities are among the most common, and the number of co-op programs in health care fields is growing. Colleges make information about co-ops available through admissions and academic departments.

Riza Liu/PSU Vanguard

Show Me the Money

Don't let the paperwork scare you away. If you're not already receiving financial aid, be sure to investigate all the available options. Also remember that your institution may offer scholarships or grants that you don't have to repay.

QUALIFYING FOR AID

Most financial assistance requires some form of application. The application used most often is the Free Application for Federal Student Aid (FAFSA). Every student should complete the FAFSA by the earliest deadline of the colleges you are considering. Additional forms, such as the College Board's Profile form and scholarship applications, might also be required and will be listed in colleges' financial aid or admissions materials or by organizations that offer scholarships. The box on page 264 outlines the steps you must take to qualify for most scholarships and grants, especially those sponsored by the federal government or state governments.

The amount of financial aid that you receive will depend on the cost of your academic program and what you or your family can pay as determined by FAFSA. Cost includes average expenses for tuition and fees, books and supplies, room and board, transportation, and personal expenses. The financial aid office will subtract from the cost the amount that you and your family are expected to pay. In some cases, that amount can be as little as zero. Financial aid is designed to make up as much of the balance or "need" as possible.

HOW TO AVOID LOSING YOUR FUNDING

If you earn average or better grades, complete your courses each term, and finish your program or degree on time, you should have no trouble maintaining your financial aid. It's a good idea to check with the financial aid office before you drop classes to make sure that you will not lose any aid.

Some types of aid, especially scholarships, require that you maintain full-time enrollment and make satisfactory academic progress. Dropping or failing a class might jeopardize all or part of your financial aid unless you are

STEPS TO QUALIFY FOR FINANCIAL AID

1. Enroll half-time or more in a certificate or degree program at one of the more than 4,500 institutions that are certified to distribute federal financial aid. A few aid programs are available for less than half-time study; check with your department or college to see what your options are.

2. Complete the FAFSA. The first FAFSA that you file is intimidating, especially if you rush to complete it right before the deadline. Completing the FAFSA in subsequent years is easier because you need to update only items that have changed. To make the process easier, get your personal identification number (PIN) a few weeks before the deadline. You'll use this same PIN throughout your college career. Try to do the form in sections rather than tackling it all at once. Most of the information is basic: name, address, driver's license number, and things you will know or have in your billfold. For most undergraduates the financial section will require your own and your parents' information from tax materials. If you are at least twenty-four years of age, married, have dependents of your own, or are a veteran, your tax information (and that for your spouse, if married) will be needed.

3. If your school or award-granting organization requires it, complete the College Board Profile form. Review your college's admission information, or ask a financial aid adviser to determine if this form applies to you.

4. Identify any additional applications that are required, such as scholarship applications with personal statements or short essays. The organizations, including colleges, that are giving the money will provide instructions about what is required. Most have Web sites with complete information.

5. Follow all instructions carefully and submit each application on time. Financial aid is awarded from a fixed pool of funds. When money has been awarded, usually none is left for those who file late.

6. Complete the classes for which you were given financial aid with at least a minimum grade point average as defined by your academic department or college or the organization that provided you the scholarship.

---

enrolled in more credits than the minimum required for financial aid. Full-time financial aid is often defined as twelve credit hours per term. If you initially enrolled in fifteen credit hours and dropped one three-hour course, your aid should not change. Even so, talk with a financial aid counselor before making the decision to drop a course, just to be sure.

Remember that although the financial aid office is there to serve you, you must be your own advocate. The following tips should help:

- File for financial aid every year. Even if you don't think that you will receive aid for a certain year, you must file annually in case you become eligible in the future.

- Meet all filing deadlines. Students who do not meet filing deadlines risk losing aid from one year to the next.

- Talk with a financial aid officer immediately if you or your family experiences a significant loss (e.g., loss of a job, death of a parent or spouse). Don't wait for the next filing period; you might be eligible for funds for the current year.

- Inquire every year about criteria-based aid. Many colleges and universities have grants and scholarships for students who meet specific criteria. Such aid might include grants for minority students, grants for students in specific academic majors, and grants for students of single parents. Sometimes a donor will give money to the school's scholarship fund for students who meet certain other criteria, even county or state of residence. Determine whether any of them fit your circumstances.

- Inquire about campus jobs throughout the year because jobs become available after the beginning of the term. If you do not have a job and want or need to work, keep asking.

- Consider asking for a reassessment of your eligibility for aid. If you have reviewed your financial aid package and think that your circumstances deserve additional consideration, you can ask the financial aid office to reassess your eligibility. The office is not always required to do so, but the request might be worth your effort.

Achieving a Balance between Working and Borrowing

After you determine your budget, decide what you can pay from savings (if any), and take your scholarships and grants into consideration, you might still need additional income. Each term or year, you should decide how much you can work while maintaining good grades and how much you should borrow from student loans.

ADVANTAGES AND DISADVANTAGES OF WORKING

Paid employment while you are in college can be important for reasons other than money. Having a job in a field related to your major can help you develop a credential for graduate school and make you more employable later because it shows that you have the capability to manage several priorities at the same time. Work can help you determine whether a career is what you will really want after you complete your education. In addition, students who work a moderate amount (fifteen hours per week) typically get better grades than students who do not work at all.

On the other hand, it's almost impossible to get great grades if you work full-time while trying to be a full-time student. Some students prefer not to take a job during their first year in college while they're making adjustments to a new academic environment. You might find that you're able to work some terms while you are a student but not others, and sometimes family obligations or challenging classes can make the added burden of work impractical or impossible.

The majority of students today find that a combination of working and borrowing is the best way to gain experience, finance college, and complete their educational goals on time.

STUDENT LOANS

Although you should be careful not to borrow yourself into a lifetime of debt, avoiding loans altogether could delay your graduation and your progress up the career ladder. For most students, some level of borrowing is both necessary and prudent.

The following list provides information about the most common types of student loans. The list reflects the order in which you should apply for and accept loans to get the lowest interest rates and best repayment terms.

- **Subsidized federal student loans** are backed by the government, with interest paid on your behalf while you are enrolled in undergraduate, graduate, or professional school. These loans require at least half-time enrollment and a submitted FAFSA application (see p. 263).
- **Unsubsidized federal student loans** may require that you make interest payments while you are enrolled. If not, the interest is added to the amount you owe, called "capitalization."
- **Parent Loan for Undergraduate Students (called PLUS loans)** are applied for and owed by parents but disbursed directly to students. Interest is usually higher than that on federal student loans but lower than that on private loans. Parents who apply for PLUS loans must provide information on the FAFSA.
- **Private student loans** are offered through banks and credit unions. Private loans often have stricter credit requirements and higher interest rates than federal loans do, and interest payments on private loans begin immediately.

Student loans are a very important source of money for college, but like paid employment, loans should be considered carefully. Loans for costs such as books and tuition are good investments. Loans for a more lavish lifestyle are likely to weigh you down in the future. As one wise person put it, if by borrowing you live like a wealthy graduate while you're a student, you'll live like a student after you graduate. Student loans can be a good way to begin using credit wisely, a skill you are likely to need throughout your life.

Managing Credit Wisely

When you graduate, you will leave your institution with two significant numbers. The first is your grade point average (GPA), which represents the level of academic success you attained while in college. The second, your credit score, is a numerical representation of your fiscal responsibility. Although this second number might be less familiar to you than the first, it could be a factor that determines whether you get your dream job, regardless of your GPA. In addition, twenty years from now you're likely to have forgotten your GPA, while your credit score will be more important than ever.

Your credit score is derived from a credit report that contains information about accounts in your name. These accounts include credit cards, student loans, utility bills, cell phones, and car loans, to name a few. This credit score can determine whether or not you will qualify for a loan (car, home, student, etc.), what interest rates you will pay, how much your car insurance will cost, and your chances of being hired by some organizations. Even if none of these things is in your immediate future, now is the time to start thinking about your credit score.

Although using credit cards responsibly is a good way to build credit, acquiring a credit card has become much more difficult for college students. In May 2009, President Barack Obama signed legislation that prohibits college students under the age of twenty-one from obtaining a credit card unless they can prove that they are able to make the payments or unless the credit card application is cosigned by a parent or guardian.

UNDERSTANDING CREDIT

Even if you can prove that you have the means to repay credit card debt, it is important for you to thoroughly understand how credit cards work and how they can both help and hurt you. Simply put, a credit card allows you to buy something now and pay for it later. Each month you will receive a statement listing all purchases you made using your credit card during the previous

FREQUENTLY ASKED QUESTIONS ABOUT CREDIT CARDS

Here are some answers to common questions about credit cards:

☐ **I have a credit card with my name on it, but it is actually my parents' account number. Is this card building credit for me?** No. You are considered an authorized user on the account, but your parents are the primary account holders. To build credit you must be the primary account holder or at least a joint account holder.

☐ **I choose the "credit" option every time I use my debit card. Is this building credit for me?** No. Using the credit function of your debit card is more like an electronic check because it is still taking money directly out of your checking account. Even if your debit card has a major credit card (Visa, MasterCard, etc.) logo on it, it is not building credit for you.

☐ **I have a few store credit cards (Target, Kohl's, Best Buy, etc.). Are these accounts included on my credit report?** Yes. Although they will affect your credit score, they do not carry as much weight as major credit cards (Visa, MasterCard, etc.). It is OK to have a few store credit cards, but a major credit card will do more to help you build credit.

☐ **Where can I apply for a major credit card?** A good place to begin is your bank or credit union. To obtain a card, remember that you will have to prove your ability to make payments. Use your credit card to build credit by making small charges and paying them off each month.

☐ **If one credit card will help me build credit, will several build my credit even more?** Research shows no benefit to having more than two major credit cards. Also, even if you're able to pay the required monthly amounts, having too many accounts open can make you appear risky to the credit bureaus determining your credit score.

☐ **What if I forget and make a late payment? Is my credit score ruined?** Your credit report reflects at least the past seven years of activity but puts the most emphasis on the most recent two years. In other words, the farther you get from your mistakes, the less effect they will have on your credit score. There is no quick fix for improving a credit score, so beware of advertisements that say otherwise.

☐ **If building credit is a wise decision, what's so bad about using credit cards to buy some things that I really want but can't really afford right now?** It is not wise to use credit cards to purchase things that you cannot afford. Living within your means is always the way to go.

☐ **Where can I get my credit report?** You can keep an eye on your credit report by visiting the free Web site **www.annualcreditreport.com** at least once a year.

thirty days. The statement will request a payment toward your balance and will set a payment due date. Your payment options will vary: You can pay your entire balance, pay a specified amount of the balance, or pay only a minimum payment, which may be as low as $10.

But beware: If you make only a minimum payment, the remaining balance on your card will be charged a finance fee, or interest charge, causing your balance to increase before your next bill arrives even if you don't make any more purchases. Paying the minimum payment is almost never a good strategy and can add years to your repayment time. In fact, if you continue to pay only $10 per month toward a $500 credit card balance, it will take you more than seven years to pay it off! Assuming an 18 percent interest rate, you'll pay an extra $431 in interest, almost doubling the total amount you originally charged.

Avoid making late payments. Paying your bill even one day late can result in a finance charge of up to $30; it can also raise the interest rate not only on that card but also on any other credit accounts you have. If you decide to use a credit card to build credit, you might want to set up online, automatic payments to avoid incurring expensive late fees. Remember that the payment due date is the date that the payment should be received by the credit card lender, not the date that you send it.

If you decide to apply for a credit card while you're in college, remember that it should be used to build credit and for emergencies. Credit cards should not be used to fund a lifestyle that you cannot otherwise afford or to buy wants

In Case of Emergency

It is a good practice to have a credit card for emergencies. What might warrant the use of credit is paying for critical expenses to care for yourself or your family, dealing with an auto accident, an unforeseen medical expense, or a last-minute need to travel to handle a crisis. Remember that spring break is *not* an emergency.

© Britt Erlanson/cultura/Corbis

TECH TIP PROTECT YOUR IDENTITY

Gone are the days when people stashed their money under a mattress and called it a day. In today's credit- and tech-driven world, being financially responsible includes protecting yourself from identity theft. In this insidious and increasingly common crime, someone assumes your identity, secretly opens up accounts in your name, and has the bills sent to another address.

Hugo Felix/Shutterstock

1 ▸ THE PROBLEM

Identity fraud is on the rise, and you're not sure how to protect yourself. The 2013 comedy *Identity Thief* tells the story of an identity theft victim (played by Jason Bateman) who confronts the thief (played by Melissa McCarthy). But if identity theft happens to you, it's not so funny.

Bob Mahoney/© Universal/Courtesy Everett Collection

2 ▸ THE FIX

To thwart cybercrooks, you have to stay a few steps ahead of them.

3 ▸ HOW TO DO IT

1. Be password savvy. The more sensitive the information, the stronger your password should be. Aim for eight to fourteen characters, including numbers, both uppercase and lowercase letters, and if allowed, a few special characters like @ and #. Never use an obvious number like your birthday or anniversary. Don't use the same usernames and passwords for every site. Try to change the passwords to your online credit card or bank account at least once a year. If you must keep a written record of your usernames and passwords, keep the list in a secure place at home, not in your wallet.

2. Beware of scams. Lots of them are out there. A few tips:
- Be sure to research a company or organization before submitting your résumé.
- When communicating with a potential employer, don't e-mail any personal information (social security number, bank details, credit or debit card numbers, passwords, etc.) that could put you at risk of identity theft.

- Don't answer questions about vital personal information over the phone if you didn't originate the call.
- Don't reply to e-mail, pop-ups, or text messages that ask you to reveal sensitive information.
- Don't send sensitive data by e-mail. Call instead and deal only with businesses you trust.
- Never click on links in unsolicited e-mails or paste URLs or lines of code into your browser bar. If an offer sounds too good to be true, it probably is.

3. Keep tabs on your credit report. Regularly reviewing your credit history pays off in major ways. It alerts you to any new accounts that might have been opened in your name. It also lets you catch unauthorized activity on accounts that you've closed or haven't used lately.

Feng Yu/Shutterstock

Note: Everyone is entitled to one free credit report a year from each of the three major credit bureaus. Make sure to order yours from the Web site **www.annualcreditreport.com**. Sites offering "free" credit reports usually require paid memberships for additional credit products, so save your money and use it to pay your bills instead!

PERSONAL BEST

Your online identity is as important as your financial one. Choose secure passwords for your social networking sites and course sites where your grades might be listed. While you're at it, limit the amount of personal information available on your Facebook profile, ratchet up your security settings, and accept friend requests only from people you know. Remember that even Facebook creator Mark Zuckerberg's Facebook page was once hacked. It's wise to try to maintain a little mystery.

(see the section on budgeting earlier in this chapter). On the other hand, if you use your credit card just once a month and pay the balance as soon as the bill arrives, you will be on your way to a strong credit score in just a few years.

DEBIT CARDS

Although you might wish to use a credit card for emergencies and to establish a good credit rating, you might also look into the possibility of applying for a debit card (also called a checkcard). The big advantage of a debit card is that you don't always have to carry cash and thus don't run the risk of losing it. Because the amount of your purchases will be limited to the funds in your bank account, a debit card is also a good form of constraint on your spending.

The only real disadvantage is that a debit card provides direct access to your checking account, so it's very important to keep your card in a safe place and away from your personal identification number (PIN). The safest way to protect your account is to commit your PIN to memory. If you lose your debit card or credit card, notify your bank immediately.

Planning for the Future

It's never too early to begin thinking about financing your life after graduation. Here are some tips that could open future opportunities and help you avoid future problems:

- Plan now for your next step, whether that's additional education or work. Get to know faculty members by visiting them during their office hours to learn about their specific areas of study and ask their advice about your career. Faculty members frequently mention that they wish more students came to talk with them, instead of just meeting them when a problem occurs.

- Keep your address current with the registrar even when you have finished your degree or program and especially if you stop classes for a term. This notification is doubly important if you have student loans; you do not want to get a negative report on your credit rating because you missed information about your loan.

- Make a point of establishing a savings account and adding to it regularly, even if you can manage only a few dollars a month. The sooner you start, the greater your returns will be.

Your education is the most productive investment that you can make for your future and that of your family. Research shows that completion of programs or degrees after high school increases earnings, opens up career options, leads to greater satisfaction in work, results in more engaged citizenship such as voting and community service, and greatly increases the probability that your children will go on to college. College is a big investment of both time and money, but it's an investment of proven worth.

CHECKLIST FOR SUCCESS

MONEY

☐ **Make learning financial literacy skills a key college success skill.** Financial literacy is a specialized form of information literacy.

☐ **Create a budget and then live on it.** Remember that it's your budget, tailor-made by and for you.

☐ **Act on some of the suggestions offered in this chapter for cutting your costs.** For most college students, cutting costs is even more important than increasing their income.

☐ **Learn as much as you can about the different types of financial aid.** Find out what is offered to U.S. college students and by your particular college, even though the term has already started. It's never too late to take advantage of these opportunities.

☐ **Carefully consider the pros and cons of working while in college.** If you do work, consider how much and where. Realize that students who borrow money and attend college full-time are more likely to attain their degrees than those who use a different strategy.

☐ **Remember that you will finish college with two key numbers: your GPA and your credit score.** College is therefore a time to learn how to use credit wisely. Potential employers will be checking your transcripts and your credit reports!

☐ **Learn the strategies in this chapter for wise credit card management to stay out of this trap.** Credit card companies troll for bait on college campuses; you do not want to be that bait.

☐ **Take advantage of help offered on your campus to learn financial management skills.** You can't help it if you didn't learn these skills before; you may not have had any money to manage!

BUILD YOUR EXPERIENCE 1 2 3 4

1 STAY ON TRACK

Successful college students stay focused. They "stay on track." They know what they have to do to be successful, they set goals, and they monitor their progress toward their goals.

Reflect on what you have learned about college success in this chapter and how you are going to apply the chapter information or strategies in college and in your career. List your ideas.

1. _____

   _____

   _____

2. _____

   _____

   _____

3. _____

   _____

   _____

2 ONE-MINUTE PAPER

This chapter covers a lot of information about financing your college experience and managing your money. Planning ahead is an important part of managing your finances. What did you find to be the most useful information in this chapter? Did anything that was covered leave you with more questions than answers? If so, what?

Now that you have read and discussed this chapter, consider how you can apply what you have learned to your academic life and your personal life. The following prompts will help you reflect on chapter material and its relevance to you both now and in the future.

1. Sometimes it's hard to plan for the future. Describe two ways that you can save money each week, such as using public transportation to reduce the expense of owning a car.

2. Money is a difficult subject to talk about, and sometimes it seems easier not to worry about it. Ask yourself hard questions. Do you spend money without much thought? Do you have a lot of debt? Describe your ideal financial picture.

4 BUILDING YOUR PORTFOLIO

Credit Cards: A Slippery Slope   Do you remember the saying "There is no free lunch"? That is a good maxim to keep in mind as you consider adding credit cards to your financial picture. College students are often targeted by credit card companies through an offer of a free T-shirt or other novelty if they sign up for a new card. Although it might seem harmless at the time, signing up for multiple credit cards can have you in financial trouble, and fast!

A big factor in effectively managing your credit card debt is being aware of the terms and conditions that apply to each account you have.

1. If you already have credit cards, find your most recent billing statement. If you do not have a credit card, do an Internet search for "college student credit cards." Choose one of the Internet offers, and find the terms and conditions and do the exercise in #2 as practice for when you do get a credit card.

2. Next, to understand the fees associated with a credit account, create a spreadsheet with the following headers (see **macmillanhighered.com/collegesuccess/resources**):

   - Card Issuer and Card Type
   - Credit Limit
   - APR (Annual Percentage Rate)
   - Default APR (A default APR may be used when you fail to make the minimum payment on your credit card account or exceed your credit limit by a certain amount. The default APR is always higher than the stated APR for the credit account.)
   - Due On
   - Late Fee
   - Over Credit Limit Fee

3. List each credit card you have, and enter the associated fees.

4. Save the file and refer to it regularly.

5. Update the file any time you open or close a credit account.

For more on this topic watch
French Fries Are Not Vegetables and Other College Lessons

WHERE TO GO FOR HELP . . .

ON CAMPUS

> **Your Institution's Financial Aid Office** Be sure to visit your institution's financial aid office to take advantage of financial aid opportunities and how to apply for scholarships.

> **Local United Way Office** If your college or university doesn't offer credit counseling, look online or in the telephone book for credit counseling agencies within the local United Way.

> **Campus Programs** Be on the lookout for special campus programs on money management and sign up for one. These programs are often offered in residence halls or through the division of student affairs.

> **Business School or College** Faculty or staff members within a school or college of business or a division of continuing education sometimes offer a course in personal finance. Check your college catalog or Web site, or call the school, college, or division office to see if there are options that you can take advantage of either this term or next.

> **Counseling Center** If money problems are related to compulsive shopping or gambling, be sure to seek counseling at your institution's counseling center.

ONLINE

> Budget Wizard: **http://www.cashcourse.org**. The National Endowment for Financial Education (NEFE) offers this free, secure, budgeting tool. See the In the Media feature on page 258 for other tools that you can use to build a budget.

> Free Application for Federal Student Aid: **http://www.fafsa.ed.gov**. The online form allows you to set up an account, complete the application electronically, save your work, and monitor the progress of your application.

> FastWeb: **http://www.FastWeb.com**. Register for this free scholarship search service and discover sources of educational funding you never knew existed.

> Bankrate: **http://www.bankrate.com**. This free site provides unbiased information about the interest rates, fees, and penalties associated with major credit cards and private loans. It also provides calculators that let you determine the long-term costs of different kinds of borrowing.

OTHER

> Knox, Susan. *Financial Basics: A Money-Management Guide for Students*. Columbus: Ohio State University Press, 2004.

MY INSTITUTION'S RESOURCES

_____

_____

_____

_____

_____

_____

_____

GLOSSARY

abstract A paragraph-length summary of the methods and major findings of an article in a scholarly journal.

academic freedom The virtually unlimited freedom of speech and inquiry granted to professors to further the advancement of knowledge as long as human lives, rights, and privacy are not violated.

accommodators Individuals who prefer hands-on learning and are skilled at making things happen, rely on their intuition, and might use trial and error rather than logic to solve problems. One of the learner groups of the Kolb Inventory of Learning Styles.

acronyms A memory device created by forming new words from the first letters of several words.

acrostics A verse in which certain letters of each word or line form a message.

active learning Learning by participation, such as listening critically, discussing what you are learning, and writing about it.

adaptability The ability to adjust your thinking and behavior when faced with new or unexpected situations.

analysis The process of breaking down material into its parts so that you can understand its structure. One of the six levels of Bloom's taxonomy.

annotate To add critical or explanatory margin notes on a page as you read.

aptitude Natural talent or an ability an individual has acquired through life experience, study, or training.

application The process of using what you have learned, such as rules and methods, in new situations. One of the six levels of Bloom's taxonomy.

argument Reason and evidence brought together in logical support of a claim.

assimilators Individuals who like to develop theories and think about abstract concepts. One of the learner groups of the Kolb Inventory of Learning Styles.

attention deficit hyperactivity disorder (ADHD) A disorder characterized by difficulty organizing tasks, completing work, and listening to and following directions.

aural learner A person who prefers to learn by listening to information. One of the preferences described by the VARK Learning Styles Inventory.

autonomy Self-direction or independence.

bias The tendency to hold a certain perspective when there are valid alternatives.

biorhythms The internal mechanisms that drive our daily patterns of physical, emotional, and mental activity.

Bloom's taxonomy A system of classifying goals for the learning process, now used at all levels of education to define and describe the process that students use to understand and think critically about what they are learning.

bodily/kinesthetic learner An individual who prefers learning by moving around and is good at sports, dance, and acting. One of the eight intelligences as described by the theory of multiple intelligences.

chunking A previewing method that involves making a list of terms and definitions from the reading and then dividing the terms into smaller clusters of five, seven, or nine to learn the material more effectively.

citation A source or author of certain material. When browsing the Internet for sources, use only material that has citations crediting the author, where it came from, and who posted it.

cognitive restructuring A technique of applying positive thinking and giving oneself encouraging messages rather than self-defeating negative ones.

comprehension Understanding the meaning of material. One of the six levels of Bloom's taxonomy.

content skills Cognitive, intellectual, or "hard" skills acquired as one gains mastery in an academic field. They include writing proficiency, computer literacy, and foreign language skills.

convergers People who enjoy the world of ideas and theories, and are good at thinking about how to apply those theories to real-world, practical situations. One of the learner groups of the Kolb Inventory of Learning Styles.

co-op programs Programs offered at many institutions that allow students to work in their field of study while enrolled in college. They offer valuable experiences and an excellent preview of what work in the chosen field is actually like. Also called cooperative education.

Cornell format A method for organizing notes in which one side of the notebook page is designated for note taking during class, and the other as a "recall" column where main ideas and important details for tests are jotted down after class.

credit score A numerical representation of your level of fiscal responsibility, derived from a credit report that contains information about all accounts in your name. This score can determine your loan qualification, interest rates, insurance rates, and sometimes employability.

critical thinking Thoughtful consideration of the information, ideas, observations, and arguments that you encounter; in essence, a search for truth.

culture The aspects of a group of people that are passed on or learned. Traditions, food, language, clothing styles, artistic expression, and beliefs are all part of culture.

database A database is an organized and searchable set of information. Like a special search engine, a database is often classified by a certain subject area, such as chemistry or U.S. history.

deep learning Understanding the why and how behind the details.

discipline An area of academic study, such as sociology, anthropology, or engineering.

discrimination The act of treating people differently because of their race, ethnicity, gender, socioeconomic class, or other identifying characteristics rather than on their merits.

divergers Individuals who are adept at reflecting on situations from many viewpoints. They excel at brainstorming and are imaginative and people-oriented, but sometimes have difficulty making decisions. One of the learner groups of the Kolb Inventory of Learning Styles.

diversity Variations in social and cultural identities among people living together.

dyslexia A widespread developmental learning disorder that can affect the ability to read, spell, or write.

emotional intelligence (EI)   The ability to recognize, understand, use, and manage moods, feelings, and attitudes.

episodic memory   An aspect of long-term memory which deals with particular events, their time, and their place.

ethnicity   An affiliation assigned to a specific group of people historically connected by a common national heritage or language.

explanatory writing   Writing that is "published," meaning that others can read it.

exploratory writing   Writing that helps you first discover what you want to say. It is private and is used only as a series of steps toward a published work.

extraverts   Individuals who are outgoing, gregarious, and talkative. They are good communicators who are quick to act and lead. One of the personality preferences described by the Myers-Briggs Type Indicator.

evaluation   The ability to judge the value of ideas and information you are learning according to internal or external criteria. The highest level of Bloom's taxonomy.

feeling types   Individuals who are warm, empathetic, compassionate, and interested in the happiness of others as well as themselves. They need and value harmony and kindness. One of the personality preferences described by the Myers-Briggs Type Indicator.

financial aid   Monetary sources to help pay for college. Financial aid can come in the form of scholarships, grants, loans, work-study, and cooperative education.

freewriting   Writing that is temporarily unencumbered by mechanical processes, such as punctuation, grammar, spelling, context, and so forth.

gender   A continuum that accounts for many different ways of identifying oneself based on the things a person says, does, or wears.

grants   A form of financial aid awarded by the federal government, state governments, and institutions themselves. Students meet academic qualifications for grants by being admitted to the college and maintaining grades that are acceptable to the grant provider.

humanities   Branches of knowledge that investigate human beings, their culture, and their self-expression. They include the study of philosophy, religion, literature, music, and art.

inclusive curriculum   A curriculum that offers courses that introduce students to diverse people, worldviews, and approaches.

Information Age   Our current times, characterized by the primary role of information in our economy and our lives, the need for information retrieval and information management skills, and the explosion of available information.

information literacy   The ability to find, interpret, and use information to meet your needs.

intellectual property   Ownership over nonphysical creative works such as slogans, artwork, and inventions. Copyright, trademarks, and patents are kinds of intellectual property.

interdisciplinary   Linking two or more academic fields of study, such as history and religion. Encouraging an interdisciplinary approach to teaching can offer a better understanding of modern society.

interpersonal   Relating to the interaction between yourself and other individuals.

interpersonal learner   An individual who likes to have many friends and is good at understanding people, leading others, and mediating conflicts. One of the eight intelligences as described by the theory of multiple intelligences.

intrapersonal learner   An individual who likes to work alone, has self-understanding, and is an original thinker. One of the eight intelligences as described by the theory of multiple intelligences.

introverts   Individuals who like quiet and privacy and who tend to think a lot and reflect carefully about a problem before taking action. One of the personality preferences described by the Myers-Briggs Type Indicator.

intuitive types   Individuals who are fascinated by possibilities, the meaning behind the facts, and the connections between concepts. They are often original, creative, and nontraditional. One of the personality preferences described by the Myers-Briggs Type Indicator.

judging types   Individuals who approach the world in a planned, orderly, and organized way. They strive for order and control, making decisions relatively quickly and easily so they can create and implement plans. One of the personality preferences described by the Myers-Briggs Type Indicator.

keyword   A term used to tell a search engine what you're looking for. Keywords are synonyms, related terms, or subtopics of your search topic.

kinesthetic learner   A person who prefers to learn something through experience and practice, rather than by listening or reading about it. One of the preferences described by the VARK Learning Styles Inventory.

knowledge   Remembering previously learned material. Knowledge includes arranging, defining, memorizing, and recognizing. The bottom level of Bloom's taxonomy.

Kolb Inventory of Learning Styles   A learning model that focuses on abilities we need to develop so that we can learn. This model divides learners into four discrete groups: divergers, assimilators, convergers, and accommodators.

learning disabilities   Disorders such as dyslexia that affect people's ability to either interpret what they see and hear or connect information across different areas of the brain.

learning styles   Particular ways of learning, unique to each individual. For example, one person prefers reading to understand how something works, whereas another prefers using a "hands-on" approach.

list format   A method for organizing notes which is most effective in taking notes on lists of terms and definitions, facts, or sequences. This format is effective in combination with the Cornell format, with key terms on the left and their definitions and explanations on the right.

logical/mathematical learner   An individual who likes to work with numbers and is good at problem-solving and logical processes. One of the eight intelligences as described by the theory of multiple intelligences.

long-term memory   The type of memory that is used to retain information and can be described in three ways: procedural, semantic, and episodic.

mapping   A preview strategy of drawing a wheel or branching structure to show relationships between main ideas and secondary ideas and how different concepts and terms fit together and help you make connections to what you already know about the subject.

marking   An active reading strategy of making marks in the text by underlining, highlighting, or writing margin notes or annotations.

merit scholarships Scholarships based on talent that do not require you to demonstrate financial need. Most of merit scholarships come through colleges and are part of the admissions and financial-aid processes.

mind map A review sheet with words and visual elements that jog the memory to help you recall information more easily.

mnemonics Various methods or tricks to aid memory, including acronyms, acrostics, rhymes or songs, and visualization.

multiculturalism The active process of acknowledging and respecting the diverse social groups, cultures, religions, races, ethnicities, attitudes, and opinions within a community.

multiple intelligences A theory developed by Dr. Howard Gardner based on the premise that all human beings have at least eight different types of intelligence, including verbal/linguistic, logical/mathematical, visual/spatial, bodily/kinesthetic, musical/rhythmic, interpersonal, intrapersonal, and naturalistic.

musical/rhythmic learner An individual who likes to sing and play an instrument and is good at remembering melodies and noticing pitches and rhythms. One of the eight intelligences as described by the theory of multiple intelligences.

naturalistic learner An individual who likes to be outside and is good at preservation, conservation, and organizing a living area. One of the eight intelligences as described by the theory of multiple intelligences.

need-based scholarships Scholarships based on both a talent and financial need.

outline format A method for organizing notes that utilizes Roman numerals to represent key ideas and subsequently uppercase letters, then numbers, and then lowercase letters to represent the other ideas relating to each key idea.

paragraph format A method for organizing notes that consists of writing summary paragraphs when you are taking notes on what you are reading.

perceiving types Individuals who are flexible, can comfortably adapt to change, and tend to delay decisions to keep their options open to gather more information. One of the personality preferences described by the Myers-Briggs Type Indicator.

periodical A resource that is published multiple times a year, such as a magazine.

plagiarism The act of taking another person's idea or work and presenting it as your own. This gross academic misconduct can result in suspension or expulsion, and even the revocation of the violator's college degree.

prejudice A preconceived judgment or opinion of someone based not on facts or knowledge, such as prejudging someone based entirely on his or her skin color.

prewriting The first stage of the writing process. It may include planning, research, and outlining.

primary sources The original research or documentation on a topic, usually referenced either at the end of a chapter or at the back of the book.

procedural memory An aspect of long-term memory that refers to knowing how to do something, such as solving a mathematical problem or playing a musical instrument.

race A term that refers to biological characteristics shared by groups of people, including skin tone, hair texture and color, and facial features.

read/write learner A person who prefers to learn information displayed as words. One of the preferences described by the VARK Learning Styles Inventory.

revision The last stage of the writing process, which involves polishing your work until it clearly explains what you want to communicate and is ready for your audience.

semantic memory An aspect of long-term memory that involves remembering facts and meanings without regard to where and when you learned those things.

sensing types Individuals who are practical, factual, realistic, and down-to-earth. Relatively traditional and conventional, they can be very precise, steady, patient, and effective with routine and details. One of the personality preferences described by the Myers-Briggs Type Indicator.

service learning Unpaid volunteer service that is embedded in courses across the curriculum.

scholarly articles Articles written by experts in their fields, such as researchers, librarians, or professors, and then assessed and edited by other experts in a process called peer review.

short-term memory How many items you are able to perceive at one time. Memory that disappears in less than 30 seconds (sometimes faster) unless the items are moved to long-term memory.

stacks The areas in libraries containing shelves that are full of books available for checkout.

stereotype An oversimplified set of assumptions about another person or group.

Supplemental Instruction (SI) Classes that provide further opportunity to discuss the information presented in lectures.

syllabus A formal statement of course requirements and procedures or a course outline provided by instructors to all students on the first day of class.

synthesis The process of combining separate information and ideas to formulate a more complete understanding. Also, a level of learning on Bloom's taxonomy. Synthesis includes collecting, organizing, creating, and composing.

thesis statement A short statement that clearly defines the purpose of the paper.

thinking types Individuals who are logical, rational, and analytical. They reason well and tend to be critical and objective without being swayed by their own or other people's feelings. One of the personality preferences described by the Myers-Briggs Type Indicator.

transferable skills General skills that apply to or transfer to a variety of settings. Examples include solid oral and listening abilities, leadership skills, critical thinking, and problem solving.

VARK Learning Styles Inventory A sixteen-item questionnaire that focuses on how learners prefer to use their senses (hearing, seeing, writing, reading, experiencing) to learn.

verbal/linguistic learner An individual who likes to read, write, and tell stories and is good at memorizing information. One of the eight intelligences as described by the theory of multiple intelligences.

visual learner A person who prefers to learn by reading words on a printed page or by looking at pictures, charts, graphs, symbols, video, and other visual means. One of the preferences described by the VARK Learning Styles Inventory.

visualization A memory technique used to associate words, concepts, or stories with visual images.

visual/spatial learner An individual who likes to draw and play with machines and is good at puzzles and reading maps and charts. One of the eight intelligences as described by the theory of multiple intelligences.

INDEX

Note: Boxes, figures, and tables are indicated by *(b)*, *(f)*, and *(t)* following page numbers.